BRITISH SOLDIERS
OF THE KOREAN WAR

BRITISH SOLDIERS
OF THE KOREAN WAR

IN THEIR OWN WORDS

STEPHEN F. KELLY

This book is dedicated to all the brave men (and women) who served in Korea and especially to those in this book.

Stephen F. Kelly is a writer and broadcaster. Born in Birkenhead, he was educated at Ruskin College, Oxford, and the London School of Economics, and has a PhD in oral history. He was for many years a political journalist with *Tribune* magazine and Granada Television before becoming an academic at the University of Huddersfield where he was Director of the Centre for Oral History Research. He has published more than twenty books, many on sport as well as oral history. His last book, *You've Never Had It So Good*, was an oral history of the 1950s and is also published by The History Press. He is Visiting Professor of Journalism at the University of Chester.

First published 2013

The History Press
The Mill, Brimscombe Port
Stroud, Gloucestershire, GL5 2QG
www.thehistorypress.co.uk

British Library Cataloguing in Publication Data.
A catalogue record for this book is available from the British Library.

ISBN 978 0 7524 8727 4

Typesetting and origination by The History Press
Printed in Great Britain

CONTENTS

Acknowledgements   7

Introduction   9

1. Call-Up   17
2. Welcome to War!   47
3. Life in the Trenches   88
4. News From Home   127
5. The Casualties of War   134
6. Prisoners of War   176
7. Welcome Home!   194

Conclusion   219

Index   223

ACKNOWLEDGEMENTS

THERE ARE NUMEROUS people I would like to thank for their help during the course of writing this book. First and foremost I owe a debt of gratitude to the British Korean Veterans Association. The Association cares for and organises events for all those in the armed services who fought in Korea. It does a magnificent job in keeping the memory of the war alive. But inevitably its numbers are now seriously dwindling as its old soldiers die off. All are now over the age of 80, many considerably older. Within another ten years the likelihood is that there will be only a handful of veterans remaining who played a part in the conflict. The purpose of my book has been to ensure that their memories and stories are not lost forever but remain for successive generations to read and understand the horrors they went through. Sue Hurst, secretary of the Veterans Association, and her husband Bill, were both helpful and enthusiastic in helping to find interviewees. I should also like to thank the various branches of the association who allowed me into their monthly meetings in order to try and find potential interviewees. Everyone was always courteous and helpful. There were, of course, some who chose not to be interviewed. Although it was disappointing that I could not record their memories I totally understand and respect their reasons for remaining silent.

Above all, however, I would like to thank all those I have interviewed. They all allowed me, a total stranger, into their homes, and happily plied me with tea and biscuits before settling down to recount their days in Korea. Their memories and their stories are quite remarkable. It could not have been easy for any of them. Many also lent me photographs and memorabilia, some of which appear in this book.

A small number of interviews and photographs have been taken from the Britain's Small Wars website and I would sincerely like to thank them for giving me permission to use them. Their first-rate website is important and well worth viewing. I would also like to thank my publishers, The History Press, and in particular Shaun Barrington, who believed in this project from the start and who battled for its publication, and my editor Chrissy McMorris.

My gratitude and love, as ever, to my wife Judith, who has had to live with this project for more than a year but always remained interested in the tales I have recounted to her on returning from each interview. And to my children, Nick and Emma, thank you for just being around.

Stephen F. Kelly
Manchester

INTRODUCTION

IT HAS BEEN called the 'forgotten war'. And with much justification. Today, few people remember the terrible conflict of the Korean War and even fewer men and women are still alive who served there between the years 1950 and 1953. Indeed people are still astonished to learn that British troops were even involved in the three-year conflict. Instead people associate the war with America; perhaps mainly because of the American produced television series *MASH*.

In 2012 we rightly remembered the 30th anniversary of the Falklands War with parades, commemorative services and acres of newsprint in our daily papers. In all, around 28,000 troops were sent to the Falklands with 255 British serviceman giving their lives, along with three Falkland Isles civilians and 649 Argentinians. And yet, when in 2010 Britain commemorated the start of the Korean War, there was little in the way of publicity or commemoration. Hopefully that will be rectified in July 2013 when Britain remembers the sixtieth anniversary of the ending of the war.

And yet the awful truth is that British troops, including the RAF and navy, were involved in an appalling conflict fought in atrocious weather conditions with many British troops taken prisoner by the Chinese and with the possibility of a nuclear attack being seriously planned by the Americans.

The statistics alone are startling. More than 100,000 British soldiers served in the war with 1,078 being killed. For the Americans it was even graver with over 300,000 soldiers involved and 40,000 killed. A further 2,000 soldiers also died from other countries serving with the United Nations. In all, fifteen nations sent troops as part of the UN command with America providing 90 per cent of the soldiers.

And that was only part of it. On the other side at least 350,000 North Korean troops were killed along with 150,000 Chinese troops and almost 300 Soviet soldiers. Civilian casualties are impossible to estimate but a figure of 2.5 million is probably a conservative guess. Much of Korea was destroyed. What cities there were lay in ruins with almost every building devastated by the incessant bombing, while the countryside lay peppered with craters from mortar attacks. Villages had been burnt down and the luscious vegetation destroyed by napalm bombs. That South Korea should resurrect itself into a mighty industrial nation within forty years, and act as host for the Olympic games, was indeed an economic miracle.

Perhaps most surprising of all to the layman is that the vast majority of British troops were conscripts; national servicemen, carrying out some of their two-year stint in Korea. Mostly they were teenagers, just 18, 19, 20-year-olds, straight off the streets of Glasgow, Manchester, Liverpool, London and elsewhere. As their eighteenth birthdays loomed they awaited the arrival of the letter telling them exactly where to go and enlist with some trepidation. Few imagined, however, that within a short period of time they would be heading for Hong Kong before being shipped to Korea. Even fewer seemed to have much idea of what the war was about, let alone where Korea was. None of them seemed to have even thought much about the politics. Why were we there, what was the point of fighting a war so many miles from home?

In fact, national servicemen were not supposed to be on the front line until they were 19 years old but there is plenty of evidence, not least from the testimonies in this book, to reveal some were clearly underage and should never have been there.

John Smith from Liverpool managed to beat the authorities twice. He had decided that he was going to sign on full-time as a soldier rather than wait for his national service call-up. But there was a problem. First, he was underage, only 17, but the army seemed to overlook that although it's hard to believe that they didn't realise. And secondly, he signed up for the Argylls even though he had not been born in Scotland, nor had a Scottish parent. But he had set his heart on the Argylls and when he told the recruiting sergeant that it had to be the Argylls or nothing, the sergeant told him to put down that he had a Scottish father. And so, they signed him up.

The Korean War was very much the beginnings of a cold war that would last a further thirty years as relations between the West and the East became strained to breaking point. The Korean conflict ended in a stalemate that precipitated an even wider stalemate until the Berlin Wall was torn down in 1989. On the one side were the communist nations, headed by the Soviet Union and China with all their satellite allies, including North Korea, whilst on the other side were the United States, Britain and Western Europe.

The war fell into two distinct phases. The first phase, lasting roughly a year, was one of advance and retreat, north and south, with heavy casualties suffered by both sides. In the second phase after the summer of 1951, troops retreated to their trenches and bombarded each other. It became a stalemate with troops holed up defending their positions around the 38th Parallel. Not unlike the First World War, there was plenty of action but few territorial gains. Eventually both sides realised the futility of each other's positions and a ceasefire was agreed, but not a permanent peace treaty.

The conflict in Korea had its roots in the Second World War. Korea had been occupied by Japan since 1910: a brutal occupation that continued throughout the Second World War until 1945 when the USSR and the USA agreed on a two-pronged attack on Korea in order to oust the Japanese. The Soviets would attack from the north whilst American troops would invade from the south, with the two superpowers meeting halfway at the 38th Parallel. The invasion was a success and the Japanese were routed. The Allies further agreed to allow each of their sectors to be governed as they wished. It was to prove to be a major diplomatic error. When the two superpowers pulled out in 1947 they left behind two starkly different regimes; in the north the Soviets had shaped a communist government under Kim Il Sung, whilst in the south the Americans had installed a brutally nationalist regime under the authority of Harvard graduate Syngman Rhee.

Both Rhee and Kim Il Sung were fiercely nationalistic and both were determined to one day unite their divided nation under one ruler. Incursions across the border dogged the next few years, until, at 4 a.m. on 5 June 1950, 135,000 communist troops invaded the south and overran the unsuspecting South Korean and American forces. The American Government in Washington regarded the attack as a threat to the region's peace and, along with British support, tabled a motion at the United Nations which was duly passed and led to the creation of a United Nations force which immediately headed for Korea.

Within days, North Korean troops had captured Seoul, just 30 miles south of the 38th Parallel. Terrified Korean refugees from the north began to sweep southwards but were stopped in their tracks when South Korean forces began the destruction of bridges. But they could not hold the communist forces back as they continued to sweep through the peninsula towards the port of Pusan in the south-east. The American army was forced back so that they held only a corner of Korea around Pusan on the east coast.

General MacArthur, at the time leader of American troops in the Pacific, then came up with a plan to invade Korea at Inchon on the west coast, not far from Seoul. Although it was a daring plan, it was to take the communist forces around Seoul by surprise, and gave the Americans a vital foothold that allowed them to push north, take Seoul and cut off the communist forces around Pusan. Before they became surrounded, however, the communist forces fled back north. MacArthur scurried after them, pushing them right back into North Korea and towards the border with China. What MacArthur did not know, however, was that more than 300,000 Chinese troops had massed on the border, and in November 1950 the Chinese leader Chairman Mao Tse Tung ordered Chinese troops to attack, claiming that the UN forces were a threat to China. The UN forces, mainly Americans, were then pushed back well south of Seoul.

MacArthur was by now planning an extreme solution – using atomic weapons. He saw the war as a moral crusade against communism and if needs be he was prepared to drop an atomic bomb. 'I would have dropped thirty or so atomic bombs … strung across the neck of Manchuria,' he confessed in an interview some years later. And there is no doubt that the United States not only seriously considered an atomic strike but actually had its planes loaded and on standby in Japan in case the Joint Chiefs of Staff gave the go-ahead. Even President Truman, although painted as an opponent to the use of atomic weapons, announced that he was fully prepared to use them if necessary. In the event he did not give the go-ahead, partly because British Prime Minister Clement Attlee flew to Washington to warn him that Britain would not sanction such at attack. Truman agreed that he would consult with Attlee in the event of a likely nuclear strike, although interestingly he still did not rule out such a strike. Fearful that MacArthur might take unilateral action and that he was not deploying the right military tactics in Korea, Truman sacked his leading general in May 1951 and replaced him with General Ridgway. Again, although Ridgway has been painted as more of an appeaser than MacArthur, it was not altogether true. Ridgway was just a prepared as his predecessor to use nuclear weapons. In the event no nuclear attack was sanctioned.

It is usually assumed that the closest we have ever come to a nuclear war was with the Cuban missile crisis in 1962, but the evidence would suggest that, on the contrary, during the spring of 1951, the United States came within a whisker of ordering a nuclear attack on Korea and China.

Under its new commander, General Ridgway, UN forces finally advanced north once more and by mid April they were back, close to the 38th Parallel, as the Chinese launched a spring offensive close to the Imjin River. At what was to become known as the Battle of the Imjin River, the Gloucestershire Regiment narrowly escaped annihilation as the 27th Commonwealth Brigade beat off Chinese attacks. For three days, 750 men of the battalion repelled successive assaults by a force seven times larger. Surrounded, with no hope of rescue, running short on water and ammunition, they fought literally to the last bullet and grenade. Some 620 failed to make it back to friendly lines. A third of the battalion were killed or wounded, the survivors spending the next two years in Chinese or North Korean prison camps. They would forever be known as the 'glorious Glosters'. The UN line held, then moved north again. This time, there was no reckless advance into the north. Instead the line stabilised in the general area of the 38th Parallel and for the remaining two years the fighting consisted of a stand-off until July 1953 when an armistice was reached to end the fighting.

The final two years of the war made for repetitive reporting with Fleet Street's editors as well as the public, soon growing bored. Korea seemed a long way off and with little or no press coverage, Korea was even more remote.

Press coverage of the war was generally sparse. After all it was over 5,500 miles away and few newspapers had correspondents over there, relying instead on either American sources or news agencies. As a consequence there was little reporting. And photographs were, of course, few and far between. Technology limited opportunities so that photographs were always well behind events, with television and cinema pictures even scarcer. There were no evening news television bulletins detailing the death and destruction as there would be with the Vietnam war ten years later. American TV was still in its infancy, whilst in Britain hardly anyone owned a TV set. If pictures of Korea were to be seen then it was on the black and white newsreel at the local cinema and these were always a week or more out of date, sandwiched between the B-movie, ice cream and the main feature.

And where there was news, the war was portrayed in hard, cold war political language. North Korea and China were seen as the communist aggressors with the United States, Britain and the United Nations as the free world peacemakers. The communists of North Korea were vilified although, in truth, the puppet regime of Sygman Rhee was just as repressive as Kim Il Sung's dictatorship in the North.

Over the sixty years since the war ended, much has been written detailing the politics and strategy of the war, although even this is sparse when compared to other more recent wars. But, most surprisingly, even less has been written of the everyday activities of the ordinary soldier. Much work has been done in the United States where servicemen have been extensively interviewed with their memories and stories published in a number of textual and electronic formats. But the same is not so true of the United Kingdom. The Imperial War Museum has conducted some interviews and whilst these are freely available from their archives, few of them have been published. As a consequence, the story of the ordinary soldier remains largely untold. And that is the point of this book.

The purpose is not to retell the history, strategy or politics of the war. That has been done by various eminent military historians and in far greater detail than this book can ever provide. Instead, the intent here is to tell the soldier's story, to detail what life was like on a daily basis for those who served. Where did they come from? How did they get there? And once they were there what did they do? It's the simple things which can often be of most interest: What food did they eat? What were toilet facilities like? Did they get to wash every day? Were they frightened? How did they cope with the intense cold? Did they come into contact with the Chinese, Americans, Koreans? Did they fight alongside other Europeans serving with the United Nations forces? Did they receive letters from home or newspapers? How did they get on with their colleagues? Did they ever get any leave? And how did they feel about the politics of the war and about their colleagues who were injured or killed in the conflict? These are the ordinary soldiers – kingsmen, privates, artillerymen, engineers; few of them were officers, and most of them were national servicemen rather than fully signed up regular soldiers. And what about when they returned home: was there a hero's welcome with showers of gratitude, parades and medals?

It is a portrait of human hardship, the likes of which – thankfully – few of us have ever experienced. An armistice remains in place but no peace treaty has ever been signed. Korea remains a divided nation. The North with its grey, authoritarian regime mirrors the worst days of Stalinism, while the south thrives in consumer goods and burgeoning wealth. More than 28,000 American troops remain stationed in South Korea, an astonishing number considering the fighting ended sixty years ago, whilst who knows how many are gathered on the other side of the border. Mostly the troops just eye each other through powerful binoculars across of the 38th Parallel. Quite what they do with the rest of their time is anyone's guess.

1. CALL-UP

'I hadn't heard of Korea but I thought it would be an adventure.'

INTRODUCTION

PERHAPS THE MOST astonishing fact about the Korean War is that the vast majority of soldiers who fought there were conscripts. As many as 70 per cent of those arriving in Korea during the three years of the war were national servicemen, and mostly under the age of 20. They were young lads straight off the streets of the big cities, towns and rural villages of the nation. Some came straight from school, others were in menial jobs.

When national service was introduced in January 1949, it was initially for just eighteen months, but with war looming in Korea it was suddenly increased to two years. National service was obligatory for all young men over the age of 18. The only exemption, and then it was only a temporary exemption, was for those at university or in an apprenticeship. As soon as they had completed their apprenticeship or education, they were called up. In theory no man under the age of 19 was supposed to serve in battle, but there is plenty of evidence to suggest that there were many, as the evidence in this book shows, who fought on the front line when they were underage.

So, shortly after your eighteenth birthday (in one case actually on the day!) a brown envelope would drop behind the door informing you of your 'call-up', and telling you when and where to report. Steve Hale remembers the stunned silence when his uncle's call-up papers arrived, and the tears when the moment came for him to actually leave home. Within days you would be off, taking a train or bus to one of the call-up depots. From there you would be dispatched to a training camp for a period of intensive training. Everyone knew it was going to happen and dreaded the inevitable letter arriving, but there was nothing you could do about it. It was simply a matter of accepting your fate and, as one interviewee says, getting on with it and getting it over and done with as soon as you could so that you could get back to normal life.

But there were some who saw it as a temporary escape from the drudgery of life or poorly paid, tedious work. For them it was an adventure. And for most the prospect of going abroad seems to have been exciting, going to places they had only read of in books. You have to remember that barely any of these young men would have travelled beyond their home-town let alone abroad in the early 1950s. And certainly none would ever have travelled to the Far East.

But whilst most of the conscripts accepted their fate with some trepidation, there were those who dreaded it. Rather than wait for the letter to arrive, thousands mysteriously disappeared when it came to their call-up. Others, having had a taste of square bashing and the brutal sergeant major went AWOL and were officially listed as deserters. Emanuel Shinwell, the Labour Government's Minister of Defence, announced in the House of Commons in 1950 that there were almost 20,000 absentees; a staggering number, although some of these may have been listed for a number of years. There were also suicides, although the statistics were heavily camouflaged to also include accidents and so forth so that the true numbers of suicides were known to only a few. After all they didn't want to demoralise the conscripts any further.

Almost all those interviewed for this book testify that when they were called up they had little or no inkling that they would be sent to Korea. There was some talk of Malaysia as a possible venue, where a conflict had recently erupted, but most assumed they would not be sent to any front line. After all they were really just amateurs, off the streets and with only a basic training. As far as they were concerned they imagined they would remain at a training camp in the UK, or perhaps be posted to Germany or Austria which appear to have been popular destinations with the average soldier. None of them knew where Korea was and would never have been able to point to it on a map. Even fewer had any idea of the conflict or the reasons that lay behind it.

Although more newspapers may have been read in 1950 than today, news from Korea was sporadic. There was virtually no television; only the occasional newsreel at the cinema and that always tended to be upbeat rather than having anything to do with war. Once into the war there was little reporting. Conditions were difficult, and getting the news from Korea back home was complicated and expensive. And anyhow people in Britain didn't really want to know. After six years of world war everyone simply wanted to forget about conflict and get on with making the peace and returning to normality.

Mostly the conscripts were assigned to the army while some, though not many, joined the RAF or navy. Training was not fun. It was square bashing, cleaning and taking orders from brutal sergeant majors who seemed to delight in making life as hard as possible for the young men, most of whom came from ordinary working-class backgrounds. It was while they were on training that the order came to go to Korea. There followed a short period of embarkation leave before making for either Southampton or Liverpool and a troopship bound for Hong Kong. But of course there were already those who were serving in the armed forces who were ordered to travel to Korea. George Stirland, for example, had been in the Royal Navy for a few years when he found himself sent east. And Eric Peters had been serving with the army in India and on the Khyber Pass before going to Korea.

The British army was already well positioned in various parts of the world, supposedly keeping the peace. The vast majority of its soldiers were stationed in Germany and Austria, maintaining a watchful eye after the war; others were in Malaya, Singapore and Hong Kong which would soon become the staging post for the battle in Korea.

The journey to Hong Kong was always by ship, usually a designated troop-ship, but at times a requisitioned German liner. Conditions varied: some were dilapidated relics from the Second World War full of cockroaches and long overdue the scrapyard, others were more up to date and luxurious. On the troopships especially, beds were few and far between, with most soldiers sleeping in hammocks slung from the underside of the deck or in bunks crammed into small cabins, often with six or eight occupants. And once they were into hotter territory many of the soldiers dispensed of the hammocks and crammed conditions in favour of sleeping on deck. Toilet facilities were nearly always appalling. They were simply inadequate for the numbers. There were no en suite facilities, with the result that everyone had to use the small number of communal toilets and bathroom, with long queues in the morning to shave and wash. And as Geoff Holland remembers, when you did get to the sink it was often full of sick and the toilets were even worse.

The ships sailed mainly from Southampton or Liverpool and made their way via Port Said, Aden, Singapore and Colombo on a four or five-week voyage that would take them to Hong Kong. There were stopover points en route as troops were allowed some shore leave but few disembarked at Aden – the stench seems to have put them off. Singapore and Colombo, however, were a different matter, and after a couple of weeks on board, putting your feet on solid earth, even if it was for just a few hours, was more than welcome. Of course there were jobs to be done whilst on the ship, although with hundreds of servicemen the work could be spread thinly. It was hardly arduous. Eventually, after four weeks or so, they arrived in Hong Kong and were usually sent promptly to a further training post, often up in the New Territories.

Hong Kong was popular. The weather was good and dress was informal, just shorts and shirts throughout the warm summer. Plus there was plenty of entertainment and sport. It was also cheap with decent food, beer and, of course, girls. Nevertheless, for many, the news that they were about to be sent to Korea came as a shock. But most seemed to have accepted their fate stoically, perhaps not fully understanding what might await them. Maybe because war had been just a few years gone and all their families would have fought, they imagined it was simply their turn. Whatever the reason, they got on with it and boarded yet another ship, in many instances an American ship, and made the short journey from Hong Kong to war in Korea. Little did they know what they were about to encounter.

Bill Fox

I was born in Collyhurst in Manchester on the 17 January 1928, so I am now 85. I volunteered to join the army but they took me on as a national serviceman. When the Korean War started they asked for volunteers who had just come out of the army. They wanted them because they were already trained and fit. Anyhow, I volunteered for eighteen months. Now for me going to a place I'd never heard of before seemed marvellous. It was on the other side of the world and to fight under the uncrowned King of the Pacific, General MacArthur,[1] was a big adventure. He was the big hero of the war but we all believed that the British army was the best in the world and we could do no wrong. I'd seen all these American films fighting the Japs and Germans and I wanted to be a part of it. I was too late for the Second World War, but when the chance came for me to go somewhere to fight for just eighteen months I was really keen. Remember, this was before the Chinese had come into it so it was just a civil war between the North Koreans and the South. What a marvellous experience I thought, what a marvellous chance. I thought, great. I had gone into the army in 1945 and had been demobbed in 1948, so I had missed all the action. After I had been demobbed I had gone back to my old job, working in a timber firm, as a driver's mate going all over the country. I enjoyed that but to get the chance to go abroad was exciting and romantic, a great adventure. So, I went down and volunteered as a reservist. They gave me a choice of one of three infantry regiments. I was undecided but picked the Glosters. They consisted of roughly a thousand men; of those only a third were from the original Glosters. The others were volunteers and reservists called up from the Second World War. The reservists thought it would all be over in next to no time, by the time they got there, but had they realised the Chinese were going to get involved, they wouldn't have gone.

---

1   General Douglas MacArthur, 1880–1964. American General and Supreme Commander Southwest Pacific during the Second World War. Effective ruler of Japan after the War and United Nations Commander in Korea until removed from office by President Truman in April 1951.

Before we left for Korea I was based in Colchester and met some-one called Derek Ball who became a great friend. He had a real country yokel accent and I used to take the mickey out of him and he'd take the mickey out of me calling me Frank Randle.[2] We left Southampton in early September 1950 on the *Windrush*,[3] a German ship confiscated by the British at the end of the war. It was a lovely trip, seeing places I'd never been; it was marvellous to go all round the world. We saw Gibraltar, we bypassed Malta and saw all the British naval ships signalling to us through the night, saying good luck. Then it was on to Suez and we saw all the British soldiers on the banks of the canal, all waving to us. It was like Britain was everywhere. Then we went to the Red Sea; I'd heard so much about that and how romantic it was. There were the deserts and mountains and then we stopped at Aden, and then to the Indian Ocean, stopping at Colombo where everyone was so nice and friendly. Then we stopped at Singapore; that was great. We had shore leave and we couldn't get ashore quickly enough to see all the sights. We went to the dancehalls and they were a bit different to Manchester. Back in Manchester you had to ask the girls very carefully and politely if they would dance with you, but here they all wanted to dance with you. They gave you tickets as well. If the girl danced with you, then you had to give the ticket to the girl and she would get paid commission. From Singapore we sailed straight to Korea, we didn't go to Hong Kong, as they did later, I think they wanted to get us there as fast as possible.

Jim Lucock

I was born in Liverpool, in the Dingle, on the 21 May 1932. I left school in 1946 at the age of 14 and became an apprentice plumber. But because I was an apprentice my national service was deferred until 21. However,

---

2   Frank Randle, 1901–1957, was a popular Lancashire comedian.

3   The *Windrush* was a former German ship, built and launched in 1930 in Hamburg and named the *Monte Rosa*. The ship was captured by the British towards the end of the Second World War and converted into a troopship. It is probably better known as the ship which brought the first wave of West Indian immigrants from Jamaica to the UK in June 1948. The ship sank in the Mediterranean in 1954 after a severe fire.

I also played football and was in two cup finals and because of that I was not going to night school. A man from the deferment board came to see me and told me that I had to go to night school otherwise my deferment would be cancelled. Anyway, a few weeks later he returned and said, 'You still haven't been going to night school, so your deferment in cancelled.' Ten days later I got a letter telling me to go down town and have a medical and ten days after that I was in the army. I was 20 at the time. I had broken the deferment agreement so they put me in the army straightaway. This was June 1952.

I wanted to go in the Parachute Regiment but you needed to sign on as a regular for that and I said I wasn't going to sign on until I had found what it was like, so I was put into the Lancashire Fusiliers and sent to the Wellington barracks in Bury. I was only there an hour and I was told I was going to the King's Own Regiment in Lancaster, so they took us down and put us – there must have been about forty of us – on a train to Bowerham barracks. When we got there, the next morning, they said, 'You're not staying in the King's Own Royal Regiment, you're going to the King's Regiment in Liverpool and you're going to Korea.' We all looked at each other and said, 'Korea?' And they said, 'Yes, you're going to Korea.' That didn't bother me because my father and grandfather and cousins and uncles had all been in the King's Regiment in Liverpool going back to the First World War. I knew about the war in Korea because I had seen it on the news at the cinema, so I knew what it was about basically but I had no idea what the conditions were like. We did our six weeks basic training. It was a good camp, no bullying, lots of shouting of course, but the NCOs were good.

After that I went down to Aldershot to do a para course but going up on a catwalk I slipped and did my knee in. I went to see the MO and they examined it and said this is going to take a while to heal up so we're going to return you to your unit, so I went back to Bowerham barracks and they said all your crowd have gone to Formby, so I ended up going down to Harington barracks in Formby on my own. Of course the lads were all a month in front of me by then so they put me with an entirely different set of fellas. So we did our basic training there and our continuation training and then they decided to give us some embarkation leave and we were on our way down to Southampton. The battalion had already gone to Korea.

Roy Cox

I joined the army in 1948 when I was 17 and three-quarters. I was living in Oxford at the time. What happened was that my sister gave me a book called *Wing Dagger* and it was about the SAS and I read it and, of course, fancied the idea of dropping behind lines. So I went to the recruiting office and said I want to join the SAS and they said, 'No you can't, not straight away, they come from other regiments.' So I said, 'OK which regiments?' and they said, 'Well a lot of them come from the Parachute Regiment.' So I said, 'OK, I'll join the Parachute Regiment.'

'Oh no you can't do that,' they said, 'to get in the Parachute Regiment you have to join the infantry first.' So I said, 'OK, I'll sign on for the Oxfordshire and Buckinghamshire Light Infantry.' So I signed on for them and I was sent for basic training. There were only two of us who were regulars and under 18. Now if you were under 18 you had to go and get half a pint of milk every day to drink from the canteen. All the blokes used to take the mickey, babies having their milk, cissies. We used to skip it a lot.

Anyway, when we'd finished all our training, which was basic weaponry stuff, they said the national servicemen are going in the ox and buks which is in Germany at the moment cos they were only doing eighteen months at the time, and the regulars, they said, were going to Malaya and you will be drafted into the King's Own Yorkshire Light Infantry. So we had a week's leave and the two of us said, 'Goodbye Mum we're not coming back for three years.' We got a fortnight's embarkation leave but a week after we were brought back and they said, 'You're actually joining the Kings Shropshire Light Infantry.' And I said, 'Where's that?' and they said, 'Buckingham Palace, they're on guard duty.' Well that was the last thing I wanted, all that bullshit. Anyhow, we went there, we were at Chelsea barracks, there was all this belt and buckle cleaning and I thought if there was a good way I could get to France I would desert and join the French Foreign Legion but I couldn't think of a good way. I was a bit mad at that age.

Anyhow, I did my posting there and I did Windsor Castle duty as well. But the sheer bull of everything! Everything had to be so polished. I finished that and went to Borden camp and got ready for going abroad somewhere. They then put us on a train to Liverpool and shipped us out to

Hong Kong, as they thought the Chinese nationalists might invade Hong Kong. We were just going to Hong Kong, this was before the Korean War had started and I did eighteen months there. We were given jungle training as they thought we might then go on to Malaya. Then suddenly we heard about the Middlesex going to Korea because there was a war starting there. We were all asking where's Korea? We had never heard of it. We were told it was somewhere up near China. After the Middlesex had done twelve months in Korea we went in 1951.

So we got on an American attack transport ship, it had a fairly flat bottom so it could get on the beaches. But it was bad for seasickness and god did I get seasick. The toilets on the ship had no doors on them so you had to sit there with everyone walking past.

Eric Peters

I left school when I was 14 and became a coal porter – not as in the man who made the music! No, I used to carry the coal for a coalman. I've still got the letter off the coalman, dated September 1944, when the army asked him about my character. In fact I've still got all my army records. I worked on the coal wagons for £1.50 a week. My mate's brother was in the Loyal Regiment. He had escaped from the Japanese and then later been killed, so we all decided to join up. We didn't all get in but I was old enough and got in, signing up for seven and five, that's seven years in the colours and five in reserves. I signed up on the 1 January 1945, at 17 and a half years of age. That was the minimum age but I didn't have a proper regiment at first. Instead I was sent for training with the 27th Infantry Training Regiment at Derbyshire for three months and it was only after that that I ended up joining the Black Watch. I teamed up with a lad from Wigan and he was joining the Black Watch and he persuaded me to go with him. I had no Scottish relations and knew nothing about the Black Watch. I didn't have to lie about being Scottish, it was about 60/40 English to Scots, that many Englishmen – cockneys, lads from Birmingham, all over.

I went to Germany on the 6 January 1946, the war was over by then but there was still so much devastation. I was in Düsseldorf, Osnabruck, then back down to Belgium where the lads who were being demobbed had to go. All the documentation to allow you to be demobbed had to be right and I helped with all that. The German prisoners of war came in every morning to clean the place out. No sheets or bedding, you just had blankets. They'd march down to our camp under their own NCOs. I was only a private at the time but I was in charge of this block. They brought me a revolver one day. A few weeks later I put a bullet in it to see if it would work and pointed it out of window and fired. It blew up in my hand, only the butt was left!

Then one day the major called me in and said, 'I've got bad news, you've got a war office posting and you're going to India.' Bloody hell! It's the other side of world, I thought. Anyhow, I went back to Scotland and after three months we were on our way to India and landed in Bombay. Then we went up to Peshawar and the Khyber Pass and to a hill station called Cherat. On the way up there you can see the Black Watch badge carved on a big rock, about 14ft tall, saying Black Watch 1907, so we carved into it 1947. We were up there for about eight or nine months. I was in the rear party ready to hand it over, about fourteen of us, when one night we heard a hell of a row. They said there was trouble, and told us to stay in our room. So we stayed there all night and then the next morning went down to the bazaar. Now normally all the Indians slept on the doorsteps of the shops, but this particular morning they were all there but they were dead, they had been killed, slashed to pieces, even the dogs and horses were dead. Killed by Muslims or Hindus. Terrible.

After that we went down to Karachi on the trains and you could see on the trains coming the other way all these bodies piled high. It was the start of Independence and the terrible fighting between the Hindus and Muslims. We marched down into Karachi to the docks and we came home, or so we thought. When we got to Egypt they cut the battalion in half, one lot going to the Highland Light Infantry and the other half went to the Argyll and Southern Highlanders. They did it alphabetically. Fortunately me and all my mates were at the back end of the alphabet, so we all went into the Argylls and were sent to Palestine.

We spent our time stopping the Jews doing harm. The Arabs were fine, no trouble whatsoever. But the Jews, they were firing from orange groves and we sent the tanks in smashing all the orange groves. It takes thirty years to grow orange trees and they were all smashed. We were guarding the tanks. After that I went to Egypt for a few months. Later we went to Hong Kong. I was stationed there for eighteen months before I went to Korea. I also went to Singapore, then I had words with my sergeant major and I threw in my two stripes. I'd had enough of him. I was up before the company commander. The sergeant major was ranting and raving at me and threatening to take my stripes away so I beat him to it and gave them to him. I told the major that the sergeant major hated my guts and I hated his, so they accepted my stripes. I then went before the company commander and I dropped from corporal to private. This was all in Hong Kong after I'd come back from Singapore, so I then had to go to another company. Two months after that I was sent to Korea on HMS *Ceylon*, a cruiser, and the Middlesex lads were on HMS *Ocean*, an aircraft carrier there as well. This is August/September 1950, the war in Korea had just begun.

Jim Houghton

I was 18 and 4 months when I got called up and was expecting it. I was living in Walton in Liverpool and was a trailer mate working for a trailer and haulage firm here in Widnes. It was long distance driving to London, Newcastle. I finished my training in York with the Duke of Wellington's Regiment, we were all part of the Northern Brigade. The Dukes were going nowhere, the fusiliers had gone to Korea, another had gone to Malaysia and, I thought, well, I'm not going to be going to Germany next year, so I thought I'll go to Korea. So I agreed to go and signed the forms. At that time they wouldn't take any infantrymen out there who were on national service. They would take regular soldiers and some of them were signing up for a second term in Korea, mainly because you got a bonus of £150. What they did was they had to get them fit enough, and that would take them two months, and then it would take them a month to get there. By the time they got there it was time to come home. It was quite a popular thing. But quite a few of them started getting killed so it wasn't quite as popular then as they thought it would work out. National servicemen had to ask to go so I agreed to go. I thought I'm not going to stay here messing around in York and then go to Germany. I thought this sounds more interesting, so I went there.

Steve Hale

I remember the Korean War well. Life was just plodding along nicely in Liverpool and I just remember getting up one morning and there was this strange hush in the house and my Uncle Peter had got his call-up papers to do national service. He was only 18. I, in fact, later learnt that it was expected. It was more or less given that he would just do some training, as the Korean War had just started, and would then be put on a ship and out to Korea. And that's exactly what happened. The barracks of the old King's Regiment are still there on Townsend Avenue and he walked up there to sign in and from there he was taken in an army lorry to the camp at Altcar near Formby. He did six weeks solid training there. He then came home for two nights and I remember that because we had a great big shindig. It was a big party and all the street came in because he was, at the time, the only lad who had been called up and was going to Korea. But everyone in the street at some point during the night came into our house to the party. So he had two nights at home and was put on a ship and it took six weeks to get to South Korea. That was the last we saw of him for two years. Peter had literally just had his eighteenth birthday and within a few days he'd had the call-up. I remember my nan crying and asking my mum why she was crying. Nan feared that he'd not come back because he'd be right amongst it all fighting.

George Stirland

I joined the navy in September 1945, the war had just ended. I was 16 in the December so I was about 15 and a half by the time I started the paperwork and was down at the *Ganges* by September. The *Ganges* was a boys' training ship establishment for boy seamen and signalmen only. It was down south close to Ipswich, Felixstowe. I had never given joining the navy a thought. My father said I've got a good job for you at the waterworks in Preston. It has a good pension but at 14 years of age a good pension didn't mean much to me. It does now! I wanted to go on farming. I'd worked on farms during the war and fancied that but my dad said, 'No this is a better job.' Anyway, I started it and after about twelve months said, 'No, this is not for me.' Why I then said I wanted to join the navy I haven't a clue. There was someone who lived opposite me who was in the navy and he used to come home with his hat on and his badges and I thought, right, and he was an Oerlikon gunner and I thought that's for me. He was one of these lads on one swivel gun, strapped in. I fancied that, so I joined up.

I had this kitbag filled with clothes, never had so many clothes, four meals a day, couldn't beat it. I was never a star man down there but equally I was never the one who couldn't manage it. I was in the middle and just did it. We were boy seamen, seamanship one week, gunnery the next, twelve months training. In the afternoon you had sport, sailing or whatever. In the evenings we had dogwatches, and classes. The whole thing from getting up to going to bed was seamanship or gunnery. It was very strict, kids now wouldn't do it. This was all done at *Ganges*. We were allowed to be birched, flogged. You would get nine cuts, that was the punishment. But you could get up to 12. I didn't get it, I kept out of trouble. Showers were cold and you had them early in the morning. It was really strict but you left being very fit. And we were all only 15. One of the things we had to do was climb a mast 140ft high. We had to climb it every day and the first time you were allowed to go through the lugers hole, but after that you had to go on the outside. One or two did fall. They said it was the only concentration camp in England. It was as strict as hell.

After that I joined the fleet. We packed our bags and hammock and took a train to Portsmouth and sailed out via the East Indies. There were three or four hundred boys who had completed the course together. And we went out on a carrier that had been in the Pacific but couldn't have planes on it any more. So it was used for trooping. We went out and joined a cruiser. Ours was HMS *Glasgow*. I was on there for twelve months then came home. A lot on the men on it were HOs – hostilities only – and had done D–Day and were ready for demob. For every boy joining they let one man go home. In 1947 the whole ship came home.

I was in barracks at the time and nearly missed Korea. I was in the field guns crew who do all the Royal Tournaments. I was in that and normally being a member of that stopped all drafts as it was so prestigious but this time they said no, they didn't have enough men for Korea. When we got on the troopship the HMS *Devonshire* to go out, there were three or four full crews plus all the army men, RAF, Marines.

Ivan Williams

I was at Cowley grammar school in St Helens until I was 18. As soon as I left I had an army medical and I was called up in mid July 1950. I knew I was going to get called up; everyone did unless you did two things – one was to get an apprenticeship and the other was to be going into further education, i.e. a college or university, but there was no attraction in that for me. At the end of that you were still called up, so it only delayed the inevitable. It did not excuse you from military service. I looked at it as inevitable, something that had to be done and got out of the way so that I could then come home and start the rest of my life. I preferred to do it then rather than after three years at university or after an apprenticeship. I knew nothing about the war in Korea which had just started although there were jokes about going to start your new career! I didn't even know where Korea was, it was something that had never even entered my mind. It never even entered my mind that I might have to go to Korea.

I joined the army and after two weeks of sorting out at Oswestry, I was sent to the school of survey at Larkhill, Salisbury Plain, on an artillery surveyor's course. The course lasted about three months and at the end of it we knew that we were going to the Far East and to Hong Kong. We liked the idea of that because at the time there were two good postings; one was Germany, the other was Hong Kong. The posting nobody wanted was Malaya because the Malayan conflict was going on at the time. But before we went we were delayed a month and sent on a sound ranging course. I was with the Royal Artillery but was still with the training regiment up to the time we left. Then

I was posted to a regiment for when we arrived in Hong Kong. We were then sent on leave and then for embarkation leave and left from Woolwich before going to Southampton and setting sail on the *Empire Fowey*.

It took four weeks to reach Hong Kong via all the postings on the way such as Suez, Aden, Colombo and Singapore. It was all a brand new world to me. Although I was well educated I was totally green as grass. I'd never been on a boat before apart from going to New Brighton on the ferry and here we were on what had been a liner. Although there were a lot of people on it there was plenty of room to move around. We could sunbathe on the decks and there weren't many duties to do as there were thousands of troops on board so the duties were spread fairly thinly. It was all very pleasant and to see all these places we'd only ever read about. Nobody went ashore at Aden because the smell was terrible, but places likes Colombo and Singapore were fascinating. We had a day ashore at each of these while the ship refueled. They unloaded troops who were going here and put on troops who were going back.

We eventually arrived at Hong Kong. The harbour was enormous, the entire British fleet could have got into Hong Kong harbour and we were then posted to a unit on Kowloon which is the land opposite Hong Kong Island and I was posted to the 59th Medium Regiment Royal Artillery, but I had nothing to do with the guns. The guns were up in the New Territories and I was stationed at a place called Gun Club barracks in Hong Kong which is like all the barracks you've ever seen in the Indian Mutiny pictures. They had one design and it was a good one so they built them all over the world. I was part of headquarters company there, which included people like the CO's drivers, cooks, all the people who served the rest of the regiment. I was made very welcome there and got on with them.

At the time it was winter and we were wearing long trousers until the end of February and after that the temperature was wonderful and the dress was shorts, long stockings and boots; that was the regimental dress. I had arrived just before Christmas 1950, so most of this is 1951 and I stayed there until I went to Korea in December 1952, so I was there nearly twelve months. The regiment worked to a very peculiar shift. As it got very warm in the afternoon, we started early, we worked from seven in the morning to twelve. Then the afternoon was recreational and if there was anything to do in the evening we worked, but there seldom was. I found that with the training I had there was little for me to do so I was available for any jobs that were going. I was station policeman for a week which was the daytime guard on the camp. I also officiated at the Hong Kong Bisley rifle competition on Stonecutters Island where I was a spotter for one of the people who were firing. I had a telescope and I told them whether they had missed or not. I was also scorer for the regimental cricket team and occasionally played twelfth man for them although I was not very good at it. But my main job there – they needed to put me somewhere where they knew I was all day – was that I was officially sports storeman. We used to blow up footballs, paint hockey balls, cricket balls, clean football boots. It was a very pleasant life given that the temperature was always in the 70s-plus all day and stayed warm at night. All the afternoons were free so we used to go swimming four afternoons a week. You might ask what's wrong with Wednesday? Well on a Wednesday we played cricket; it's what British people do when aboard. So Hong Kong was very pleasant. Also it was the only time I've been well off in my life because the British army had an overseas allowance system that applied worldwide and it was three and a half times your salary, and the cost of living in Hong Kong was about a tenth of what it is in the UK, so suddenly you had money that you didn't want to spend. And that's not happened to me before or since.

John Hegarty

In 1949, I had been a radar plot instructor at the RP School, HMS *Harrier* in west Wales. It was a good job and with a fair complement of WRNS at the base, life was good. Certainly, I had no inkling of any 'draft' coming my way for some time to come. We had read of HMS *Amethyst* and the Yangtse incident[4] with admiration but, that was far away, and my priorities did not include thoughts of the Far East.

---

4   In April 1949 the British frigate HMS *Amethyst* was fired upon by Chinese communist troops whilst she was sailing down the Yangtse River and was forced to drop anchor. The ship remained trapped until July, when she made a daring and successful break for open waters. It became known as the Yangtse incident and was later made into a successful film.

So it came as something of a surprise when I was informed of my posting to HMS *Jamaica* once I had taken draft leave in the UK. *Jamaica* had been stationed in the West Indies, considered by most to be a rather cushy number, so of course I was not the only one crying in my beer when the ship was moved to the Far East station as a result of the tension and uncertainty in that area. *Jamaica* was to replace HMS *London*, which had suffered considerable damage during the Yangtse affair.

There followed some hectic domestic arrangements that included such minor matters as getting married to Bernice, my WRNS fiancée, with a short honeymoon in a wet and stormy south coast town. I joined HMS *Ocean* at Devonport for the month-long passage to Hong Kong where I joined HMS *Jamaica*. It was November 1949. I soon settled in and my main duties were coxswain of the ship's motor boat, and at sea in charge of one watch of the Action Information Organisation under the ship's direction officer.

John Smith

I was born in Liverpool in December 1930, off a well known road in Kirkdale and went to school in Huyton, St Alowious. I left school in 1944 at 14 and I worked in a butcher's shop for three years in Old Swan[5] training as a butcher. At first I was just an errand boy, then did a bit more as the men were away at war. I was working in the shop, serving behind the counter. When I was 17 and 4 months I joined the army but I gave the wrong age. I should have been 17 and a half. I went down to Pownall Square in Liverpool, near where the Liverpool Stadium[6] used to be, that was the recruiting place for the army. I wanted to join the Argylls. My grandmother was from Musselburgh, near Edinburgh, and the chap who lived next door to us was a sergeant in the Argylls during the war. So, I thought I'd join the Argylls. So I went to the recruiting office and there's an Irish Guard sergeant and he wanted me to go in the Irish Guards. He

---

5   Old Swan is a part of Liverpool.

6   The Liverpool Stadium was a well-known boxing venue in Liverpool.

says, 'Why does a big fella like you (and as you can see I'm over 6ft tall) want to go in the Argylls when you would be ideal for the Irish Guards.' So, I said, 'No, I just don't want to be into the Guards. I've made up my mind, I want to join the Argylls.' He then told me that you can't go in a Scottish regiment unless your parents are Scottish. I said, 'Well my parents aren't Scottish but my grandmother is from Musselburgh.' He said, 'Well you'll have to go in the Irish Guards cos they won't take you in to the Argylls.' I said, 'Oh well then, I'm not bothered, that's it.' He said, 'Oh come on, sit down, sit down.' He said, 'Put down that your father is Scottish.' I'll never forget this as long as I live, because when I enlisted I went up to do my training up at Fort George with the Argylls. I realised that I wasn't the only Sassenach cos there was another chap from Liverpool, lots of chaps from Manchester and the Cheshire area. They were all in the Argylls and a lot of the band in the Argylls as well weren't Scottish. And then I realised that because I was tall he had wanted me in the Irish Guards. So I got into the Argylls on two counts of deception!

Anyhow, I settled down very well. I had good friends, another chap from Netherley who I met up at Fort George. I was 17 and he was about 22. He showed me all the ropes, what to do and what not to do. I settled in very well. We finished training and one day I was approached by a colour sergeant in the Black Watch and he said, 'Are you from Liverpool?' and I said, 'Yes', and he said, 'Well I'm looking for someone to work with me.' He said, 'It's sort of prisoners' escort.' He said, 'What we do is go around and pick up deserters in police stations and that and take them back.' And he said, 'The reason I'm asking you is because if you live in Liverpool and I live in Manchester I can work a couple of nights at home.' He said, 'We can work it so we have a night or two at home.'

I used to like dancing a lot and we used to have highland dancing on a Saturday night in a little village not far from Fort George in Inverness-shire. Anyrate, I went on this dancing one night and I met a young girl – I'm 17 myself then – and I ask her if I can take her home and she says, 'Yes, certainly John.' Dilys her name is. So, we leave the dance hall and we're walking through the village and I ask her where she lives and she says, 'Oh I live up here', so we're walking up the lane and she says, 'I turn right here'. I said, 'Do you live here?' And she said, 'Oh yes, you probably know my daddy.'

I thought, hang on this is the officers' quarters. I said, 'Who's your daddy?' And she says, 'Oh, he's the major!' I thought, 'Oh I don't believe this.'

I went back to the Fort and I was on guard the next day with my rifle and Dilys comes up to me and says, 'Hi, good morning, John, did you enjoy last night? I might see you again some time.' She says, 'I'm just going to the kirk, I might see you on the way back.' I looked across my shoulder and there was the guard commander, sergeant. He came over to me and says, 'Do you know who the lassie is?' I said, 'Yes sergeant I do know.' He says, 'Don't go with her, you'll be in trouble.' I never saw her after that!

About 1948 there was a shortage of RMPs[7] so a few of us said we'd have a go, so we went and had a go and because we were regulars in the army we didn't have to go down and do the training. All we had to do was a five weeks' course in a place called Blackford near Gleneagles golf course. So we were there riding motorbikes and doing bits and pieces. I was then posted to Maryhill barracks in Glasgow and then other camps. Eventually I was put on draft for Hong Kong and that would be 1949. Apparently the Chinese communists were advancing on Hong Kong and coming in from the mainland and they decided to form a division. Anyrate, we got out there. It was the 40th Infantry Division. When I was out in Hong Kong I ended up in the same brigade of the Argylls which was 27 Brigade. I thought I can't get away from this lot!

That went fine and then I got sent to 28 Brigade and then I heard about this thing in Korea. Well, nobody knew anything about Korea. I was in 28 Brigade but 27 Brigade went out to join and they went on the HMS *Ceylon* to Korea. Time goes by and eventually it was decided that 28 Brigade would relieve the 27 Brigade in Korea. I was told they would be sending an advance party of just four of us. That was April 1951. The war had already started. Off we go in the trucks to the ferry at Kowloon. When we got there, there was this American warship which was called the USS *Montrose*. I remember going aboard and there was this commander-in-chief, Commander John Harding and he spoke to us all once we got aboard and he said the reason you're going to Korea is to stop the communists.

---

7   Royal Military Police.

Jim Grundy

I was born in Eccles, Manchester, precisely where this block of flats is today. It used to be John Shaw Street but they knocked them down and built this. When I was a kid I was in an orphanage in Padgate in Warrington. When I came out of the orphanage they put the girls into service and the lads went onto farms in Derbyshire. I was that badly treated by the farmers that, when I was 18, I walked away and the farmer rang up the authorities and told them that I was now eligible for national service. So in October 1949 I was called up. I did one year's national service and then I went in as a regular soldier. I was originally with the Army Catering Corps. I went in there because when I had my army medical they found something wrong with my spine, something I had never had any problems with in all my life. My first choice had been the Royal Artillery but I was forced to go in the Army Catering Corps.

My mother died when I was 3 and my father wouldn't have anything to do with us. There were nine of us so we all got put in different orphanages over Lancashire. So from the age of 9 I had people shouting at me. When I joined the army and had some sergeant major shouting at me, it didn't bother me; it had stood me in good stead for when I joined the army.

In February 1951 I went to Korea. I was a regular soldier by then. I got enlistment orders in December 1950, and after having a month's embarkation leave January came around and we were shipped from Aldershot to Southampton, and then in early February we went on the *Empire Lancashire* to Korea, that was a troopship. We went to Kure in Japan, near Hiroshima, and we went to Hiroshima as well. By then Hiroshima was built up but we did see lots of photographs of what had happened and some of the devastation. I was in the depot there in Kure doing training and then got sent to Pusan in Korea, it's now called Busan. I was supposed to be a cook but I never even made a cup of tea the whole time I was in Korea! In fact, I didn't make one until I got back to Manchester.

Brian Daly

I was born in Salford, Manchester. I left school at 15 and started off as an apprentice joiner and then when I was 18 I got called up for national service. I signed on for three years though I don't know why. This was 4 December 1951. I was sent to Catterick, then York, then volunteered in 1953 to go to Korea. I thought it was an adventure. I hadn't even heard of Korea but I thought it would be an adventure, something different. I had no idea at all what was going on in Korea and I think most soldiers were like that. You heard bits and pieces from those who came back but I never realised what had happened in the first place. I initially went into the Royal Signals as a wireless operator. I didn't want to do this, however. I was sat there all day listening and doing Morse code. Not for me. And that's when I decided to go to the police, so I joined the Royal Military Police. It would be July 1952 when I transferred. I was sent to Woking in Surrey to do my training. I left there on 2 March 1953 to go to Korea, via Southampton.

Geoff Holland

For obvious reason I was known in the army as 'Dutch'. I was 21 when I got called up. I had just finished my apprenticeship. The call-up age was 18 but I got deferred until I had finished my apprenticeship as a joiner in Rochdale. I've been a joiner all my life. The first two weeks I was train- ing at Oswestry in North Wales and then we were posted to Rhyl where we did fourteen weeks training. From there it was down to Woolwich to get ready to go abroad as we were going to Hong Kong. I went down to Woolwich and we got fourteen days embarkation leave and we sailed from Southampton at the end of November, arriving in Hong Kong on the 21 December 1950.

When I joined the army I certainly never thought I would be going to Korea. In fact I'd never even heard of it. Actually, I got my papers on my birthday, 17 June 1950, so along with all my birthday cards I got my call- up papers. I thought, well, this is good. I went in the army on the 6 July.

So, as I say it was back to Woolwich after embarkation leave and we sailed away on the *Empire Orwell*. The Korean War started on, I think, it was 26 June. I had no idea where Korea was, but we knew we were going to Hong Kong, but there was no talk of going to Korea. It took twenty-eight days to get to Hong Kong. We were six in a block with three bunks each side in a small cabin the length of a bed and the width of two beds. There were hundreds of troops on the troopship. The toilets were awful, no en suite; you had to queue up to go for whatever, wash, shave, toilet, it was just a big washroom with basins and toilets. When you got to the sink it was usually full of sick. It was a bit rough.

We did get off the ship at various points. The first stop was Port Said but we weren't allowed off there. We stayed in port but couldn't go off. Then we went to Aden and got some shore leave there. It was an awful place, it was roaring hot, I don't think there was a blade of grass in the place. But it was nice to have a walk on dry land. From there we went to Ceylon as it was then, Sri Lanka now. I enjoyed that, although we only had a day there. Then, from Colombo we went to Singapore and we went ashore there. The next stop was Hong Kong.

We had no money. They put us in the barrack room and it was coming Christmas, we were asking, 'When do we get some money?' and they were saying, 'Well it isn't pay day until next week.' In the end they did give us about 15 shillings, that's about 75p now, isn't it? But it was quite good, Hong Kong. We thought we were in Utopia. There was no rationing whereas there was rationing here in Britain – we got a bar of chocolate a week, we had cigarettes, we could have whatever we wanted, we were over the moon. I was stationed first at a place called Cape Collinson which is on Hong Kong Island. After that I was posted to the New Territories and the barrack was right in the centre of town. It was great, we were out at night in the various service clubs – my favourite was the China Fleet Club where you could get a really good slap up meal for a few dollars. I've actually been back to Hong Kong and that club. Hong Kong was good. I did about ten months there but after ten months they then must have decided I needed livening up! Go to Korea!

Terry Moore

I joined the army in 1945 for my two years' national service. I had asked to go to an Irish regiment because of my heritage, so I was sent, in the wisdom of the army, to the Queens Own Cameron Highlanders in Inverness! And that, of course, is not an Irish regiment! This was just after the war had finished. I was in a platoon there drilling and one day and an officer came over to me and said, 'We are putting you in a squad to go to WOSBE.' I didn't know what WOSBE was – War Office Selection Board – for a commission. I hadn't thought about it as I'm not desperately ambitious. We went down to the south of England overnight by train where we did four months and I got a commission. I was then commissioned to the Royal Irish Fusiliers, so I got my wish in the end.

I was immediately sent by the army, in its wisdom again, to the Royal Ulster Rifles whom I joined in Austria as part of the army of occupation. I stayed there for eighteen months or so doing various jobs. I had a very nice commission in what was known as the PFZ – the Prohibitive Frontier Zone – which was an area of land across a river called the Drau in Southern Austria between that river and the Yugoslav border. The dispute was over the Yugoslavs saying that we were on your side during the war and this used to be our natural boundary and we'd like it back! The West was saying, well hang on a sec. Anyhow, I was in charge of this area where the British army had in its company prisoners of war awaiting trial. I had a lovely time living in a requisitioned hotel that had its own swimming pool, well that's where the soldiers lived and I lived in a separate villa about half a mile away with a Swiss lady doctor who had retired there. Her husband had died so I stayed up in the mountains there for a while. And that was it. Then I came home and returned to civilian life and my previous job where I had worked in a laboratory in the north end of Birkenhead.

I was on the RARO – Regular Army Reserve of Officers – I joined that at the instigation of General Templer, later Field Marshall Sir Gerald Templer. I became very friendly with him and he asked me to sign up on the reserve and this resulted in my recall to the Korean War.

When I was recalled, my employers had no choice. I didn't even discuss it with them, but I do remember that it was a rushed affair and I joined a ship in Bidston dock in the north end of Birkenhead – a troopship – I was a mile and half off my home but they wouldn't let me off to go and see my parents! The ship then moved to the Liverpool landing stage and it sailed from there. I had no idea how long I would be recalled for. I, of course, knew I was going to Korea. The politicians were a bit sniffy about it. The United Nations had agreed to send a force and the British were a major part of it but there was nothing in the press about it, very little. In fact one of the things that has always niggled me – and I have been through the press records – is that after the first big battle we were engaged in, called Happy Valley, when we had about fifty men killed in the space of a few hours, nothing was reported in the press back home in the UK. Was it political censorship of the press? I don't know. But so much never made the press and I have checked and checked.

Brian Hough

I was born in Manchester in 1933 and raised in the West Gorton and Ardwick area of the city. I started school at 5 and left at 15. I was one of the first lot to have to go on until 15 and I thought that was a disgrace. I wanted to get out working at 14! By the age of 18 I was an apprentice sheet metal worker and welder. I hated every minute of it, but as my dad used to say, you need a trade. My dad had suffered the indignity of three or four years without work during the 1930s – just after I was born. And he never forgave the system for it. When the Second World War started he was called up and we didn't see him for another four or five years.

They used to announce on the radio or in the papers that men born before such and such a date with surnames starting with the initials … A to G or whatever had to register for national service on a particular date. But, just by coincidence, the day I had to register just happened to be my eighteenth birthday. But that was just a coincidence. We went down to the main labour exchange in Manchester and we registered there. You waited then until you were called for a medical which happened after a few weeks and if you passed your medical you then waited for your call-up papers. And then you were sent to wherever the MoD wanted you to go. My mates who all lived nearby were all the same age and getting their call-up papers and going here, there and wherever, Inverness, the south coast, they were going all over the place. I thought this sounds good; I'd never been as far as Rhyl. I came home one evening after work and my mum said, 'There you are, there's the letter on the mantelpiece.' And there it was, propped against the clock, in the brown envelope. We all knew what it was. I opened it up and everyone said, 'Well, where're you going?' And it said to Ashton under Lyne! Ashton under Lyne, it was only a sixpenny bus ride away! I was ashamed, I really was. I thought I couldn't tell anyone I was only going to Ashton under Lyne. At that time it was the regimental HQ of the Manchester Regiment. Well that was a bit exciting because I did know one or two lads who were in the Manchester Regiment cos at that time they were serving in Malaya. So my initial reaction was, OK, so I'm going in the infantry, so the chances are I will go to Malaya and I will see a bit of the world. The day before I went in I was sat at home and I was due to go in the army on the 7 February which was a Thursday and the day before I was in the living room listening to the radio when programmes were interrupted and the announcer said that King George VI had died. I've always said that I was one of the first soldiers of the Queen because I had to sign allegiance to Queen Elizabeth the Second and our group was the first to do that.

On the day I went in my dad came home, he'd been on a late shift, and I really did feel ashamed going to Ashton. 'Come on,' he said, 'I'll walk you down the road to get the trolley bus.' And he did! My dad shook my hand and wished me all the best. It's something I've always remembered. That was the first time my dad had ever shook my hand.

Now initially I was told that I was in platoon number two of the King's Regiment. Now I had never heard of the King's Regiment and I thought it was something to do with the King dying the previous day. So, I went straight into the King's Regiment and not the Manchester Regiment. We had six weeks' basic training at Ashton and there were two platoons of young lads. One platoon eventually went off to Malaysia and number two platoon, which was in the King's Regiment, were told within days that we were going to Korea. That took the breath away a little bit! They said something like, this time next year you'll be in Korea fighting the Russians. I knew something about the Korean war because of my family's activities politically. We were aware because some of the dads' pals, cos of this involvement in the Labour party, were opposing our intervention and didn't agree with Clement Attlee[8] supporting the UN resolution. Some of my dad's pals were further left than he was. I knew all that because of my background. But personally I thought it was going to be a great adventure. I really did. The politics didn't bother me too much. I thought if there was a UN resolution then it was correct and I took the family view on that.

I did my six weeks at Ashton and in theory I should have gone to Harrington in Formby to train with the King's Regiment and do another six weeks before joining the battalion. But that didn't happen. We went to Formby and we were there for perhaps only a couple of weeks before joining the battalion at a place in Wiltshire, not far from Swindon. They had just come back from Berlin. We did some training on Salisbury Plain and we were given a few weeks' embarkation leave and we set sail on 4 June 1952 from Liverpool for Hong Kong. When we were there we did extensive battle training up in the New Territories on the Chinese borders. The terrain was very similar to Korea – hills and very steep.

What then happened was that Clement Attlee had lost the general election in 1951 and after the first shock of the North invading the South, Britain recalled lots of reservists for national service. In the early days there were lots of casualties among national servicemen and people began to panic – these lads were only going in for eighteen months at that time so they extended national service from eighteen months to two years and put in the proviso that no soldier under the age of 19 could take part in the war. However when I went to Korea I was only 18. A few of us were called into the commanding officer's room and told that the battalion was going to Korea but we wouldn't be going with them as we weren't 19. Anyhow, we said that wasn't fair as we'd done all this intensive training so we were allowed to sign a declaration saying that we had volunteered. And when we arrived in Korea we had been in the army just seven months. Had I known I would have stayed in the fleshpots of Hong Kong!

---

8   Clement Attlee was Prime Minister of the Labour Government 1945–51.

Bill Hurst

I was born in Ancoats in Manchester. My dad's name was William and my mum was Alice. I was brought up in Collyhurst and went to Abbots Street school and did a lot of swimming for them. I swam for the all England championships in Blackpool but didn't get anywhere because the lads who I was swimming against were about 6ft 2in. From there I worked as an apprentice bricklayer and then I worked in the cotton mills and then became a coalman up to my call-up. I was 18 on 1 October 1951 and at the beginning of February got a letter from the ministry telling me to report to Ashton, to Ladysmith barracks, Ashton under Lyne. There were quite a few of us joining up. Three platoons, we did all the training. Then one day we were all on parade and they came to us and told us to take our berets off because we had joined the Manchester Regiment. And then they gave us another beret with a red patch on and they said you're now in the Liverpool King's Regiment, and you're going to Korea. Well, the first thing we all said was 'Where's Korea? Never heard of it.' The sergeant said, 'It's a long way away, but don't worry you'll be getting plenty of training before you go.' But we had never heard of Korea, knew nothing about a war there. Although the war had been going on, it never registered. I was working and just got on with that, having a drink at night, dancing. We knew we'd get called up but you never dwelt on it, you just put it out of your mind and got on with life. We reported the day the King had died so we became not the King's soldiers, but the Queen's soldiers. We did six weeks at Ashton, then went to Formby for two weeks which wasn't much really as it was more of a staging post.

From there we went down to Swindon in Wiltshire and we were there before the battalion came back from Germany. We lived in these mizzen huts with broken windows and we had an open bag which we filled with straw and put on a wire bed. And that was our bed. We had no sheets, pillows, just a blanket on top and that's how it was for about six weeks. Then we were given embarkation leave of twenty-one days and had to report back and landed up at Liverpool docks.

Brian Hough

Although I knew quite a bit about the Korean War because of my family background I have to say that my colleagues in the army knew very little, and I'm not being rude here, but yes, they knew very little. But had you put a map in front of me and asked me to point to Korea I wouldn't have had a clue. I knew it was in the Far East but nothing beyond that. Generally, most of the lads didn't have my background so why should they know. In fact, in the early days I remember reading a newspaper and Korea in our national press was actually spelt with a C and not a K. So even they didn't know about Korea.

Our battalion was predominantly made up of Merseyside lads and the rest were mainly from Manchester, Bolton, towns in the south Lancashire area. There was no rivalry, however, between scousers and Mancs, it was never like that in those days. We got on well. It's only in recent years that this has grown up.

One of my regrets was that I sailed on the 4 June with my battalion and didn't actually take part in the march in Liverpool. When we sailed I was on the ship – I was part of the advance party. We were loading the ship and all these lads were coming aboard after the march through the city and they were gleaming. I was leaning on the rails of the ship, and the pier head and surrounding area was a mass of faces and as the ship moved out from the dockside the band struck up with a popular tune of the day – 'Auf Wiedersehen'. Petula Clark[9] had made a hit of it and they sang it, all these people on the pier head. I'm even emotional now thinking about that. Everyone on the pier head was singing. That was a lasting memory. There was a hand on my shoulder, it was that sergeant who would make my life a hell and he said, 'Come on, we better get things ready for these lads to have their tea.' And he said it so gently I thought, is this really him? So it must have touched him as well.

---

9   Petula Clark was a popular singer and film actress, born 1932.

Ken Hawthorne

I was living in Wallasey with my mum and dad. I expected my calling papers, of course, and was waiting for them. I had just become a fully fledged plumber, aged 21. I had been able to finish my apprenticeship but was then called up on my twenty-first birthday. They didn't waste any time in calling me up. This was February 1951.

I knew the war was going on and although I knew I was going in the army I thought it would be over, so I never really thought about the possibility of going to Korea. Once I was in I thought there was a small possibility but didn't really think it would happen to me. Most of the lads, after they had done their training, went to Germany and most of my mates from here had all gone to Germany, none had gone to Korea. I got my papers a week after my birthday along with a rail warrant to go to Elgin in Scotland where I was met by an army lorry and taken to the Royal Engineers. I had no choice about which regiment I might join and had to go with the Royal Engineers.

Right away we started on infantry training, which was bullying basically, though I can't say as I disliked it. We did various things including water-manship; they had some boats in the bay up there. Fortunately, one of my friends who had gone up a year before looked after all the boats, he was a sort of cocky watchman and did nothing else but looked after the boats for his whole two years. I was at Elgin until June 1951. I didn't particularly like it at the time but it's something I'm glad I went through especially the Korean War part. I then got my posting to the military school of engineering at Chatham and did a metal worker's course there for another six months until January the following year. When we'd finished the course we all looked on the blackboards one day to see where our postings would be. I looked down the postings and it was so and so Germany, so and so Germany, then I came to mine and it said Korea. I nearly died on the spot. I think only two of us went to Korea. I had a quick leave and then I went down south to an embarkation camp where they kitted us out and took all our brass off us and gave us combat uniforms. I liked that as I no longer had to clean everything. We also got commando boots. I was only there a week or so and got our injections to go abroad and then off to the troopship.

I was very surprised because not many people knew there was a war going on and those who did know were fed up with war. But we got a good send-off from Southampton, there were a lot of families there. I was to be a replacement for someone coming home. Most of the time as an engineer I was on my own. I did meet a couple of other lads I had done my training with on the boat.

I went out on the *Empire Fowey*. It was the best and quickest of the troopships at the time although I didn't like it that much. We all had hammocks but they still said that *Fowey* was the best. It was a ship taken off the Germans[10] in the war. But it was overcrowded and all the sleeping on hammocks was under the waterline. Once we got into a warmer climate, however, you could sleep anywhere and lots of the lads slept on deck. I got the job of looking after the ironing room where you could iron uniforms. I had to sweep the floor, put the irons away and then lock the door. It was an officer's job but he had past it over to me. That's what I did all the way out. We went via Gibraltar, Aden, Suez. I was only 22 at the time and I was surprised at how quickly the weather changed, we had left in the freezing cold but once we got into the Med it was so much warmer. I'd never been abroad, nobody had, so it was an adventure in one way. After Gibraltar, we went through the Mediterranean to Suez. We had to stop every few days to resupply with water and food as there were a lot of us on the ship. We weren't allowed off at Suez as there was a spot of trouble, and the infantry mounted machine guns all around the boat when we were there. But the only real trouble was from what were called the bum boats which used to come out and throw ropes up to the troops and try and get soldiers to buy things. They would throw ropes up and sometimes they just took the money and scarpered and we'd be hurling everything at them; beer bottles, anything you could get your hands on.

---

10   The *Empire Fowey* had been built in Hamburg in 1936 as a liner. It was captured after the war and refitted in Belfast in 1945 as a troopship and served in that purpose until 1960 when it was sold. It was scrapped in 1976.

2. WELCOME TO WAR!

'Something seemed to be saying, keep out of here.'

INTRODUCTION

THE VAST MAJORITY of those who ended up in Korea did so via Hong Kong, which was the principal staging post for the war. Hong Kong had long been a British military base with plenty of amenities and training facilities for the conscripts. Almost all the soldiers who spent any time there speak of it in exalted terms. Its principal attraction was that it was cheap. Cigarettes, alcohol and food could be purchased cheaper than almost anywhere. For a few dollars you could enjoy a slap up three-course meal. And while post-war Britain was grey, wet and still recovering from the ravages of war, Hong Kong was sunny, warm and fun. In Britain rationing was still enforced but there was no such rationing in Hong Kong. On the contrary you could buy whatever you wanted. Those who spent more than a few weeks there lapped up the weather and freedom. What's more there wasn't that much square bashing or arduous training. It was fairly relaxed with the hot afternoons often free for sport or whatever.

But for most it didn't last long. After a brief spell of training they were on board a ship bound for Korea. In the final two years of the conflict it was usually Pusan where they docked on the east coast of Korea. And their first memories of Pusan were unanimous – it was the smell. They all described it as appalling. Memories of arriving in Pusan are vivid, not just because of the smell but because this was their first step into the unknown.

But at least there was a warm Hollywood welcome awaiting them on the dockside in Pusan with an American band hammering out the 'St Louis Blues' or some other recognisable tune. Many of the British soldiers spotted that the band were almost all black. For some of the British troops this would have been the first time they had ever encountered black people. Their other memory of Pusan is of the train journey to the front. The trains varied from old American steam locos to more recognisable British steam trains, which had clearly seen better days. The carriages all seem to have been compartments with wooden seats to take about half a dozen people but without any passageway access to other compartments. The journey to the front was slow and painful. There was little food or water and toilet facilities seem to have generally been non-existent. The train would stop and start and seemed to frequently go past the same place on more than one occasion. This may have been an assumption on the part of the troops who were not accustomed to the geography of the land. Whatever, it was not a very pleasant welcome to Korea. But it was fun initially, a good laugh, singing along with the band on the quayside, waving to them, stumbling into the trains, all a bit inexperienced together. It was when they began to get hungry and needed a toilet that things started to degenerate.

When the train had reached a point where it could go no further they were all ushered into trucks and driven to the front line. And when they did arrive at the front line many of them were tired but were pitched into battle almost immediately.

Some of the troops arriving in the early days of the war did so at Inchon on the west coast of Korea and were thrown into some of the fiercest fighting as soon as they arrived.

Other troops made their way to Korea via Kure in Japan which was a further staging post for Korea. The American base there was also a convenient place for rest and recuperation and was used extensively during the course of the war with giant American Skymaster planes regularly flying in hundreds of soldiers for a few days' leave. There was a hospital there as well which treated many war victims. Kure was also close to Hiroshima where the first atomic bomb had been dropped in 1945 and a number of soldiers recalled visiting the city.

By whatever route they arrived, the reality of war soon settled in. Conditions were grim. Those arriving in the winter months soon discovered just how cold it could get and that there was not the adequate clothing or facilities to deal with the freezing conditions. If they arrived thinking that it was to be a great adventure, they soon changed their minds.

Bill Fox

We got there during the night and we didn't see Korea until we got up on deck in the early morning. We could only see the shape of dark hills, no lights. Everyone said nothing, there was a silence, something seemed to be saying, keep out of here. Some of the older soldiers who had seen a lot of service didn't like the look of it, something about it gave you the shivers.

At daybreak we made into the harbour in Pusan and there was an American army band to greet us playing all these catchy tunes of the day. All the Koreans came out as well, and there were lots of handshakes. The band then disappered leaving the quayside very empty. And quiet. We also began to hear rumours that the Chinese were entering the war. Anyway, we stayed there until dusk when all the cheering had long stopped, and began to disembark from the ship. We walked through the sheds and there was this train lined up for us, it was an old type of English locomotive; it looked like it had been out of service for years, it smelt musty and it was puffing and blowing like it wasn't quite right. We piled on and it helped having the regulars with us as they were telling us how to do things; put your bags on first, then get on. And although I hadn't had any education as I had been evacuated during the war and my schooling was a bit lacking, I had learnt in other ways. So, the train eventually started and then it stopped and then it was stop, start all the time.

Jim Lucock

We sailed for Korea in January 1953 from Southampton on the *Astoria*. It was terrible. It was a flat bottomed boat – what an experience! Mind you at that age I didn't worry. I was crying in my sleep at night and fellas were getting letters from home and crying and getting homesick. We'd stopped and the mail had come on and fellas were getting Dear John letters. It was an experience. I'll always remember going through the Med. We went through the Bay of Biscay and it was very, very stormy. I've never been so sick in all my life. We went down the Suez Canal, that was awesome. And then we went into Aden and then Colombo. I was offered little girls there. I was absolutely appalled. Then we went to Singapore. We got really drunk in Singapore. For some reason the six or seven lads I went with all ended up in the ship's nick at the bottom of the boat but I didn't! They were drunk and had been fighting – they were mostly Liverpool lads! And they were in there until we got to Hong Kong. We docked in Kowloon. All these sampans selling stuff and begging. And then we were taken out to the New Territories.

The ship was packed like sardines. In fact, had they been sardines they'd have had the RSPCA out! Going through the South China Sea we hit a typhoon, everything was battened down, everyone was being sick and confined in this small space. It was horrendous, the food was terrible. If there were any rats or cockroaches they would have been too scared to come out.

We were attached to the Royal Norfolk Regiment, who didn't like us. We were stroppy scousers and we called them 'swedes'. I think they thought we had too much to say, we were an unruly bunch of soldiers, we were all national servicemen who didn't want to be there. They didn't give us any training, they just left us alone. Because I was a good shot with the rifle and Bren gun, I was picked for the regimental rifle team and they wanted me to enter the Hong Kong Bisley but they wanted me to wear a cap badge and I said, 'No I'm a Kingsman,' so they wouldn't have me and all the perks I was getting suddenly stopped. I was a Kingsman and proud – still am – proud to be a Kingsman. But sadly my regiment has gone now.

Sgt Major Blood – I always remember his name – came and he said, 'You get your kit ready, you're going on a religious course.' I said, 'Me, on a religious course!' He said, 'Yes,' so I was sent to Hong Kong Island where there was a little hotel. It was wonderful, best food I'd ever had. Basically, we started in a morning, it was more like seminars. I've no idea why they chose me and they were all laughing when I went. I leant a lot about mind over matter and it was very interesting and I've been interested in it ever since. At about 8.30 in the evening a few of us would go out to the South China Fleet Club and have a few ales. We had a fortnight there and had no exams or anything like that. When we came to leave the padre said, 'Nice meting you, are you going home now?' And I said, 'No, were going to Korea.' 'To Korea!' he said, 'I didn't know that.' They were very upset to learn that and especially that nobody had told them. Anyway I went back to the Norfolks then.

So we were back up to the New Territories and then we were told we were going to Korea, but before you go to Korea you're going to Japan. So we were sent to Kure in Japan where we went to a battle school at Hara-Mura, it was a Commonwealth battle school with Canadians, Australians New Zealanders and various British regiments. We were there for a month, maybe six weeks and we had to sign a will and articles of war. It was a bit frightening at first until you got used to the gunfire. One of our lads got killed there. He was called Albert Higham and he was almost 19. You couldn't go to Korea until you were 19. He was shot – friendly fire – while practising at the battle school. We all stopped, knowing there was something wrong, but he was dead. But the army just made us get on with it. He is actually buried in Japan. I'll never forget him.

Then it was back to Kure and two or three days later they said you're going into Korea. So we went on these two ferryboats – *Esan* and *Wosan* – two little boats. There was nowhere to sleep as they were so small. They gave you a hammock but there was nowhere to hang them. We were on there for forty-eight hours and it was appalling. Talk about civil rights, we had no rights. When we landed in Pusan there was an American band to greet us. They were exceptionally smart with fancy coloured scarves. They were all black and were playing the 'St Louis Blues', marching up and down on the quayside. Then they took us to this camp. Two miles off the coast you could smell Pusan. There was no industry there as it's all agricultural. I always remember how barren it was with no trees, but it wasn't until we got there that we found that the smell was human excrement. They used to put it down a well to ferment and then they put it on the paddy fields. I never ate rice for forty years after that but I never told the wife why I did not like rice.

We went to a camp called Seaforth barracks and we had decent food some of the best I had out there. We got as much food as we wanted and proper beds. We must have been there about a week when we got on this train and we were sent north to the line. The carriages on the train just had wooden seats. There were no toilets either and some of the lads tried to sleep on the top of the train. It would stop, we'd get off, then start again. We never washed or shaved and had nothing to eat or drink. Anyhow, we ended up at Seoul. There were all different regiments on the train but when we got there we were taken to the King's. This would be March 1953. The weather was starting to get warmer but the lads who were there were saying it was so cold in the winter. But I never experienced the cold until the end of my stay but the other lads had had a terrible experience.

Ken Hawthorne

The infantry were training all the way, mainly doing shooting practice from the side of the boat. It took almost five weeks, though most of the troopships took six weeks. I had a slow one coming back. Anyhow we called in at Aden, Singapore, Hong Kong and then we went straight up to Jure in Japan. I met up there with three lads on the boat who had done their training with me and we went everywhere together. We arrived in Kure in Japan and were bussed up to the British base there on army lorries. The difference you could see in the towns. Prostitutes were everywhere, some of them even selling daughters. We noticed that and how strange it was. We only had a short stay there as they were just building the battle school where all British troops would go. I didn't get much out of that. Being an engineer they gave us a lot of military stuff on types of mines. It was then that I started to get very frightened.

Then I had the most frightening night of my life. We went over to Korea in a tiny ship although it was a troopship and the weather was atrocious. I'm not kidding you but everybody on the ship was sick, everybody. I found that if I went up to a room where you could see the sea from I wasn't sick but when you went down below the waterline, it was just appalling. You looked out and one moment you were above everything, then you were in a hollow with a complete wall of water around you. It was frightening and I was glad to get there. It was terrifying and I really didn't think we'd get there.

The first thing you remember when you get to Korea is the smell at Pusan. It was terrible. I was there one night and I met Bill Speakman[11] in the NAFFI. He was on his way home to get his medal from the Queen, I had a chat with him about his experiences but that was a bit depressing as I began to realise what it was all about.

The following morning we boarded a train. The three lads who I had been with in the engineers and who I did my training with, all got port jobs and they left me at Pusan so I went up on my own on the train with an infantry regiment, though I can't remember which one. The train didn't go very quickly, it went up to the back of the line. It took all day to get there and the sights when we went through Seoul was absolute devastation, the war had gone through it several times and there wasn't a building that hadn't been touched. Hardly anything had been left standing. This would be the end of February 1952, a year after I had joined up.

I was with another lad who I didn't know; we were replacing people who were going home, so it was different to the infantry who were moving en masse, altogether. We were moving singly. A chap picked me up at the railhead and took me right up to the back of the front. We were in tents at the time just behind the line and I got a bit of a shock as I didn't think I'd go up there so quickly. He showed me to a place in the tent which was to be mine. There was a bit of a bed made out of four pieces of wood, standing on boxes with signal wire across. I improved this myself a couple of days later when I made another. There was also a box

---

11   Sergeant Bill Speakman, born 1927, was awarded the VC in November 1951 for gallantry at United Hill in Korea.

by the side of the bed to put your personal belongings in. I felt strange and quite frightened and then when it went dark all hell was let loose and I didn't know where I was, pretty close to the front, I thought. I listened and heard a young Chinese lady talking to me and asking me to surrender. They used to put a radio on at the top of the hill and pumped this propaganda out. I got settled in and was making friends over the next couple of days. The engineers were working on the roads at the back of the line. We did this, repairing them for the next few weeks after the cold winter. I'd been there about three night and I was on guard one morning and an officer was jumping into a jeep, and he said, 'Hop in and ride gunshot, bring your rifle.' I said I had to wake the next man to take over guard duty from me and he said, 'That doesn't matter, just jump in.' I think he was just showing me what was going on. He took me up the front and when I looked at it and saw the trenches, bunkers and the valley below and the hills the other side, I thought, god, this is a hell of a place to be.

Roy Cox

When we got into Korean waters off Inchon, they said, 'Man your stations!' The Yanks were putting on helmets and so on, and they issued us with ammunition and hand grenades. I looked out of the hatch, there was these landing barges going up overhead and they started the engines while it was up in the air and then it drops into the water and is away within seconds. We got in the landing barges, I had a Sten gun, magazines, two grenades and they gave me a box of Bren gun ammunition which was as heavy as hell – and I get down in the landing craft with this on my shoulders and as soon as the boat was full, off we went and we all went into shore at the same time. We were landing at Inchon on the west coast.

Once we got settled in we were bedded down near a lake and it was all pebbles and stones and I thought, I'm not going to get much sleep here. We were just lying on a groundsheet and trying to sleep like that. The Americans were about but we were never really with them. It was much later on that we had more contact with them. The major said – Major Phillips it was – said the battalion is going to attack the Chinese in the morning, so we'll be up at 4 a.m. The road that we went up was more of a track than a road and it ran parallel to the front line. Our battlion was up there and I was going up there in a jeep with the major, but the major turned off too early, and I'm sat in the back with a signaller here with a Sten gun and the major there. I got a bit suspicious when the major suddenly said, 'When you go around this bend change into third.' And I thought why, he's on the wrong road. Then all of a sudden I saw all these flashing lights and I thought, Blackpool! All these lights, you see. Anyway, they weren't lights, they were bullets flying everywhere, one went through the canvas of the jeep. The major said, 'Shoot back,' and the major's trying to get his pistol out and I've got a Sten gun pointing here, just by the major's face and between the signaller and I nearly hit him. 'What the bloody hell are you doing?' he shouts.

The Chinese had tricks, you know. They would put barriers on the road and when you got there you'd start to turn back, but the Chinese would have then gone and crept up and put barriers behind you so that you were trapped. They did that a lot with the Americans.

Bill Hurst

We sailed on the HMS *Devonshire* which was an old troopship carrier, and we set sail for Hong Kong. I think we were six weeks on board. We did a lot of training on the boat, marching up and down, doing firing practice with rifles and Bren guns over the side of the boat. We eventually landed in Hong Kong at the end of June, then did six more weeks training there at Kowloon, on the border with communist China. We mainly did patrols, climbing up the hills and so forth. At one period we were attached to the Gurkhas and they gave us mules for carrying guns up the hills. It was just border patrols, no fighting. A lot of Chinese were trying to get across the border into Hong Kong, so if we caught them we just sent them back.

Then we set sail for Korea and landed there on the 4 or 5 September 1952. When we arrived they put us on a train at Pusan to go to the front. It took us nearly three days. We were getting shot at and then they put us in these American trucks that were driven by black American soldiers.

There wasn't a white American among them and there must have been fifteen, sixteen, seventeen trucks.

At the end of September we moved on to Yongdong. I was 19 then and was sent into the front line. I was in the front line for three months and one week, I did this extra one week so that the Black Watch could have New Year off and celebrate their hogmanay. Then we were in a rest period for a while doing some more training, mock battles with the Americans, and then we moved back again into the front line. In May we landed at the Hook, where some of the most fierce fighting ever took place. They reckon there were more shells landed on Hook than even in the First World War. Day and night there was shelling. The Duke of Wellington's was on it, the Black Watch, the King's and they all held the Chinese back, it was never taken.

When the war ended on 17 July 1953, we were in the front line. We were firing red, white and blue into the air and mortars as well. The Chinese appeared from out of their trenches and came to the wire and some of the lads went and talked to them as best they could, exchanging cigarettes and so on. We came out of the front line and went back into reserve, and in October the King's Regiment took over and we set sail back to Hong Kong. We did more training and parades there. And then at Christmas, New Year, I set sail for home and arrived back in January. I'd been away for two years and had had hardly any leave.

Jim Houghton

We got to Pusan and as soon as we got off the ship there was a train waiting for us all and that took us as far as Seoul – you couldn't go any further on the train. It took twenty-four hours because the trains ran on a single track most of the way. There was all wooden seats as well. When we got there we were in this camp for just a few hours and then lorries took us to an assembly area up north and that's where I met up with the Northumberland's. We were stationed north of the Imjin River. Most of my time was spent just north of the Imjin.

Roy Cox

We had a new CO. The first one was only there about two or three months and he was the only one who went back without being awarded the DSO. Anyrate, the sergeant said to me, 'You're going to be his wireless operator, I think you've got the same sense of humour,' though I'm not sure what he meant by that. So I became his wireless operator and had to follow him everywhere. Well he was a good CO, and always visited the positions. One day I was trotting behind him and he was with a bloke in the army gymnastics, who did all the regimental physical training and the CO had him as bodyguard so we went off to visit one of the companies. I'm walking along with a 31 Set on my back and suddenly I'm flat on my face. 'What the hell am I doing,' I thought. The CO asked if I was all right. 'I think so,' I replied. 'Didn't you hear it coming?' 'No sir, I had my earphones on.' It was a shell or mortar, and I caught the full force of it. There was a hole in the wireless set this big and there was shrapnel bouncing around in there! That was my first lucky escape.

Bill Hurst

We were called Kingsmen. I was a driver, I drove in Hong Kong, and when I got to Hong Kong I was attached to 'C' Company. We were all in trenches, at machine guns, Bren guns, all of us would be in the trench, in the front line, ready for action, particularly in the morning as the Chinese always seemed to attack at that time in the morning.

Most of the time it was boring, just listening and looking out. There wasn't constant attacking, except at the Hook. That was constant. The Chinese really wanted to take that hill as it was high. You'd think in the front line you'd be firing all the time but you weren't. The line never moved much. You might progress a bit, take a position then you might be forced back and so it went on. The first time we were on a position called Yung Dong, then we had another position, I think it was 146 or 126. Sometimes we had to take ammunition down to another company, or food or water and we would be helped by Koreans who were called Gooks, they used to have these big frames on their backs with all the stores, cans of petrol and so. We had about twenty of them and three of us would go with them, one at the front, one at the back and one in the middle. We'd go out in the middle of the night with them, making our way to the forward position, about quarter of a mile further out. We'd stop halfway to count them all just to make sure none of them had disappeared. When we got there we'd unload everything and then load up with stuff to bring back.

Personally I didn't feel scared, frightened. I just got on with the job that I had to do. The worst time for me was the winter, it was that cold you could never get warm. You'd be stood in your position and you couldn't go walking about to try and keep warm. You were stuck there for two hours. You couldn't make a noise, smoke or anything and it was 35°F below and more at times. You couldn't touch metal. If you did it would take all the skin off your fingers. The motor transport would all be parked up and they'd all be in one compound and you had to start them all up every hour just to keep them going. Inside the hutch we had little stoves. We had a jerrycan with a tube running from it and it had a little tap. You turned it on and lit it. It was petrol and it got hot and kept you warm but you couldn't have the flame too big otherwise it might start a fire.

There would be two or three of us in the hutch. We made bunks with steel pickets which were hammered into the ground and we could make beds that way. We made a frame with the pickets and there was plenty of telephone wire around so we'd wrap it around like this to make a bed and that's how we used to sleep. We always slept in everything and we never took our boots off. We had a big sleeping bag, so we might take our boots off then and get into the sleeping bag fully clothed. We never had a bath but always had a wash and a shave in the morning in the hutch. We would boil water, and use that. In the winter you could boil the water, take it outside, put it down and in a minute it would be frozen, no kidding.

All we did was sleep in the hutch, clean the rifles, do our washing, then hang it up inside the hutch near the stove. Most of the hutches were facing back, so mortars would come over. Shells would hit the doorway and sometimes we had to dig people out, most of them were back facing. If you weren't on stand-to you'd have a sleep for four hours.

We lived on C rations for four months. This was a box with four meals in it. Beans and sausages, corned beef hash and a pudding. Also you got a long tin with soup in it and you had a thing running through the middle and you lit it and it would heat the soup up. So if you were out on a listening patrol – maybe half a mile away – you could take it with you. You had a radio with you as well so that if you saw anything you could report it and they'd send a flare up first, and if they saw anything the mortars would start, boom, boom, boom.

The first time I went in I was three months in the front line, three months living in the hutch. They used to have what they called bath times; a fifteen hundredweight lorry would come up, usually driven by me, and take so many men down to the shower unit which was away from the front line. We'd just drop them off, you'd get showered, put on clean clothes and everything and then we'd take them back. It was a big tent with a shower unit in it, you might get a haircut as well. This would happen about once a month. But you had to wash your own clothes, underpants especially, long johns. It wasn't easy to dry them but we had these heaters in the hutch and you would hang your clothes up as best you could and hoped they would dry. You had three pairs of everything – three pairs of underpants, three pairs of vests, three pairs of long johns, three or four pairs of socks.

We got a tin of fifty cigarettes every time we got our C rations, or it may have been twenty, and we got our C rations virtually every day. We used to play cards for the cigarettes, some didn't smoke, so would use them. Some of the lads smoked like chimneys.

Jim Houghton

I was with the Northumberland's then and went to Korea in August 1951. I was there with the Northumberland's until October when I was then attached to the Leicestershire Regiment, the Royal Leicester's, officially from 1 November. We didn't get any special training for Korea, it was just the ordinary infantryman training. I went out on the troopship, it was one day short of six weeks, it was called the *Devonshire*. We were all in hammocks, it was a very old ship. We stopped at Port Said, Aden, Colombo, and we had route marches at all these places, then Singapore, Hong Kong and Kure in Japan. This was where the main British base was with hospitals and so on.

We didn't do much on the troopship on the way out – just hanging around. We had the odd lecture or something but in between you didn't do much at all. There was a bit of gambling going on but there shouldn't have been. In fact, when we sailed they only gave us £1 so you couldn't gamble, but one fella – he wasn't with us – finished up with eighty-odd pounds. That was a fortune in those days. I don't play cards, so I wasn't interested.

Before I went I'd heard about Korea and read about it but you didn't really take it all in, I was only 19 then. You go to any war cemetery and look at the graves and the lads are all just 19–23 years old. Anyone older than that has got more sense. It's a young man's game.

I was only in Japan for about six days and then we went overnight by train to the other side of Japan. We were in an American camp there but we couldn't go out and then at night they took us on a small boat over to Pusan in Korea. They wouldn't go over during the daytime, it was at night when it was dark as it was too dangerous to take the troopship across so we went in these small ships – about a hundred of us in each boat.

Bill Hurst

When we arrived they put us on a train at Pusan to go to the front. It took us nearly three days. We were getting shot at and then they put us in these American trucks that were driven by black American soldier. There wasn't a white American among them and there must have been fifteen, sixteen, seventeen trucks.

I had as little as possible to do with the Americans as I could. I could tell you a few tales but I'm not going there. The only time we dealt with the Yanks was when we were moving, going in convoys. The Yanks had the GMCs (General Motor Co.) – they were big. Our three tonners couldn't carry a lot of troops, so when we were moving, it was with the Americans.

The only other time I met the Americans was when we were having rest and recuperation and we went to Japan. They'd pick so many of us and we'd go to Japan for seven days or whatever. We had to go to Seoul airport to get on the big American Globemasters. You'd queue up to get on and then you'd get a big black MP would put his hand up and say, 'You've got to stop there, there's some US troops here just come out of the front line.' We said, 'Well where do you think we've just come from?' We were all nice and clean shaved because our thing was that you had to have a shave in the morning whether its freezing, snowing or what, you have a shave and a wash. But they didn't and they'd come straight out of the front line without washing; they had beards and looked untidy. I don't know that the British soldiers had a high regard for the Americans. Put it this way, the British never lost any positions out there apart from the Gloucester's, and that was because there was a big push by the Chinese, probably 50,000 of them pushing. They just got taken over and most of the Gloucester's were captured.

All the time we wondered what the hell we were doing out there. But we were British soldiers and you do as you are told, you don't say no, they tell you that when you join. But what can you do.

Ivan Williams

Because I had done this sound ranging course I became a surveyor sound ranger, and the regiment called the 15th Observation Battery Royal Artillery was stationed on Hong Kong Island and they were going to be sent to Korea to do sound ranging and they were short of personnel, so people like myself who had been distributed around the gun regiments were suddenly called back to boost numbers of the 15th Obs. I was just told one day by the sergeant, 'You probably never read orders so,' he said, 'I'll tell you, you're going up the sharp end,' which was the slang for Korea, of course, 'and you're going in the morning. So get your kit together.' And off I went. I was a bit shocked, my pleasant life was coming to an end but other parts of the regiment had gone. I'd been to a drumhead service shortly before with a group of people going out but I never thought that I'd be one of them because the regiments I was with were not destined to go to Korea. So I think I was unpleasantly surprised. But you soldier on.

I transferred to the 15th Observation Battery, as it's known, about two months before we left. We were brought up to speed on surveying, which I'd done nothing on for nearly twelve months, and sound ranging. We were allocated to the sections we were working in. There were two sets of sections, a left and a right section with a headquarters behind them and we went out before Christmas. We were transferred onto an American freighter, this is 1951. The funny thing about it is that the truce is on at this time, they are already talking and there was an accord that if troops were replaced they had to be replaced like with like, so the movement of our sound ranging battery was against that accord. We were just a battery of the Royal Artillery as far as everyone was concerned. But in all truth we shouldn't have been allowed to go there because we were a specialist unit, but rules are there to be broken.

We arrived in Inchon two or three days before Christmas 1951. We went by an American armed freighter. We slept in the hold, which was not as unpleasant as it sounds as it was next to the engine room, so was quite warm. We were accepted by the Yanks with some curiosity, 'We got a boat-load of goddam Limeys here!'

When we got to Inchon we disembarked over cargo nets over the side of the boat which was going up and own and we had a full kitbag, and rifles slung around us, so we climbed down this net. I'd never been on a cargo net in my life before. I was very relieved to hear an American voice say, 'You're down Limey, put your feet down.' But one of our lads fell off the net and broke his leg and was put back on the same boat and sent back to Hong Kong! His trip to Korea lasted as long as it took him to fall from the net to the quayside.

From there we were sent by lorries to a transit camp at Inchon. At that time the line must have been 10 or 15 miles north of Inchon. So we did about three or four days there and got kitted out. Many have complained about the kit they had but we had the very best because we had the full American winter gear which was very good indeed. We did about three days there and then we were transferred up to the line, first of all to a base camp about 10 miles back and then to an operations centre which was about 2 miles back from the front. This is December 1951/January 1952. It was in the winter and was bitterly cold. The front line was fairly static all the time I was there. It was a sort of trench warfare. The trenches weren't continuous, the hills were defended all around as opposed to a continuous line of defences, so the valleys were open season, but all the time I was there I don't think there were any major incursions into our line or their line.

So I was there with the right section of 15th Obs to do sound ranging with our whole object in life being to try and locate the enemy mortar positions because they had a 3-inch mortar which was causing a lot of trouble all along the front. And although we had spotter planes all over the lines, a spotter plane could only see them if they fired because they were easily dismountable and they only brought them out for a short period of time. They would then put them into a cave or a hole in the ground so that the spotter planes had difficulty in finding the locations. The idea of sending the battery out was to try and locate them. And that was our reason to be there. We were in action shortly after we got there. It didn't take us long to set up.

The idea of sound ranging is that you have a line of four microphones a set distance apart, maybe 150 yards apart, in a straight line and they are all surveyed very accurately and each of these microphones has a landline to HQ which was about 2 miles back and these microphones are about half a mile from the front line. To activate the set-up you had to have someone who heard the sound before the microphones did, so we had an advance post on the front line. We called it an AP, an advance post, but for anybody else it was more like an observation post. The lines from the microphone were fed into what was then quite a high-tech system. It was a recorder that had four pens like a seismograph and it burnt an image with a high voltage pen onto metal back paper. The paper measured the difference in the intervals the sound hit the various microphones. You could then plot, and by plotting – there was then a formula – and you could then plot a line from the gap in each microphone and the wires. And where the three wires met, that was where the location was. This could be done very quickly. The starter was the man in the AP who had to press a button to start the recorder going before the sound wave hit the microphones, and then the recorder was switched off at the other end when the film had finished and the sound was like a little kick on each line. And it had various characteristics so if there was more than one bang going you could pick up a particular one because it had a characteristic sound wave.

Our duty pattern was that we did one week in the advance post doing two-hour shifts, two hours on and four off, for a week, and then two weeks at the command centre at the receiving end of all this information. We were all trained to do every job. At the AP there was a signaller and a surveyor on three shifts, so there were three surveyors and three signallers, and at the other end there must have been about another dozen surveyors, signallers, drivers, backup staff. There was a landline from the AP to the command centre, a telephone line and, besides, the line that controlled the microphones. There was also a wireless and I've often wondered why as we used the wireless a lot and didn't use codes, it was open and when information got back to our command centre there was then another line back to headquarters which must have been 12 or 15 miles back and they passed on the locations to the gun regiments who would try and take them out as quickly as they could. And that's what I did for six months.

I suppose some of it was dangerous as there was all sorts going overhead both ways. On the front line we were with the local infantry, at first we were with the Canadians. The infantry people were there all the time and we had a bunker at the backside of the hill. Four of us slept while the other two were in the AP; the Canadians manned the front line all the time. They had their own observation post next to ours and the defence of the position was in their hands.

I was on Hill 159 at first then moved after two months to Hill 355, for what reason I don't know. The thing is that when you are there you have no real idea where you are apart from your immediate surroundings, but I had no idea of the relative positions to anything. We were out of sight of the sea and there were no real landmarks, but we moved position just the once during the time I was there. I actually left Korea from Hill 355.

I think we constantly wondered, 'What on earth are we doing here'. We came into contact with very few Koreans. The only Korean I ever really saw was a lad in the cookhouse whose name was Kim – I think all Koreans were named Kim. There was a ROK (Republic of Korea) division situated behind the lines and occasionally when we were going back to our rear headquarters we would drive past their camp but we never saw any of them. Once a party of villagers came across the lines. How they managed that I don't know. We were told to stand-to as we could see these villagers.

The head of the villagers had national dress on with a high hat. They had escaped from North Korea and had crossed the Chinese lines and our lines. How on earth they managed it I don't know. We just waved them through and they disappeared. Mostly they were women and children and they were the only Koreans I saw. The only Chinese I saw were through binoculars. At the advance posts you could see them just as well as they could see us. Unlike some of the people I now meet I never got involved in anything in close quarters. As I say the line was static.

We had no interest in the politics of the war. I think the main thing was keeping in one piece and doing the job as best you could. We were very disdainful of the peace talks. We could see it from both positions, the searchlights from the peace talks at night where they were talking, and of course they're still talking. We thought they were wasting their time.

The other strange thing was that the King died while I was there, George VI and we were taken – at a lot of trouble – back behind the lines to swear allegiance to the new monarch, Queen Elizabeth. That surprised me. Of course, when we joined we all swore allegiance to the King and now the King was dead. It was quite a formal little parade. Some high-ranking officer told us that the King had died and we had to repeat after him … our allegiance to the Queen. And that was the nearest to the politics that we ever got.

The Americans were next door to us with a similar sound ranging set-up. We would barter trade things with them. God bless them. They had the best food, clothes. We had a cookhouse at the back and we had a chef who could make bread – he must have been the only chef who could – so we had an abundance of bread and cheese and we would swop it with the Americans for peanut butter, Hershey bars and tinned fruit. In fact, Hershey bars were like currency. We had chocolate but it was Boer War stuff. It was dark chocolate but the Hershey bars were a nice chocolate. We traded with the Americans and got on well with them. But they didn't like the Canadians. They hated them. They called us the Limeys; they never knew our names, Limey if you were on your own, Limeys if more than one.

The WVS also gets forgotten about. When I drew my hat out of the bag, I went on leave and there were two WVS ladies there to meet me. They must have been in their thirties, I guess. Now they didn't have to be there.

They had volunteered and their whole object in life was to make us feel at home. Now we had to be there but they didn't and the conditions they were in were just as bad as ours. It was just as cold as it was in Inchon. Since leaving Hong Kong I hadn't seen a woman of any description. It was quite a shock to see these ladies. I'm sure that they don't get the plaudits they should. I suspect they are in every battle theatre. They did their best to be mum, sweetheart and daughter to us. They were just company. They never seemed to sleep, always wore their green uniform. It was only afterwards that I thought about it. They weren't safe, there was no guarantee the line would stay where it was, they were only 2 or so miles behind the line.

Peter C Le P Jones

We landed at Pusan in South Korea to be greeted by a hysterical, noisy welcome from the Koreans and an American band of some doubtful ability as musicians, but certainly not lacking in enthusiasm. The Argylls disembarked but there was much difficulty keeping the sailors from joining us and at least one sailor was found by the naval police hiding under a seat – they wanted to join their army friends.

As I remember it, the journey to the front line was not far, but took rather a long time due to the unwillingness of the engine driver to go more than short distances and then go to sleep. He eventually had to be forcibly made to continue by an officer standing with a drawn gun to persuade him. At the end we finished up in an apple orchard, with the most delicious apples that could be picked from where we slept on the ground. The next morning everyone who had eaten the apples had upset stomachs and it was discovered by our medical officer that the apples had been sprayed with arsenic against insects – removal of the powder relieved the problem. This was a short break before business began.

Our first position was on a hill beside the Naktong River, which overlooked a road running alongside the river. The enemy (Gooks, as they became known) were on the other side of the river well within small arms (rifle and machine gun) range. Our arrival at this point was to take over from an American unit.

At the dead of night my unit, 'C' Company, reached this position by a somewhat circuitous, dangerous and not recommended route – we had got ourselves lost. By moving down no-man's-land along the road between the Americans and Gooks (North Koreans) who held positions over the river, we were in considerable danger from both sides. This was all something we did not realise fully until later (what price the fog of war) and was done with considerable luck and all without attracting the enemy who were some two/three hundred yards away.

We eventually found where we should be. The Argylls, who were keeping quiet as is normal, were suddenly met by the Americans – all hell let loose with great welcome greetings being shouted mainly by the black American troops who made up the majority of the unit. The object was not to let the enemy know what was going on and the greeting certainly frightened the Argylls who did not usually conduct war in this way.

Soon we were to discover that American combat units (equivalent to our battalions) were in many cases a very undisciplined lot, but their Airborne, Marines and some combat units were excellent. One American was heard to call in a loud voice, down into a dip in the ground, 'Who dat down there?' and the reply, 'Who dat up there calling who dat down there?' The enemy must have heard this, as they machine-gunned in our general direction and the Americans left rapidly. Our platoon and one other took up positions at the top of the hill, while another platoon took up positions at a location nearer the bottom.

There was much patrolling and a good deal of exchange of fire. One patrol lost two dead, with Captain Neil Buchanan and his batman both badly wounded, managing to bravely give covering fire to allow the rest of the patrol to withdraw with several wounded.

During the next two nights the 'Gooks' sent patrols against our Vickers machine guns within the lower platoon's position. They wounded some men on the first night, but on the second night when they returned just before dawn no one fired until the light grew stronger. Then the sergeant ordered them to fire and the 'Gooks' lost ten dead and several more were seen to be wounded. This was all teaching us about the 'Gook' and was to stand us in good stead for the future. After some two weeks we were relieved. Next started what was to be very much the story of Korea;

climbing in trucks, travelling with tanks as escorts, moving forward and clearing locations of enemy and then on again.

Terry Moore

So we sailed for Korea. I never felt unhappy about that. It wasn't in my nature. I wasn't married and I felt it was what men had to do in those days. However, a lot of the reservists who were called up were ordinary men who were married and had children. When we had casualties we had to write to the mother of children, not just the mother of a son who had died, to explain that a father had gone. The average age of our brigade was older than the average age of an infantry brigade in the previous 1939–45 war. So the average age was 23, 24 because of them being reservists, more married men and, of course, more orphans.

We landed in Korea in the November so we probably sailed early October 1950. I can't remember the name of the ship, it may have been one of the empire boats, but it had been a liner and was now a troopship and it had some rearrangement done with sandbags on the deck. When we were sailing through the Mediterranean, I think they were worried about air attacks because we mounted Bren guns on the aft of the ship in case of air attack while going through the Med.

We had some fun in Aden. We came back to the boat rather drunk and one of the Irish soldiers was ascending the ladder – we were anchored out in the bay a bit. He got to the top of the ladder and an officer said to him, 'You're filthy dirty, get down below and get washed.' So he just jumped off the boat and into the sea, swam around the ship and came back up! We went into Aden, Colombo, Hong Kong and then Pusan. We did rifle drills, had lectures, even a route march in a desert somewhere. Officers received info about the country we were going to. We were told it was about the size of the UK but had only 32 miles of tarmac in it. But when we got there we discovered that the American tanks had destroyed that too. But they never really talked to us about the war and what it was about. It was discussed below ranks but we never discussed the political side of the war at all. The main interest for us was the half a dozen nurses on the boat!

We got to Pusan and were greeted by the inevitable American jazz band, marching up and down playing 'St Louis Blues'. Lovely stuff. And then we shipped out of Pusan to I know not where and we started to get used to the country and the chilliness that pervaded it. It wasn't quite the height of winter, but within a month there was snow everywhere.

We moved up south of the capital city and it was probably December when we first went into the line but we never saw an awful lot of action. But then the Chinese came into the war and there was quite an assault, running backwards by the Americans who came flooding back and eventually said we've got to stop here. And in January they came flooding down again and our brigade on 3 and 4 January was engaged in its first action which saw quite a few casualties in our battalion, the Ulster Rifles, and quite a few in the Northumberland Fusiliers.

I was a lieutenant at this time, on the front line. We never had trenches at first because the ground was so hard you couldn't dig. The trenches came later when the ground thawed. So you just put something down and slept on it. We would raid the villages that had been destroyed and take the straw from the straw roofs and put this down to lie on – hence all the bugs that made us itch and scratch. That was how we kept warm. The small rivers were frozen so anyone who wanted to could wander across them in the night, so if anyone wanted to infiltrate you all they had to do was walk across the river. You couldn't guard every inch of it. The front line wasn't dug in and it was not defined. So we were very exposed and because the Koreans and Chinese aren't daft they didn't have a front line either and were equally exposed so they also tended to sleep in old ruined houses or under straw. It was all a bit of a dream, almost a nightmare really.

We came across the Americans although we were not with them as such. We never had any transport of our own – trucks and such things – so if we ever wanted to go any distance the Americans supplied transport and that was our main point of contact with them. They had an annoying habit though which happened in the 3/4 January battle. We were told that they were behind us, about a mile away, but in our phased withdrawal we discovered that they had disappeared into the night and we had to walk.

We came across other UN forces though quite frequently. The Turks were nice people. I remember later on when things thawed and we were out of the line, we arranged a football match with the Turks. We were taking over an area they had held – there were some houses on it – and when we got there the Turks were busy cleaning it. They had broken branches off trees and were using them as brushes to sweep up and remove all the dirt from the place. They were good people. We also had the Belgians and they were the ones we mainly came into contact with.

While we were on the front line we were fluid. The Americans would shell a place, then get in their wagons and rush north, but eventually we took our positions on what was the 38th Parallel which became the line of the truce. And it was there that the Imjin River battle took place where the Gloucester's fought and had so many casualties.

It was seven months before I got any leave and then I got my five days in Tokyo with Tony Trevor Roper, brother of the historian.[12] We stayed, as everyone did, at the Australian officers leave hotel, a lovely, famous hotel, where we were entertained admirably and fed. The first night we went there we both went straight to our room, and the first thing we did we had a shower and collapsed on our beds. I woke in the morning to giggling and there were two little Chinese girls who had brought tea to us.

The only aerial bombardment was by the Americans! They landed some napalm on us one day because we were sitting on a hill and they were flying in strafing us with napalm. This plane came flying over and started strafing us and a lot of our incendiaries were going towards him so he overloaded his napalm about 50 yards ahead of us and he got the hell out of it. He was obviously worried about getting hit and didn't want to be hit himself with a load of napalm on board, so he just got rid. It hit some of our soldiers and they got badly burned. The Americans were perhaps not as disciplined as the British were at that time. They bombed where they shouldn't. After that the war settled down a bit.

---

12   Hugh Trevor Roper, 1914–2003, Professor of Modern History, Oxford, made a life peer in 1979.

George Stirland

I was in barracks at the time and nearly missed Korea. I was in the field guns crew who do all the Royal Tournaments. I was in that and normally being a member of that stopped all drafts as it was so prestigious but this time they said no, they didn't have enough men for Korea. When we got on the troopship the HMS *Devonshire* to go out, there were three or four full crews plus all the army men, RAF, Marines.

I went out on *Devonshire* in August 1951. We were going to the China station for two and a half years, but as Korea was there we spent all our time out there. China station was in Hong Kong. We joined HMS *Cockade* in Hong Kong and that was the ship I spent all my time on. We then went on to Japan. We couldn't land in Korea so our base was in Japan in Sasebo or Kure.

The main thing we did was to guard the carriers. In the Pacific in World War Two, the only airfields were carriers, there were no airfields on land. When a carrier is out at sea it's not alone, it always has two or three destroyers around it because there would also be submarines around. You cover it all the time. I never saw any submarines, they would of course be Chinese or Russian subs but I never saw any. We stayed up the coast from Sasebo for a month and then back to Sasebo, three or four days in Sasebo, refuel, re-ammo and then out again, same thing. Ships were coming back and going out all the time. We were with the United Nations and we had Europeans with us. We covered the west coast of Korea, the Americans had the east coast, they had enough ships and didn't need us. I was on *Cockade*, a C-class destroyer, for two and a half years. It had gone out there at the end of World War Two and stayed out there until it came home for scrap. It was a rough ship. Mind you, we were in our twenties. It was grim though. They weren't built for the Arctic and all the ice and we had a lot of ice. At night all the condensation in the cabins froze and by morning there was that much ice on the bulkheads. We slept in hammocks then and you slept anywhere. You were allocated a place and we were in the mess, some were in passageways. There'd be twenty blokes, tables, some lockers for your kit. But there could also be a passageway going through. The food was grim as well.

I've never seen as many cockroaches. We used to get the food, we'd have four sacks of spuds in our mess and white bread and after a couple of weeks at sea the water would get in and a loaf that size would finish up an inch or so. The cook would then start baking bread. You get one slice a day. The cockroaches, the ship was full of them. They got behind the trunking. There was insulation but they used to get behind it and they came out at night. You'd have a sack of spuds then someone would switch a light on and suddenly the bulkhead would be black with them all disappearing up into the trunking and everywhere. You didn't see much of them during the day because they didn't come out. But the spuds would be eaten inside with just the skin left. I can't remember seeing any rats though. They probably would have gone in the stew anyway! Cockroaches were the biggest thing. When we went into Singapore they deloused the entire boat.

If we were at sea we were at action stations, then after an hour they would switch around, some manning guns, at engine room and so on. There would always be so many guns manned. At dusk, we'd all be at action stations until it went dark and then we were at cruising station. We didn't see much action though.

Eric Peters

We were the first British troops into Korea, us and the Middlesex. Then the Australians joined us and we became the first Commonwealth brigade, the 27th Commonwealth Brigade. We went to Pusan and were fighting within twenty-four hours. There's a 30-mile perimeter around Pusan. We were taken off the boat and put onto trains, they were really rough trains, rackety things, it was a poor country. And that was when the Yanks bombed us.

We went up the first hill, we were lucky, we were 'A' Company and we took it. The next morning across the valley we see 'B' and 'D' Company going up the next hill. We're sitting on the top. We had dug in our trenches and we were watching. They're fighting and then the planes come over and start bombing and strafing them. Then they strafed us but only killed one person in our platoon – Paddy Dempsey. He's in the trench with Digger Nixon who comes from Wrexham and there wasn't a mark on Digger but Paddy was blown to bits. These were the Americans. They hadn't napalmed us but they had napalmed the other two hills, they thought they were North Koreans. They killed 35, I think, all British. This was well before the Gloucester's were all killed, they hadn't arrived. We got so far up and then they flew us to Inchon and we advanced then to within 17 miles of the Manchurian border. We'd lead one day, then the Yanks the next and the Middlesex, then us again, we'd leapfrog each other. The Aussies had a lot of bad luck, they always seemed to hit something, seemed to lose a lot. We didn't lose so many, though we did lose our platoon commander one day.

We'd only be in the trench for a day or so as we were advancing all the time. At times there was hardly any opposition, just a few snipers. But at Sariwong we had a big do. The Koreans were moving down towards a crossroad and we were coming down from another road. They waved to us, shouting, 'Ruskie, Ruskie,' they thought we were Russians, then it suddenly clicked and they opened fire. All the guns were firing. We didn't lose anybody but they lost a lot.

When we got to Inchon, the Chinese came into the war and we went back fast, a lot faster than when we had come. We were on tanks and we had to keep walking around them, your feet were getting burnt on the exhaust. We never stopped. This was the big Chinese advance. MacArthur was sacked and Ridgway[13] took over. He said we stop here, not going any further, and we began to make our own gains until winter set in. During the winter we stopped, nothing moved. MacArthur wanted to bomb China,[14] all the bridges, armament depots and so on, but we were never aware of this at the time, not until a long time later.

---

13   General Matthew Ridgway (1895–1993) took over from General MacArthur in April 1951 and became responsible for resurrecting the United Nations war effort.

14   General MacArthur had drawn up a plan for a nuclear attack on North Korea and China and was pushing for its implementation. President Harry Truman, strongly backed by the British Prime Minister Clement Attlee, opposed the plan and MacArthur was controversially sacked from his position.

We had Yankee gear. Much better than ours; they had these hoods with fur on them. Our gear left your ears exposed. Our lads knew how to fight a war. But not the Yanks, we'd go up a hill to see if anyone was there but not the Yanks, they'd bomb it to hell before anyone went up.

I had only been there for two months and I became a corporal again. I didn't want it. But it was more money and I was with a different sergeant major who was a smashing man. We came out in May or June 1951, I was there almost a year. I was then shipped back to Hong Kong and did another eighteen months there. No infantrymen did two tours, just the one tour. But if you were miles back serving in huts you could do half a dozen winters. We were only ever dug into a trench for short periods, always moving on. It wasn't until later when there was a stalemate that they were dug into the trenches for long periods. We were under American orders as well although these orders would be relayed to our brigadier. But they fed us and gave us gun support, etc.

People never talked to us about why we were there, we just saw it as a fight against communism, simple as that. We used to see prisoners being marched back. The only time we saw the Chinese was when we shot them. But not prisoners of war, we had nothing to do with them. If we captured anyone they were shipped back.

I was married and the wife came out to Hong Kong. I got married under special licence at Heswall church as they knew I was going to go to Hong Kong. Anyrate, three wives came out because they met up and came out together. I was on embarkation leave, 1951. I hadn't seen her for a couple of years and the family for three and a half years.

I had one experience. I was a corporal and told to take some men and go across a frozen river and go around to the next village just to see if there was anybody about. If it was occupied, you don't go into it, you had to listen to see if there were any dogs barking or the sound of other animals. I asked if there was anybody else out and I was told, no, we were the only ones out that night. We went off, walked across the frozen river, found the hill, climbed it and the village was just down below. Not a sound. Deadly, no signs of life. Coming back, halfway down, we spotted people walking along on the edge of the frozen river. They were silhouetted and stood out. Had it just been water we would not have seen them but the ice made it different. So we went further down and I said to the others, don't any of you fire until I do. There were four of us. There were about half a dozen of them. We waited until they were really close and I yelled out, 'Halt, who goes there.' And they told us. They used the password. They were ours! As soon as I got back to camp I went straight to the platoon commander and said, 'We were told there was nobody else out tonight.' I said, 'It's scandalous, we nearly shot all our own men.' They were really annoyed as well. I was worried, if I had lost any of them, that's what you worry about. But if someone did get killed we never went to any funerals. We just said, 'Oh so and so's been killed, he was a good lad.' And then you just got on with it. You didn't look back. But yes, plenty of my mates did get killed.

George Stirland

You could only send so much mail, signals were restricted. At night it was so dark, no lights, no cigarettes on the upper deck, everything was battened down in case you got hit. The cold was the main thing, 15°F below; in them days nobody knew what the chill factor was. You do now. You're charging along at 30 knots, 10°F below, that makes it 40°F below. You go on deck, and wow it's like someone's chopped your head off. There was plenty of ice about on the sea. The ice would break up but there were no glaciers. The ship got some damage, but you were plodding through the ice. Once clear of land mass there was no ice, it was just a mile or two off land.

We'd have four days or so off when we went back to base and we'd get a couple of days off ship and then it was back to normal. The one good thing was that, being war conditions, there was no cleaning brass or anything like that, none of that bullshit. We had about 250 men on the *Cockade*. I was a torpedo man. At *Ganges*, I'd done gunnery but when you left there you specialised – radar, gunnery, torpedo, whatever. We only fired torpedoes in practice and when we did that we had to go and recover them. It was like a ton and a half bobbing up alongside you, like a porpoise coming up. We'd bring it back on board, strip it down, grease it and put dummy warheads on. We didn't have warheads on all the time.

We were out there in Korea until the end. It was December 1953 when we came home. We were still on patrol when the ceasefire was signed on the 25 July. I was on the *Cockade* the whole time but came home on another troopship. Altogether the number of ships that took part were hundreds. The Admiralty said thank goodness it's over, it didn't serve any purpose. I loved the navy, it gave you an insight into what the lads did on Russian convoys. That was horrendous. The main thing were the carriers and keeping them planes flying. The other ships didn't see much action, just protection work. The planes were flying all the time, going off to the coast dropping bombs whatever.

When we finished we went to Hong Kong. By then the ship was a shambles, the decks were paper thin, and they needed new decks, we took the funnel off, even the guns had been taken off. But they refitted it and it did a few more years. Once the cold war was on everything became anti-submarine work.

Geoff Holland

I sailed for Korea either end August or beginning September. We sailed on the *Empire Pride* and it was a terrible ship. The sleeping accommodation was a hammock slung off the roof or underside of the deck. I had difficulty getting into my hammock so I slept outside on the deck. I just couldn't get in the damn thing, everybody was taking the mickey out of me. The ship was absolutely crawling with cockroaches and it didn't help much sleeping on deck, but it was only for three days.

Training was running up and down the hills and there were plenty of them. In Hong Kong we were originally a light ack ack battery, 40mm Bofors. They were for shooting planes down but they were getting a bit archaic at the time as there were jet fighters. By the time you got your gun lined up it had gone. So they split us, two ack ack batteries went up the Imjin River guarding the bridges and we went as a mortar battery. All I was doing was running up and down the hill with a big mortar. It weighed a ton, setting the sights on the mortar. They asked for volunteers for signalling. They used to say in the army never volunteer for anything but

I thought, I'm just a labourer here, so I volunteered. The course was taken by a bombardier. I really enjoyed it, I just took to it. I finished up being promoted to bombardier and the bombardier who had been taking the course was demoted. We trained on rifle shooting, we had an Enfield .303s, Sten guns, Bren guns. Oh, and we did a bit of grenade throwing as well. I could really throw them, though obviously they were not live grenades. We'd put caps down on the floor and throw them. I got quite good at that. But when it came to lobbing the live ones it was a case of get rid of it quick. We went to a place called Stonecutters Island which is just off Hong Kong and that's where we practised throwing live grenades.

I was in the Royal Artillery Regiment. We were joined by the Canadians, Australians and New Zealanders and we were all part of the same division. They were good some of those lads. As a signaller you could be a wireless operator which is what I was. Other signallers were what was known as line signallers, you'd have a telephone in your dugout and there'd be lines going to another troop 3 miles away over the hill and the line signallers would be going out at all times. If there was firing going on, the Chinese or North Koreans or whatever, and the wires got blown away and they'd say can't get hold of so and so, so the linemen would get hold of the wire and follow it until they found the break and obviously repair it.

As a wireless operator I was listening in to our own messages and sending them but I wasn't listening into the Chinese or North Koreans, it was just our own. We were all connected. The wireless sets we had were nothing like they have today. It was a 91 Set. There was a 31 Set, 62 Set, and 91 Set, I think it was, and that was a big one, as big as that screen on the television. They were Russian, made for Russian tanks during the war and that's what we were using. Having got that job I was promoted to bombardier in charge of signals and I more or less ran the show. And the best part of it was that you were in a command post which was just a hole in the ground but there was a heater in there. I'd be taking the messages from the observation post up in the hills. They would send through the map references for firing from the guns or whatever you were firing at. So while the lads on the guns were stood there freezing, I was warm. And that's why I think it was the best thing I ever did getting into signals. I really did enjoy it. I took to it. I could go through the alphabet now, although it's been changed now. I knew it all off by heart.

When we got to Korea we landed at Pusan. You knew you were in Pusan because it stank. You could smell it, and I'm not exaggerating, long before the ship got into the harbour. They spread human waste onto the paddy fields and the stench was terrible. After we got off the ship we were put on a troop train and it was the worst train I have ever seen in my life. They were just wooden seats and there weren't separate carriages. They were like the old trams. We all had our kitbags, all your webbing and stuff, rifle, tin helmet and you're all thrown in together in this train. And the lads were all asking, 'When are we going to get something to eat?' They came round and I am not exaggerating, they gave me a tin of corned beef hash and that was between two of us. And that's all we got. It was about a ten-hour train journey. I had no idea where the train was going. It was dark, night-time. You were looking out of the window and seeing a town and then an hour later you'd be passing through the same town. They were shunting us around, I don't know what they were doing. Anyway, we eventually got off the train. And the toilets on that train! Well you just can't describe them. It was just an iron pot and there must have been a few hundred soldiers on that train. If you went to the toilet it was just absolutely impossible. It was filled to the top with you know what. Ugh. Eventually we got to Britannia Camp and from there they were sorting you out where you were going. We were there about two or three days and we were going in the line the day after. And that night a big attack came in from the Chinese, so they held us back until things had got sorted out. And that's the night Speakman won the Victoria Cross and we went into the same position where Speakman had been. It was between Hill 355 and 227. I'll never forget them. He was in the King's Own Scottish Borderers, though he came from Altrincham. He ran out of ammunition and was charging the Chinese throwing beer bottles! We went in the day after and I remember they put us into army trucks and we went down this road which had been camouflaged and it was known as camouflaged road. I can remember it vividly. We got down to the bottom and they said, 'Right lads, you're crossing this valley and you're in full view of the Chinese so run!' And we did run. And we were carrying ammunition, rifles, all your kit and we had to run about 150 yards across this valley. And you do run! Anyway, we got across and that's where we dug in. And we were there for about four months. Hill 355 and 227.

There was a troop of about thirty men and we got together as signallers and we dug our own hole. Sounds rough and it was rough. But being a joiner I was quite handy and I did make it, I wouldn't say comfortable, but it was reasonable. I even made a door out of ammunition boxes and put it on. You were just dug into the hillside. We covered the roof with timber and soil and sandbags. There would be four or five of us in the one hole. Very cosy and we had a heater! We made it. Actually they were illegal. We had a can of petrol on the roof of the dugout and we had a hose and it came down through the roof of the dugout and into a jerry tin which had a hole in the bottom and had a corned beef hash tin with holes punctured into it. This tube had some copper pipe going to the hole in the tin. We made a chimney onto the jerry tin. It was very Heath Robinson.[15] You had a jubilee clip so you could squeeze the tube so that it was just dripping. And when you lit it, it was good. The tin would be burning hot. We used to brew up and all sorts. They reckon there were more killed by them heaters than by the Chinese!!!

I suppose we knew why we there. The UN said that any country who was attacked, the UN would send a force in to stop it. The American soldiers who went at the beginning were based in Japan – an occupation force. They were living it up. They were barely trained and they got slaughtered.

I had two lads who got killed, although they were killed after I had left. We had three days leave at Inchon, just a bit of a camp where there was a bar and barracks and where we could get a decent night's sleep not worrying about a bomb coming through the roof. But that was the only break I had apart from five days leave in April in Tokyo. One bloke refused to go unless his mate went and the sergeant major said he's not going, so he said he wasn't going, so they asked me. You got on these American Skymasters with seats down the sides with us all sitting either side of the plane looking at one another. When we got to this leave camp in Tokyo they made you strip off all this rubbish you had on and it absolutely stank.

---

15   William Heath Robinson (1872–1944) was an English cartoonist and illustrator, best known for his eccentric drawings of machinery.

If you're in a place where everybody's stinking you never noticed. We stripped everything off and just threw it in a pile. They sprayed you with DDT.[16] Now that's not allowed these days, a lot of soldiers have died since, after having being sprayed with DDT. It's not used now. You got that when you were going home as well. You have these occasional checks, FFI, Free from Infection. They looked for scabies or anything else you might have picked up. You couldn't get on the ship if you had any disease.

Brian Daly

We went to Japan initially and stayed there for a while before going to Pusan. I was stationed there for a short while but we left there and went further up to the banks of the Imjin River and I was there until I finished my time. The war had a couple more months before it ended. I didn't see any fighting or anything like that. I was part of the peace-keeping operation most of the time. There were still a lot of soldiers out there. I was based at Pusan then up onto the Imjin River. The camp was a bare plot of land with tents and we lived under canvas most of the time. It was a bit rough. There was nothing there except the military. The part I was in was exclusively a Royal Military Police base for about thirty or forty of us.

We were guarding a building where all the officers used to go to do their business and we were outside the place guarding it, checking who went in, who went out. I was also on the bridge going over the Imjin. I was on duty there guarding that although there was nothing to guard on the bridge just bits of traffic. I was never guarding prisoners. I never saw any prisoners; I have no idea where they were.

16   DDT (dichlorodiphenyltrichloroethane) is an organochlorine insecticide. It was used extensively for the treatment of malaria during the Second World War but was later discovered to be harmful and was subsequently banned.

Brian Hough

We docked into Pusan harbour and for most of the people who went to Korea, one of their lasting memories was the smell. It was awful. Because it was so strong, I think that's why it stayed with us. People said it was all the stuff that had been thrown into the water because it was a harbour. But it wasn't, sadly. It was the country and that does sound awful. I don't want to be disrespectful but they didn't have any real sanitation. They really didn't and of course hundreds of thousands of troops coming from all over the world didn't help. It was an awful place.

As we left the ship we were greeted by an American army band. I thought it was great. Being a Stan Kenton[17] fan at the time, I thought it's not bad this. They were playing jazzed up military music. Certainly our regimental band didn't play like that.

So we left the ship and they put us on board a train. We were given packages of sandwiches, stuff like that, and we went on this train. The actual train that pulled the carriages along looked like it was out of one of John Wayne's films. It was a typical old American railway train with a large stack at the front and cow rails. It was a cowboy train! When you got into the carriages they were just wooden seats. And we sat there and we sat there and we sat there! Anyrate, eventually we moved off. I think by that time most of us had eaten the sandwiches we had been given. We were in a very small compartment, sat opposite each other, like in the old carriages but very close together. The train moved off and it took us almost thirty hours to get just north of Seoul, and without toilets. Now it's quite an achievement and quite hilarious to watch grown infantrymen trying to do their toilet out of the carriage window! You can imagine some of the comments! The train would travel for half an hour and then it would stop. For what reason, we never knew. We'd be there half and hour and then off again, and so it went on. Every now and again they'd give us food when the train stopped. It was always Americans who supplied us with hot drinks.

I do remember one incident. We'd stopped and we were told not to get out of the train – you mustn't leave the carriage – every time you stopped,

---

17   Stan Kenton, 1911–79, American pianist and bandleader.

kids appeared, youngsters, and we were giving them stuff until one of the sergeants came round and started playing hell with people because they were giving them socks and such stuff. Now I thought I'd seen poverty in Ardwick but believe me we hadn't. Now one particular stop we were told to get off the train – it was just a field like. A couple of hundred yards away there was a road and parked along this road was a line of American trucks and food wagons. So we went up with our mess tins and they lobbed stew or whatever into them. We walked back to sit on the grass in this field and all of a sudden there must have been twenty, thirty children arrived and they just stood there looking at us. That was tough. We all thought we were hard lads, Jack the Lads, all scousers and Mancs together like. The kids didn't beg, they just stood and looked until someone moved and gave them some food from his mess tin. I think most of us eventually gave some of our food to them and we fed these children. That was the first time I'd seen starving children. It wasn't the last. And that to me was the sad thing about Korea – the children. Cos I don't think at that time that the UN had any agencies like the UN High Commission for Refugee Agency to help them. Well, I certainly didn't see any. If the children had lost their parents or their parents had been killed, they were left on their own. There would be gangs of children walking about the countryside. It was awful. Even as a silly 18-year-old it ripped me apart. It really did. Again, it is a lasting memory. They were all orphaned.

Eventually we left there and went on to just north of Seoul. We were taken off the train, put into trucks and taken to a camp of tents and told that we would be moving up into the line within forty-eight hours and we had to prepare all our weapons, clean our rifles and so on. I had a Bren gun then – so we cleaned it to make sure everything was spick and span.

Two days later, at night, we moved up into the line. We got in the trucks and drove for half and hour or so, then we got out of the trucks and walked for a couple of miles or so with all our kit on. We relieved a battalion of Australian soldiers to begin with. I was carrying the Bren gun and we were going up and the Australians were coming down. And as we passed each other we stopped to allow the Australians to get past and I've got this Bren gun across my shoulders and one of the Aussies says, 'Here's the guy with all the brass and all the money.' I said, 'What?' Apparently if you're a Bren gunner in Australia you got another 10 shillings a week. I said, 'I think I'll join your lot, cos we certainly didn't get any extra.' There was lots of banter like that among the men passing each other. So we found ourselves in the front line and basically it was as simple as that.

At the battle of the Hook, the Duke of Wellington's Regiment took a terrific battering, and the King's Regiment. It went on for a fortnight. There had been shelling every day for a fortnight before the Chinese assault actually took place. There were 500 mortar shells a day falling on the King's and Wellington's positions. The last day before they attacked, 1,000 shells an hour were raining down on our positions. Now I didn't count them but it is in the MoD official history of Korea. We had mainly shrapnel wounds. We were there thirteen months, but the last ten months before the ceasefire, and in that ten months the King's lost I think it was 30 men and over 200 wounded. And that was from shelling mostly.

But I went on leave to Tokyo, five days R & R. The Americans organised that and the Americans can certainly organise things, there's no two ways about that. And we met American personnel then, it was the first time I had ever spoken to Americans, and yet, during the Second World War, there was an American army base at Belle Vue close to here in Manchester, right on my doorstep. We were taken in trucks to Seoul, ushered into this huge aircraft, a Globemaster. I thought it would never get off the ground. There were 300 of us packed into it – British, Americans, Australians, everyone from the UN forces. We went to Tokyo, and remember Japan was an occupied country then, and we went to this camp hotel and we all had a shower and were given clean clothing, had our rifles taken off us and had them registered, and we were shown to a barrack room. And there were white sheets on the beds! We couldn't believe it. Wonderful. We were given a bed and there was a reception and a hot meal. The Americans had organised it all. There was this huge Canadian sergeant and he told us what we could do over the next five day. He said, do what you want, if you like you can stay in your bed for five days, I don't want to see you, just make sure you're back for 18.00 hours on Thursday, or whatever it was. If you want a woman don't just go picking one up off the streets. And he gave all the lads a list of all the brothels they could attend. They were registered hotels with legal prostitutes and the girls working in these hotels were inspected every other day and they had a card that was stamped. He said please your-self what you do but before you go to bed tell reception what time you want breakfast. This was unbelievable, breakfast whenever we wanted, and before breakfast some Japanese girls came around and gave us tea in bed. All organised by the Americans. I would never call the Americans.

John Smith

So we were on the USS *Montrose* about five days and I always remember what a lovely place it was to be on because the Americans seemed to have everything. There was a cinema on board and the food was great, the Americans were great. And they were giving us inoculations of all kinds. I remember the American doctors weren't like ours. Ours were more gentle. You stood one side of the table, the Americans the other and they just jabbed you. But it was OK and we enjoyed that little trip. Every morning the Yanks would be on this tannoy – 'Now hear this, hear this! Today we have two more baseball players'. And on our final day it came over, 'We now have three cricket players.' I asked this American what's all this about. And he said, 'It means there's three British guys who've got VD!'

Anyhow, we eventually pulled into a place called Inchon; that's April 1951. We get there and it's just like a John Wayne film with the Yanks on the tannoy all the time, 'Now hear this.' I hadn't a clue what was going on. We got on these trucks and ended up where the New Zealanders were. All hell was let loose. Twenty-five pounders going off. There were all these Chinese prisoners with their hands on their heads, some were wounded. This was Inchon. I always remember one of them shouting something and there was an interpreter there and I said, 'What the hell is he going on about?' and he said, 'He wants to go to the toilet.' 'Yes, that's OK,' I said, 'he can go down there in that crater.' Well the chap goes down there, drops his trousers and he's looking at me and I'm looking at him. I've got a Sten gun – you've got to be careful, can't take any risks – and he starts yelling out in Chinese. 'What's he saying?' I asked. 'Well, he thinks you're going to shoot him,' was the reply. I remember me saying to him, 'You tell him we are the

British army and we do not shoot prisoners of war.' And you should have seen his face light up and I looked across to my right and I could see the other twenty-nine fellas, their faces lit up as well. They thought if I was going to shoot that man then they would be next. You could see the relief on their faces. Eventually we handed them over to the Yanks and they took them off to some prisoner-of-war camp somewhere.

I was on the move all the time. The sergeant came up to me and said things were not looking very good at all. We were relieving 27 Brigade and on our left were 29 Brigade. They were getting a hammering with the Gloucester's. The sergeant said, 'Look there's a chance we're going to get taken prisoner here. Don't forget you only give your number, rank and name. And that's all you give them and no more.' But, as it was, it didn't occur. Some reinforcements came and I knew some of them from Hong Kong and they said, 'We're glad to see you cos we were told you had been killed.'

But then things got a bit more organised. There was always lots of gunfire. Eventually, we got working on the bridges on the rivers. We did a lot of convoy work, putting up a lot of signs as well. I remember one day I was in a jeep picking up some signs and there's a jeep coming towards us. There's a an officer sitting in the front seat and he says, 'Corporal, go this way down this road cos round this corner there's thousands of Chinese, so don't be going down there.' So we turned back.

In November 1951, I was sent for and they said, 'By the way, you have qualified for five days rest and recuperation in Tokyo.' Not bad that, very handy. So we went to Tokyo. The Yanks flew us out and we were put up in a hotel and we were looked after. We were just drinking and having a get together. We were with the Australian lads at a bar in Tokyo. Then a bunch of American MPs came in and had someone up against the wall and one of the Aussies said, 'Come on, I'm not having this, let's go and disarm them.' I said, 'You will not disarm them. Just sit there and leave this to me. Don't you dare move unless you want to spend your five days in a guardroom.' I went over and had a word with the Americans. It all got sorted. I heard a story about the Aussies who were digging in front of the Russian embassy in Tokyo before I went there. They got up to some tricks. They'd pinch the Kiwi's vehicles and such stuff.

We never got trouble from our own lads, never. We weren't really keeping law and order at all. We slept in big tents, we stayed there and worked from there. Sometimes we were sleeping in smaller tents if we were on the move but we were never digging in like the ordinary infantry, although we did get close up to the front line and the trenches on occasion. I remember getting warned off once cos I had a peak cap on and one of the lads said, 'Get that hat off, there's snipers here and if they see that hat they'll think you are an officer and they'll go for you.' Fair enough but that was life. Another time there were mortars coming over the road but we weren't in the front line as such.

We had a football match against the Indian ambulance. We had our army boots on and they played in their bare feet. And you know what, they beat us 10-0. They were fantastic.

Brian Hough

We arrived in Korea in September 1952 and within ten days we were in the front line and didn't move out until January 1953. In November 1952 the Black Watch Regiment took a pounding on the Hook. They reckon there was more blood spilt on that hill than anywhere in Korea. If you knew your battalion was going on the Hook, your heart sank. After November 1952 we took the place of the Black Watch and we should have been out by Christmas but because of the Black Watch situation it was decided to keep the jocks out of the line so that they could at least celebrate the New Year, then they'd go back in, so we were there until 4 or 5 January.

We would be out of the front line for just twenty-four hours. That was on rotation but that was about once every three weeks. We had a shower and change of clothing about once every two weeks. We must have been a right passive lot, we just accepted it.

There was fear. I'm not suggesting we were gung-ho but we knew there was a job to be done and if we came into contact with the Chinese it was every man for himself. You knew if you didn't get them, they'd get you. We just did what we were trained to do. The training in Hong Kong had really hardened us. There was an element of indoctrination. We got lectures and we were told some right tales about what might happen to you if you got captured. There was undoubtedly a certain amount of brainwashing.

The Chinese were brilliant at indoctrination. They were so good it cheered us up. I remember once, it was Christmas Eve 1952 and we were a couple of hundred yards from them. I was on patrol and nothing was happening. It was a case of keep your heads down and don't make a noise, it's Christmas Eve. Then all of a sudden there's this huge noise, Chinese music and then some baritone starts singing 'Rose of England', all coming across from the Chinese lines. They were sending us Christmas greetings. 'We wish you Kingsmen a happy Christmas. What are you doing fighting with these Americans, why not come and join us? The Americans will all be on a beach in Florida celebrating Christmas,' and so forth. It was good entertainment, we had a laugh. It cheered us up.

The lines were pretty static for eighteen months. We might move to another position taking over from some other of our soldiers, but that was about it. But we didn't have much movement. Sometimes we never even came into contact with our other companies, they might be only 500 yards away but we might never see them for months.

Geoff Holland

One little story: Christmas Eve 1951 and things had quietened down, it was an unofficial ceasefire. Nobody was taking pot shots at one another. On Christmas morning a bloke went around the perimeter fences and the Chinese had left us little presents on the barbed wires, little things like trinkets. I said, don't touch them. The commanding officer had said they might be booby traps. But they weren't. How the Chinese got up to the perimeter fence without us hearing them I'll never know. They left propaganda leaflets as well, saying things like, 'Your MPs will be having a good time,' and there was a picture of Churchill with a glass of wine and a big cigar. And, 'Your girlfriends will be with other fellows. Come and join us the Chinese People's Volunteer Army. You will be treated with respect.' But nobody went!

3. LIFE IN THE TRENCHES

<u>'The cold was the real enemy. We lost men with frostbite,
the Americans had men frozen to death.'</u>

INTRODUCTION

LIFE FOR THE ordinary conscript soldier serving in Korea was as difficult as it gets. It was bad enough for the regular soldiers with hardened experience, but for the young servicemen coming straight off the streets of our towns and cities the weather and conditions came as a massive shock. It led to some friction with the experienced regulars becoming increasingly frustrated by the national servicemen.

That first winter in Korea, 1950/51, was simply appalling. Temperatures dipped as low as minus 40°F and rarely got much warmer. Neither British nor American forces could have experienced such conditions or hardships for such a prolonged period. The worst conditions of the Second World War had been in Russia, around Stalingrad, but neither British nor American troops had been involved in that. Nobody had experienced anything quite like it. The weather came as something of a surprise for the

American and United Nations forces who were extremely ill-equipped for such conditions.

Throughout that winter, and indeed other winters, there was constant snow and bitter winds that raged in from Siberia. During those winters the ground was rock solid, making digging in for trench warfare all the more difficult. Indeed, the job of digging trenches had to be left to the engineers. Roads were also dreadful, little more than tracks that had to be constantly cared for. Clothing was poor and insufficient for the weather conditions. It was a case of putting on more layers rather than having anything more sophisticated. There were no duvets, fleeces, gortex or alpine clothing as there is today. Instead it was vests, long johns, flannel shirts and pullovers beneath the traditional uniform along with gloves and a hat of some sorts. The Americans had parkas – fur-lined top coats with framed hoods – which were extremely popular. In time these would become available to the British soldiers, but not significantly until the second winter in Korea. But one of the problems with layers of clothes is that it restricts movement. Many, for instance, discovered that firing a gun with gloves on was awkward. Mitten gloves especially made it difficult to perform any complex task, especially shooting a rifle. But there was little option as taking gloves off at night was a dangerous choice that could easily lead to frostbite. It only took a split second and once you had frostbite there was nothing you could do about it. Weapons also had to be serviced regularly so that they didn't clam up in the cold. Those on duty at night were obliged to constantly check their weapons to keep them operational. Vehicles also had to be started every hour or so with engines left to run for short periods so that again they would not freeze up. You would never know when you might need the vehicles as an escape from the enemy.

All the soldiers interviewed complained of the cold. It was one of their abiding memories of Korea. How they survived it only they will know. Many didn't. There was frostbite and in some instances soldiers just froze to death. Anyone lying injured or gone missing stood no chance as overnight temperatures plummeted. The main task was just in keeping warm.

The following winter of 1951–52 brought marked improvements and the third winter was almost luxury compared to the first, both in temperature and equipment. Clothing improved dramatically and the Americans introduced a small heater that could be used in the hutchies to take the place of the less sophisticated and more dangerous contraptions that many soldiers had rustled together. Lessons had been learnt. The army also realised that one winter in such conditions was more than enough and to demand that national servicemen should operate a second winter was unreasonable. Consequently, servicemen were informed that they would only have to serve one winter. On occasion, however, even this rule was overlooked.

The Korean War was almost as much about survival as it was about fighting. The Chinese suffered as well and given their numbers must have encountered even greater difficulties. Some soldiers noted that when the temperature fell, even the Chinese were reluctant to come out and fight.

Most of the time the troops lived in what they called hutches or hutchies. These were dugouts on the side of the mountain along the front line. Once a reasonable sized trench and hole had been dug then logs, sandbags and soil could be placed on the top so that they were capable of taking a mortar attack. And as long as it was not a direct hit, the hutches seemed to be reasonably protective. The soldiers would sleep and rest here. In the later stages of the conflict there were tents towards the rear of the front line. But most life seems to have revolved around the hutches. Some managed to set up a heater although it was, as they say, very 'Heath Robinson' and beds were made from telephone wire, bits of wood and anything else you could lay your hands on.

Washing facilities were virtually non-existent. Soldiers could boil up some water in the morning and just about manage a cup of tea and if they were lucky, maybe have a shave with any water left over. But that was about it. In the first winter, and indeed in subsequent winters, washing clothes was almost impossible and soldiers simply wore the same clothes for weeks on end. The problem was not just in having sufficient warm water for washing their clothes, but as much in getting them dried. Socks could be left to dry by whatever heater they had, but it was considerably more difficult with underclothes and shirts. Once decent heaters had been set up, then this became just about possible. It was a constant battle on two fronts. On the one hand fighting the enemy, on the other fighting the conditions and the weather in particular.

If they were lucky the army might give them a change of clothes once a month. But it didn't always happen. Showers were out of the question during the first nine months of the war, but as the armies settled in, and became more acclimatised and better equipped, some mobile showers were introduced behind the lines. But you would be very lucky if you could manage a shower more than once a month.

At night it was far too cold to strip off and jump into your sleeping bag. Boots might come off, but little else. As a result it didn't take long before everyone was beginning to smell, but if you smelled, then you could be sure everyone else smelled. But you didn't notice it as you soon became accustomed to the general odour around you.

The simple task of going to the toilet was also a nightmare. There were no toilet facilities. You either went to an allotted ditch, which would have a carefully placed tree log over it, or found a ditch of your own. There was no privacy, not much toilet paper and nowhere to wash your hands afterwards. It was very basic and very undignified, although again there were some minor improvements as time went on.

In the summer it was different. Temperatures rose and it could be extremely warm but few complained of the heat. Instead they took a dip in the river if there was one close by and also took the opportunity to give their clothes a good wash and dry. Indeed, the summers brought about a marked change in mood. The snow gave way to a rich green vegetation and many have remarked at how beautiful a country Korea was when the sun was shining. The ground was also softer and digging into the hillside considerably easier. Repairs could be made to the hutch, trenches could be widened, deepened or re-dug. And of course the roads, or tracks to be more accurate, had to be repaired after the winter. The snow and ice had left them in a state of disrepair with potholes and fallen boulders. At times, as in many wars, this conflict was about logistics.

Food was a further problem. There was no cookhouse a hundred yards from the front that the soldiers could take turns in visiting. Instead food had to be brought to them. Mostly it was American rations, a couple of tins of something, a chocolate bar and twenty cigarettes. Indeed, the one thing that was never in short supply was a cigarette. Of course this was a time when most men smoked and it seemed that the authorities placed a huge importance on making sure that the men had their daily quota of cigarettes. It was almost as if they feared a revolt if the cigarettes were not in ample supply. Inevitably it led to an over abundance of them with not only the Americans supplying a regular ration but the British also delivering a weekly ration. There was also the occasional beer, but it tended to be available only when there was a lull in the fighting.

And then there were the rats. Some never saw any and joked that even the rats knew better than to come out in the cold winters. But others saw rats in abundance. With bits of food around, sewage problems and some warmth from the heaters, it was little wonder that the rats appeared. Lice was a problem as well, a result of wearing dirty clothes for long periods of time and not being able to wash regularly.

The first part of the war was a moving conflict as major advances were made or retreats were necessary. As a result armies were constantly on the go with new trenches being built all the time. But after a year the war petered into a stalemate as both sides dug in. It became trench warfare, not unlike what had occurred in northern France during the First World War. The line might move half a mile forward but a few days later it would be forced back. Advances were limited but at least troops became embedded and this allowed for better servicing and organisation behind the lines. But no matter what, life in the trenches for these soldiers was as bad as it gets.

Bill Fox

The weather was beginning to get cold as it was November 1950. Now MacArthur by then had made the war a great success with his landing because the army had swept on northwards and were still pushing on. MacArthur had announced that they would advance onwards and go all the way up to and over the 38th Parallel, going north all the way to the Yalu River that borders North Korea with mainland China. He had put signs in Korean and English around saying we won't stop the war until we have washed our swords in the Yalu. So MacArthur then ordered the US Marine Corp to land on the opposite side, on the east of Korea, and to go right up near to the border and capture the North Koreans before they could escape into China. But the Chinese came in then. The Chinese soldiers were referred to as volunteers but they weren't volunteers out of the paddy fields or anything, they were volunteers out of the Chinese army, and they didn't get any choice. They were seasoned soldiers who had been soldiers for five years and were experienced in solid fighting. They knew how to survive on limited rations and so on. It was only afterwards that you learn these things. One of the things that you learn is that the most important thing is not the fighting or the generals or the strategy of war but the generals behind the lines, the quartermasters; how do they supply you up there, how are you going to get back, how do you get medical help to those people. You don't think about these things at first, you just think US Marines, we're in. But you have to have a good quartermaster being there for you, organising things. They are more important sometimes than the general in the front. They don't get the glory but they do the thinking.

While we were in Korea we were always well supplied. We sometimes got American rations because they were well established over there. The first twelve months were the really difficult time because that was the time when the North had swept all the way down to the South causing mass destruction and death and had then swept all the way back and then all the way south again when the Chinese joined in. It was that that caused so much destruction and so many deaths.

I was a Glosters' infantryman when we were in the front line and each night we had to dig in in the most suitable hill. It was bitterly cold and the ground was so hard but we'd try and dig a trench and stay there. Sometimes it was so freezing cold. We didn't have a base that we could retreat to or go to for the night, we were stuck there on the hillside and sometimes we were replacing the Americans who were already there. We had a sleeping bag but at times we had to wait for the sleeping bags to come up because you couldn't just carry it with you all day. And some days it wouldn't arrive and you'd be without anything at night. Food was also brought up to us as well. We had American rations then, in a little box called, I think, a K2. It was quite good, though it was cold of course. If you were in the trench for a few days you could get a fire going, have some tea or things like that. We had a sort of Bunsen burner; one of the lads might stay behind and get the food ready while the others were on patrol.

They weren't official cooks but they did the necessary when they could. We were moving northwards then, this was November 1950. We got up north, we got through Pyongyang, so you can see we were going way up north. We didn't stop in the capital either, we just went right through it. We were right up north and we were getting a bit worried – how far are we going before we stop? Eventually we stopped – we had the American troops in front of us – but even so we were well north of Pyongyang but I don't know how far we were from the Chinese border, they didn't tell us that, we were just privates, but we couldn't have been that far off.

So we had pushed up north and we dug in for a while. It was cold, so cold, you couldn't describe how cold it was. We were all wrapped up, thick trousers and everything. Jesus, it was cold, even now I shiver at the thought. You can read articles about the cold but let me tell you something, ah it was awful, we had to huddle together like that to keep alive. One day we saw all these American wagons coming south and we thought, what's going on here. It's only heavy equipment, they said, that they don't need and they're taking it back south. But more and more was going back south. It just kept coming. Now you don't have to be a very educated man to realise something's going on; they were pulling out and we were going to be left in the front line. That's what was happening. The Chinese were massing up and were about to attack us. The pride of the American nation, the American Marines – we were behind them – were up near the Russian border and the Russians didn't like it. The Chinese came in and cut them off. They lost the battle, although they never admitted to it. And they pulled out. How much stuff they must have left behind is anyone's guess because when the Americans go in they take everything with them including the kitchen sink. So we pulled back as well, to Pyongyang,

There was a huge American food depot there, and in this depot were the warehouses with all the food and the walls had been pulled down so that they could blow up all the food supplies. Big cans of ham, spam and the like. The American army was doing the blowing up, laying down all the wires and detonators. And there was a perimeter fence about a hundred yards away with wire to stop all the peasants coming in. We were guarding the other side of the fence to stop the starving peasants from getting in. You didn't need to understand the language; they were begging for food. We was guarding it and I was only a young fella at the time and I was a bit soft hearted, especially when you see women and kids. I was taking stuff and flinging it to them. Anyhow, I threw a good amount of stuff to the people and eventually we pulled away because they were going to detonate it all. All these bangs were going off, they blew the lot up, everything, all the food. I don't think they minded the locals having some. We got in the trucks and we crossed the main river and the Americans were ready there to blow up all the bridges, the lot was blown up. When you think about it afterwards that happened all over Korea. You think of our suffering in this country but it was nothing compared to what happened to them in Korea. Years later you think when you go to Paris or London and you see all the lovely bridges over the river Seine and the Thames and I don't think one of them was blown up during the war. The Americans smashed all the houses as well, they set fire to them to stop anyone, such as guerrillas, using them.

We pulled out and when we came out of Pyongyang, we were put on trucks and went down south for mile after mile after mile, we were glad to get out of it to be honest. Mile after mile we travelled until we were back in South Korea and we went well back down into South Korea. We were then put on a unit guarding the bridges in the south near a stream where the Americans were purifying the water for supplies. They were putting the water into big boilers to purify it. Even with the iciest cold well water you were told never to drink it cos it would kill you.

Jim Grundy

Our living conditions were absolutely horrible. We had tents that were patched up but the patches weren't waterproof. So if you were sleeping at night under a patch and it started raining it'd be dripping on you all night long, even though you also had a poncho, you'd have dripping all night. The living conditions were just terrible. There would be five of us in the tent, the team, we slept together, we went in the NAAFI together, we worked together, you kept together as a team.

Roy Cox

I got to Korea in May 1951 and by then the weather was beginning to improve and get a lot warmer. But it could still be quite cold some nights. It got a lot warmer in the summer and can be quite hot but then in August it starts to cool off again, then it gets a bit chilly in September and in October you are beginning to get into the winter. We weren't there for that first winter of 1950–51. We just did the one winter which was the following winter 1951–52 – you of course only did one winter serving in Korea. The winter we were there was nowhere near as bad as that first winter and I think that the third winter of the war 1952–53, was not even as bad as the previous winter when we were there.

Peter C Le P Jones

The winter arrives very quickly in Korea. One day it is tropical with hot nights, then hot days followed by very cold nights and soon arctic weather with minus 25°F to minus 40°F plus. We had spent the pre-winter period with frost at night in tropical clothing, a blanket and a waterproof poncho that kept us mildly warm. Luckily for us the Americans produced magnificent winter clothing, though it made marching (not often practised by the Americans) more difficult due to the bulk. British string vests – very warm although a rough garment – worn under British army shirts, draws (woollen long), battle dress trousers and top, American windproof trousers, a superb jacket, fur hat and British outer arctic gloves – then try a route march. We had American sleeping bags made of a blanket material with a zip that undid immediately in case of attack and this was inside a very good arctic British sleeping bag. Get snuggled down in that and then 18 inches of snow in two hours on top, while we slept with all our clothes and boots on – one was very warm until someone came trudging along and stepped on you to call you for the next two hours on sentry duty. Getting up entailed a mound of snow going down your neck and into the sleeping bag. Two hours off, desperate for sleep, but difficult to sleep because you only had two hours – two on and two off, or two on and four off depending on the seriousness of the situation was an extremely exhausting but quite normal life.

Bill Fox

We were there, we were doing patrols into local villages. It was a godforsaken, dirty, peasant-ridden country. It was a shame because the people weren't dirty or anything like that. But they lived under thatched roofs. I was surprised that not so many years later Korea could build itself up and hold the Olympics. Amazing. And the thatched roofs were a haven for vermin including big spiders and such. And of course rats. I honestly believe there are more rats per population per mile than anywhere else. It was infested with rats. I believe most of the rats are more or less a vegetarian rat. There wasn't much in the way of meat for them to eat. In lots of the villages you'd see rats hung up to dry and then to be eaten. I don't know if they would eat them themselves or feed them to the animals. At night you saw more rats than people. Terrible. During the summer the rats are out in the paddy fields, they were all over the place. They'd come into the huts where people lived, they were all over the place. The main floor of these Korean homes were built a foot or so above the ground, whether that was to stop water and rain getting in, I don't know, or whether it was supposed to stop the rats. But if it was it didn't work with the rats. They were everywhere. They had a form of central heating as well in their homes, with open fires on both sides of the hut and the chimney smoke went beneath so that it was warm in winter time. They always had massive bowls of water heating up as well. We got to know the villages. The people were friendly and they'd bow down to you when you came along. You couldn't be cruel to them but you never saw any young men, they'd vanished. You'd see women, kids, old men but never any young men.

At Christmas, one platoon would have its Christmas dinner one day and other men would have it the next day and you'd be excused all duties. The beer would be out as well and we had a good booze-up, we'd have a sing song and if the Americans heard they came along as well and joined in. We got along great with the Americans. I never saw any trouble with the

Americans, arguments or anything. But then why should there be. So that took us up to Christmas 1950.

Terry Moore

It was so cold that you rarely took your clothes off, even to sleep. Everyone became riddled with fleas and bugs. I can remember being in the company of a brigadier who was scratching himself like mad while he was talking to us. And he would have had his own caravan and more chance of keeping clean than we did. You got filthy, you stayed filthy, you got used to it. And later on we never took our boots off either because your feet would freeze.

Peter C Le P Jones

There were a number of occasions when we had to route march for many miles because transport did not appear for some reason or other. On one occasion in the dark and snow we walked and walked, climbed a steep, high hill with enemy all around in the deep snow. We were told that we were cut off, and had to climb down back the way we had come. We passed, in both directions, a broken-down Bren gun carrier that had thrown a track which, had they known, would have had plenty of time to get repaired.

Eventually we arrived to see a huge bonfire lit to guide us back to where transport was waiting across a solid frozen river – tanks and troops were able to cross in the dead of night. We were so crowded in the trucks that you could sleep standing up. Someone dropped a Sten gun that fired, but luckily no one was hurt. If a hand touched metal it immediately stuck to it causing a large loss of skin. Snow, when it did snow, fell with abandon, some 18–24 inches in a couple of hours. When you were on for two hours and looked round you could see no one and had to walk until you trod on someone to get your replacement for the next shift.

We were full of lice. On one occasion, in extreme cold, we had to take off all our clothes in the open and wash from hot water heated in a 45-gallon barrel laced with the medical officer's disinfectant and heated over a fire – we then put on clean clothes. The old clothes, on a stick, were taken to the first-aid post and put in disinfectant-laced 45-gallon barrels to be deloused. What a relief to be free of the lice, but this did not happen very often so you just scratched and picked.

Ken Hawthorne

We used to use a lot of explosives on the roads and anything heavy like big boulders we'd blow out of the way. One day, by 355, the Welsh regiments were on it when I was there; we were setting a charge to blow up a boulder that had fallen onto the road. The idea of blowing anything up on the road is that some of you go one way and the rest go the other way to stop anybody coming up or down. We were just about to set it off and there were only about three of us there when the sergeant came along and said, 'How you getting along?' and we said, 'We're just about to blow the rock.' He said, 'No need to go down that way, I'll stop anybody coming up.' So we set the charge and looking back we see a jeep coming up right by the explosive. We could see the fuse burning. He jumped back in his jeep and just managed to get away. We had nearly killed an officer. When we saw him we said we were sorry, but had he not passed a jeep on the way up? He said yeah, and we said he's supposed to stop you. He said he was new here and wanted to get to 355. Well 355 was a great big hill that we occupied and was part of our line so we told him how to get there and we looked and he hadn't taken the right road and he went right through the valley towards the Chinese. I think they called it the bowling alley. I don't know whether he got back at all.

Roy Cox

I was living in the dugouts, we didn't call them hutches. In the one I was with in 'B' Company I had one to myself because we took over from a Canadian regiment. There was a bit of a hole in the ground and they put these two blokes in the one with a wireless set and two blokes. I found a hole in the ground and spent the night in that but the temperature dropped terribly that night and I was outside in minus 15°F and I near froze to death.

We didn't even have sleeping bags at first, it was quite some time before we got them, maybe a month or so. By then I had a Korean who was a marvellous chap. When you lay barbed wire you have these posts that you wire. I got some of these posts and made a bed out of them. The Korean lad was a fisherman so got hold hold of some wire to stretch across the bed. Beautiful it was. When we finally got sleeping bags we were told not to sleep in them. You could lie on them but not sleep in them, this was because some American outfit had been bayoneted in their sleeping bags, so they said you can't sleep in them in case you got attacked. They later came up with a design that had two legs so you could get up and walk about! We got extra clothing for the winter which was helpful but some of it wasn't really of a good design. We had winter boots that had an insole of copper mesh to keep your feet warm and dry. They also had big cleats for walking on snow and ice, but they got clogged up and were not much use. They also gave us windproof trousers, which were cold to put on, but after a while they were okay. We didn't get much in the way of clothes to change. But it was so good to take your boots off and wash your feet. You would take your socks off, swap them around, turn them inside out, and put them back on. We must have stunk but we never realised it because we didn't have any washing facilities.

Pat Quinn

It was cold. I've never felt so cold before or since. Blood numbing. Without the American special warm clothing we were issued the British troops would have frozen to death. The battle dress and ammo boots we normally wore were not made for Siberian winters. The most warming thing was the thought of a return home or to garrison life back in Hong Kong. But that was to remain only a thought, for in October the Chinese entered the war.

Peter C Le P Jones

We became used to American 'C' rations, the top two items of which were fruit salad and a huge bar of the very best, at least as far as I was concerned, drinking chocolate. With these came twenty American cigarettes a day – Lucky Strike, Chesterfields, Camel (humpty backs), plus another 200 every Friday from the American PX (equivalent to the British NAAFI), i.e. 340 cigarettes per week per man. If we had smoked all these it could have been more dangerous than the enemy. Instead we used them to bribe the local peasants to carry heavy loads up the hills on their A-frames. Tapeworms were another jolly little hazard and our MO laced the tea with his various concoctions that were very effective. It was very alarming passing an 18–24-inch tapeworm. Was it your own guts?

Bill Fox

It was February 1951 before we moved up to the front line. We went forward then to Hill 325 or 327. This was the real action then. We were pushing the Chinese back and this hill was quite high and had gullies all over it. It was reckoned that there was a lot of Chinese holding out there just trying to delay us. The Americans had a job capturing it, so we had to come in. We captured it okay but I think the Chinese had dropped back. But we did well to capture it. We were face to face there. Our platoon officer went forward and we was waiting for him to come back to tell the rest of us to go forward. But he hadn't come back and we were wondering what was going on. Anyhow, I volunteered to go up on my own to see if I could spot him. I was crawling up, like a snake, and I could see him down on the deck and an officer in front of him. I could see the officer, then there was a huge burst of gunfire and his head went back, He'd been hit. He was dead, riddled by a heavy machine gun, not like a Bren gun. Our troops heard this and started firing back. Anyrate, we moved up and the Chinese pulled out. We got up there to the top but we had lost eight men. There was a glory in winning the hill, a feeling of 'We beat the bastards' even though we had lost eight men. I think we took a couple of prisoners. The glory of it, the excitement of winning. How different that feeling was to when I got captured, oh, I felt so alone then.

We got a rest period after this although we still had to do guard duties. We moved up then into the main line up at the Imjin River where they were expecting a massive Chinese army coming down, bigger than they had ever faced before. This was April 1951 and we were there for about three weeks.

Ken Hawthorne

Another hairy moment I had. I got quite used to the minefield work although I wasn't doing it all the time, I was also doing the roads. We were laying out minefields in front of our own forward positions. We always went out with the infantry in case any Chinese came near us. I hadn't been trained in minefields and all I got was that first week in Japan, other than that I don't think I did any in basic training. But you soon get to know. The officers had good training at Chatham. We laid the mines in patterns, there's a way of laying them so that it's difficult for the enemy. You have pathways that are not straight. You just have to know which of the patterns we were using. Sometimes we had to go out with the infantry on patrol showing them how to get round the minefields and back. We always had a password to get back in. It was pretty quiet most times but one night when we had decided to pack in I was keen to get back. I think the password was coffeepot; it changed every night. Somebody yelled something else to me and I was expecting coffee. He said, 'Its been changed mate.' They'd never told me.

Also, one night when we were out working, a fella came walking out of the shrubbery and it turned out to be an Australian sniper and he said, 'I'm glad I met you blokes cos I don't know the password to get back in.' He said, 'I've been out for three days picking off as many Chinese as I could.' Australians! I don't know!

Brian Hough

We had outer gloves, which were on a string, like the gloves kids have when they go to school. And you kept them on until you had to take them off. They were like mittens and you would take them off if you had to fire your weapons or clean them. But you only took them off when you really had to.

I remember the padre coming round one time. He was a nice guy. But he had a revolver. I was chatting with him and I said, 'You've got a revolver there, you're a padre,' and he said, 'Well if those Chinamen are going to have a pop at me then I'm going to have a pop back.'

Jim Lucock

Don't forget there were two wars. The first was up and down fighting and the second war, that I was involved in, was trench warfare. A bit of a stalemate. But what the lads who were first there went through must have been horrendous. Our war was very different to theirs.

When we arrived we were taken up to battalion HQ. The sergeant came out and I'd heard about him, he was known as the Big Mick. He'd come from the Irish Guards but he was actually a Welshman! And he frightened the lives out of us, he really did. He said go get this, go get some food and there's a Doris Day film on tonight. Now I love Doris Day, lovely singer, her and Ella Fitzgerald, Sarah Vaughan. She was one of my favourites. The next day they spilt us up into different companies. They wanted to put me in 'D' Company and although they were good lads there was one particular lad I didn't like so I said I didn't want to go in 'D' cos I was going to have problems with him. So they put me in Charlie Company. I didn't like the fella, still don't like him. One of the first fellas I met was Bill Hurst – he was slim then! It was so quiet there, you never heard birds. I was taken to a dugout, on my own, to a hutchie and given some wire and told to make a bed. It was a bit daunting being on my own. So they told me how to make a bed out of some angle iron and wire and you put your sleeping bag on there. I've never felt so alone in my life. I'm all by myself. That was my first welcome to the King's Regiment, I was left on my own. After that experience I made sure that anyone who came was not left on their own. I was on my own forever and a day, the whole time I was there, and even when I became a lance corporal and then a corporal, I always was alone.

'Don't go onto the forward slope,' they said, 'you'll get killed.' If they spotted you the Chinese would start lobbing mortars over, they were always watching you and we were always watching them.

We had a company commander, Major Dines, a gentleman he was, been in the Indian army, spoke frightfully slow. When I was a corporal he would say, Corporal Luckock, get them men to dig the trench deeper, so very precise he was. Dig em deep Dines, we called him.

I wasn't in the hutchie much of the day. There was always something to do, they made sure they kept you busy and didn't give you time to think about about anything. The next night I was told to go down to the company HQ and they said, 'You're going on patrol tonight with a corporal and three Kingsmen.' Nobody told us what it was all about but we were told to take our ammunition, some grenades, get our guns cleaned and so forth. Anyhow, when we got down and it was just going dark, the mosquitoes were just starting to bite and the frogs – massive they were – were beginning to croak away. But once they went quiet it meant nobody was coming the other way, but when they were, they all started croaking. But nobody told me that. So we went down, it was dark and I didn't know where we where. The corporal said to me, 'Come here with me,' and he took me about 30–40ft in front. He said, 'You stay here, I'm going back.' He gave me a handset and I thought, what the hell am I doing here? I'd be all right with them in numbers but I was being left alone. But that was the way it was. Anyhow, at about two o'clock in the morning I see these lights coming towards me, like someone smoking a cigarette. I had a little Bren gun and I thought, jeez who's this. There were four or five of them, so I just opened up with the Bren gun. It caused a bit of a stink later. What it was, was that it was fireflies. It just looked like cigarettes. The corporal came, 'Let's move back,' he says, 'What the hell were you doing, they were just fireflies.' 'Well how the hell was I supposed to know.' I said, 'Nobody mentioned them to me.' But I learnt from that. In fact I learnt a lot in the first few days, especially about how you should be treated. But that was the army's way of doing things. Once I got into the platoon and got to know the lads things became a bit different.

Ken Hawthorne

We were at this time living about a mile back, still in a tent. The Chinese artillery was building up quickly and they were bombarding us so living in a tent wasn't such a good idea, so we quickly changed to living in the hutchies. We built them ourselves, I'm not sure why they were called hutchies or hutches, maybe it was after rabbit hutches or what.

We were up with the Australians once and we got shelled. There were three of us outside this hutchie and the shells were landing around us so we were looking for some shelter when this little Australian appeared out of the door from a hutchie and said, 'come in here'. So we dashed in. He'd built it himself. We put logs across ours and then sandbags on top of them, but not the Australians, and there was soil coming down on us every time a mortar fell, the roof was sagging with the weight of soil. Australians – they are mad.

George Stirland

Clothing was poor. We got a pair of long johns each and they were that thick you couldn't get your other gear on, most of them took them ashore and sold them to the Japanese. It was very old stuff, half of it had First World War labels. We got an extra jersey and that was it, I think. The summer wasn't bad but we had to have long sleeves and trousers on as we were firing the guns.

Jim Lucock

You couldn't wash your clothes. You had only so much water brought up and you'd have a shave in the morning. I didn't shave then but everybody had to have a shave – it was compulsory. It was still very cold in a morning. When we came out of the line we were in tents and this water was put on in the night to warm up, so if you were last out of bed you got pea soup. Everybody would have washed in it, you can imagine the slime cos everybody had used it and nobody would wash in cold water, it was just too cold. So when we were in the line you very rarely washed. If you were lucky you would go down the Imjin River once a month where there was a mobile shower unit and you had a shower. And when it was really warm you might have a swim. I remember everybody had white swimming shorts! Their bodies would be brown but then when they took their trousers off it was all white! We didn't get much in the way of a change of clothes, but if it had been extremely wet they might bring some dry clothes up for you to change into. It was a bit different by the time I got there. Before that the lads hadn't been able to change or shower. But after a year or two things were better organised. But like everything else, you got used to it, you can get used to anything if you have to.

We had British rations, which we sometimes swapped with the Americans. But the British food wasn't bad. And we always managed to get a few bottles of beer. We would put the beer in our sleeping bags overnight to stop it freezing. We never saw newspapers unless someone's parents sent them something. There used to be a monthly paper that had bits from all the papers. Somebody would get it and it would be passed around everyone. It would be well worn by the time you got it. But I never got the football results or any other sports news.

The centurion tank regiment were always good to us although we never wanted them around half the time as the Chinese deliberately targeted them and they'd be shelling all the time. Go somewhere else we used to tell them. But the centurion tanks always had hot water because of the engine and they had hot meals and other things. So you had to be very careful with them as sometimes they'd give you a bit of hot water, make some tea or whatever. You could always make tea as we had all these makeshift heaters. But life was very harsh.

A mate of mine who went into the REME – he was serving his time as a bricklayer and he and I used to go to night school together and when I said I wasn't going because I was playing football, he said, well I'm not going either then, so we got called up the same way. Anyhow, he was in the REME and he was stationed in Seoul, so they didn't do what we did in the infantry. His time in Korea was very different to mine. As an infantryman you were entitled to moan, nobody took any notice mind you.

The ceasefire must by this time have been close. We were still doing patrols. We used to see the searchlight where the peace talks were taking place so we knew that if we could see the searchlight they must still be talking. Even the night of the ceasefire it was there, then the artillery started firing red white and blue. I felt a big sigh of relief, everybody was the same. We depended on one another, some you liked, some you didn't. We came out in October 1953 and went to Teal Bridge where we were kept in reserve in case the ceasefire stopped. Then I was given a party of men to go digging on Gloster hill, digging in more trenches. Then we finally went down to Pusan where we got smartened up, polished our boots, rifles and marched down to the cemetery. There were just wooden crosses, it was poignant. And that was it, we then went home.

Ken Hawthorne

It was quite warm inside the hutchie. When the cold weather came back towards the end of my time, we had fires or stoves supplied by the Americans. They were run on petrol, it was just an empty stove with a chimney and you just heated it up and it was lovely and warm. When we weren't at work it wasn't all warfare, we did get away from the front line. We had a little Chinese boy joined us who was 15, or so, and he used to do all our washing for us. He was a good little lad and we kept him fed. But it did get very cold just before I left. When I arrived it was getting warmer and it was quite nice, the scenery was lovely.

Geoff Holland

I had a bed that I had pinched off the Yanks. It was like a camp bed. Otherwise you just lay on the floor. I always remember one night. Being signallers, someone had to be on the radio every minute of every day. Sometimes lads would be sleeping during the day as they had been on the radio all night. This particular night it was bloody freezing, minus 30°F to minus 40°F, and you couldn't hold your rifle with your bare hands as it would rip the skin off. When we went at first we had no winter kit although we did eventually get really good winter kit. But this particular night they issued us with sleeping bags as well, fleecy lined. You got into your bed or bunk or whatever you want to call it with all your clothes on, just take your boots off. It was just too cold to take your clothes off. This particular night we'd had a meal – there was a cookhouse in this little valley where we were – and I'd been down and come back with my mess tin. I'd made a shelf in the wall – I'd knocked some pegs into the earth and put an ammunition box lid on – and was using it as a shelf. So, I was having this meal, stew I think it was, and I said to the lads, 'I'm getting my head down now.' I'm lying there and it's pitch dark and I heard this scratching. It was a bloody rat and it jumped and ran all over me. I think I was more frightened of the rats than the Chinese. It really frightened me, it did. I cringe even now thinking of this blasted rat crawling all over me. We got a lot of rats, it was absolutely walking with rats. I suppose it was the dead bodies everywhere. We had a Korean who used to walk around with one on a string! There were loads and loads of them – everywhere. But I never saw any mice. It was all winter that I was there – I left in May and then you got mosquitoes, millions of them. You had to take paludrine which is actually still used. Just a tablet for malaria. In a morning you'd have this parade and an officer would come round with this Paludrine and you'd have to eat it while he was watching. It was called the Paludrine parade.

The toilet was a hole in the ground – a box with a hole in – although there was a bit of a shed around it. We never got away much from our hole. We had our own cookhouse and the NAFFI would come around with cigarettes, beer and chocolate. We must have gone months without changing our clothes and without a shower. Everything was just frozen. You could get a bucket of snow and melt it but you only finished up with a bit of water. We did have water but sometimes you'd run out of it, so you'd get a bucket of snow and make a brew.

We were in the hole twenty-four hours a day, seven days a week. It got quite boring. In that twenty-four-hour spell you were more or less on duty the whole time, not like a holiday camp. But it was usually four hours on duty, two hours off.

The area where we were, we put perimeter wire around and we had trenches dug on the edges of the wire so that you could defend your own position. You'd each have your own trench – it was probably about 4ft deep – and you'd be stood in this trench waiting for them to come. And out in the freezing cold it was not much fun. You didn't go on guard on your own in Korea. You had to keep watching one another for frostbite. You had all the gear on – big parkas – and you could pull the chords together so that they just left a slot for your eyes. And you had big mittens. How you were supposed to fire a rifle I don't know. We had long john underpants, string vest, fleece-lined trousers, and then wind proof trousers on top of them, then a wind-proof jacket under your parka and an old army shirt. You were well looked after but you could hardly walk about. You had to have it or you'd freeze to death. I think the first lads who went broke through and got almost to the Chinese border, and when the Chinese came in they routed ours and there was a big retreat. They suffered in the snow in that first winter. We suffered but not to their extent.

Brian Hough

It was trench warfare at that time. After the spring offensive of 1951 it became static for the next eighteen months. The only way I would describe it – and no way would I suggest that we suffered like they suffered in the First World War – but it was very like it. I've seen pictures and film of the trenches and it was like that. We just dug holes in the hillside. We had to make sure that the trench was deeper than we were tall. Into the side of the hill you would dig out a space for living quarters. It was called a hutchie, I think it must have been a Korean name. We would prop it up with timber and we used to live in that hole in the side of the hill and when it rained it got flooded and it was full of rats. Now that is my biggest fear – rats. They were awful. It was overrun with rats. You'd be lying in your hutchie and we'd made beds from angle iron and telephone wires. That was to sleep on, a bit like a hammock and we had sleeping bags. You didn't take your boots off or anything. Half the time you were standing-to. You could be as close as 200 yards from the enemy and you certainly couldn't move about cos they had very good snipers. You certainly wouldn't show yourself in the day, well not intentionally anyrate. We were thrown into that kind of environment straight away.

The rats could crawl all over you. We'd been on patrol one night with a good pal of mine, one of the lads I'd joined up with, and nothing had happened. We were having a moan cos we'd been up all night, so we came back to the hutchie and the first thing you do is to clean all your weapons. We were sat down and this lad from Moston, Stan Jackson, lays down full length in this slit trench. I'm sat with my knees up and my back against the wall of the trench and there was a Welsh lad on the other side. Anyrate, I'm dropping off and next minute I said, 'Look at that there!' Stan Jackson was fast asleep with a rat on his chest gnawing at his clothing. It was awful. I've got scars caused by rats. I'd only been in Korea a few weeks when I developed sores on my ankle and like a fool I ignored them, they'll go away, I thought. And, of course, they didn't go away and I had to go off sick. They had to fly me out to Kure. They were from fleas off rats. They'd spread and were all over my legs and ankles. For a few years after it would still break out in sores. But I've not had them for quite a long time now. When I reported sick our regimental medical officer he gave me a right roasting. He said I should have reported it earlier. And he was right. But at the time I thought you can't report sick with a sore ankle, you're in the army. But it was part of my thinking, you didn't complain. But of course it got worse and spread. So I was about three weeks in hospital in Kure in Japan.

Jim Houghton

When we were up there we didn't get cooked meals we had what looked like a brown shoebox called C sixes and C sevens and it was all American food and we all preferred that. You'd get a tin of spaghetti, chicken and something else – there was two tins of solids – then a tin with something sweet of some sort, a big thick biscuit and American cigarettes, that was very popular. I used to smoke Philip Morris, you got fifty free cigarettes from the British every week, everyone got that wherever you were – Senior Service, Players – and then there was twenty more in your rations every day. You could heat the tin up. We preferred that as you could eat when you wanted to. When I transferred over to the Leicester's they had cooked meals and you'd get a hot meal in the winter. The winters were very cold, bitter cold. You had the meal in the trenches, they would bring it to you. If you got any beer you only got one bottle but not very often.

The trench was 4ft by 2ft and the beauty of the British trench was that everyone would have a little shovel or a little pick which hooked into the back of your belt so you could widen it. The Chinese were far better at it than we were because the Chinese had so many people there. We used to call the Chinese the laundrymen. At night they could dig a trench all the way around the mountain overnight. A complete circle, takes some believing that. The next day you'd see another one, all round in a big circle. They would bury their own dead in the trenches, just put some soil on it. They treated their dead badly. But they treated the living well, the Chinese were always clean, always shaven, always clean clothes on them, well turned out. I remember they wouldn't even bury their own people some times. I remember being out on patrol and spotted this dead Chinese soldier in a stream and another lying just by. They'd been dead for weeks and they hadn't bothered to bury them even though it was in their own territory. One day we took some Chinese prisoners and I couldn't believe it, they were spotless, shaven clean as anything, clean clothes. We were like tramps compared to them and I thought, they don't bury the dead, they're not bothered about them. I didn't understand the mentality of that. The north Koreans were a hard people, we knew them as Gooks and the South Koreans we called ROKs (Republic of Korea) and the Chinaman was always the laundryman.

The trenches were about 4ft deep, just as long as you could stand in it, 3ft might be enough. We were living in them most of the time, certainly those in the forward position. You had a few behind as well where you had your groundsheets, at the back of the hill out of sight, and you could knock a bit of a tent up there with them. There would always be guards on the front at a night-time but if it was a quiet night with nothing going on you could sleep in your tent at the back. In the winter the ground was too hard to dig in so you'd stay in the trench. During the day in the trench you'd be doing nothing, having a cigarette, talking to each other, maybe writing a letter if you wanted. You got a free airmail letter with a stamp on it so that you could write home. Or you could just sleep if you wanted because some nights you would have been standing on guard.

If something was happening you'd be on a stand-to at night. There was always two of you, so you might have one on duty and the other sleeping and every hour you'd change over. There'd be two of you in this trench and further down there would be another two. When we advanced to a new position we always had the same people to the right and the same to the left and I always knew who was behind us. In the dark it meant that you could recognise the voice and you always knew they would be 7 or 8 yards away to the left and right. We always stuck together like that.

There were no showers up there on the front line. In the summer we could go down to a village where there might be a well. You'd go down there, draw some water and tip it over yourself, maybe every fortnight. You'd go maybe nine, ten days in the trench and then get a bit of time out of it.

Jim Daly

I just had a canvas bed at first. Outside the tent there was a 45-gallon drum of water and we had to take a bucket load inside and put it on a stove for shaving, washing and so on. Later on when we had been there for a few months we got proper beds, metal beds.

The weather was extreme. The winter was very, very cold and we had specialist equipment like parkas – that's like big duffle coats with a hood on. We had special boots, string vests and so on for when we went out on patrol traffic duties. In the bad weather it was mainly traffic duties. We had monsoons and so much rain, so we had to do road checks and only certain things like food, petrol and water were allowed to travel. The cold weather was difficult at first because we weren't used to it. We had a little paraffin stove in our tent. It was rough but we survived. We had a shower. It was a made up job. It was like a little shed with a watering can above it. The food however was good. We had Canadian rations and Australian rations which was far better than the British army food. Being in the RMP we weren't always popular but we had a job to do. We didn't have too many actual problems, no drunken soldiers or anything like that. There was a NAAFI, but no problems. We got paid £3 a week and as a regular you got more. There was nothing much to spend it on anyhow apart from toiletries and that.

There was nowhere to spend it on apart from the NAAFI. We worked different shifts; two hours on, four hours off, depending what duties you had. When we had time off we'd play cards but there wasn't much to do, it was a desolate place with few facilities. They didn't put any entertainment on – that was more the Yanks – they had movies. I never thought of it as boring because you were occupied most of the time.

John Smith

We never had showers. In fact the only showers I ever saw were in the American camps. I certainly didn't have many showers the whole time I was in Korea. As for food, well once we got in with the Canadians we started getting good food. We lost our cook. We had a heater and one day it went up in flames and he was badly burnt. I never learnt what happened to him but we then had no cook. You're moving around so much that you lose touch with what's going on.

I remember one time it was fairly quiet and they said that there was a beer ration for us, Japanese beer. Somebody had to go down and collect it so I said, OK I'd go. I brought it back and handed out the rations and while I'm there there's three black American lads. We're there drinking it from jerrycans and they said, 'Can we buy some beer off you guys.' I said, 'No, no, we don't sell our beer ration but,' I said, 'I'll tell you what I'll do with you, get those three cans there and you'll be welcome to a beer.' And they couldn't believe it because black soldiers weren't treated well in those days. We were all white lads. Anyhow, they sat there and had a beer with us and thanked us. The following day an American came up in one of their jeeps, a black fellow, and someone was shouting me, 'Corporal Smith, Corporal Smith, there's someone here to see you.' So I walked over and said, 'Yes I'm Corporal Smith,' and he said, 'You're the guy. My commanding officer has sent me up to invite you and some of your lads down to our camp to entertain you because you entertained our guys here last night.' I said, 'Ok, very good.' Anyhow, only two of us could go, so I went with someone else. We went into this camp and this black officer came up to me and said, 'Oh you're Corporal Smith are you?' He said, 'Well thank you very much.

My men have done nothing but talk about the way you British looked after them last night and wouldn't take any money for the drink.' He said, 'They had a good night with you,' so he said, 'To repay you for your hospitality we are going to put on a movie show for you tonight, and you see that 2½ ton Dodge over there, well that will be the screen, but before we have the movie we're going to provide you with a really good meal.' Well, we had chicken and all sorts.

When the evening finished the officer came over to me and said, 'Everything OK? Well before you leave gentlemen can you put the rear end of your jeep in front of that marquee over here.' He said, 'Don't worry, it's all been arranged, that is our quartermaster. Now he will fill your jeep with whatever he can get in it.' I couldn't believe it. There were Hershy bars, Babie Ruth, cigarettes – 200 Phillip Morris, Lucky Strike, 200 cartons in sacks! So I drive back to our camp and the fellas are all looking at this stuff. I said, 'Gather round, here you are lads, this is from the Americans,' and threw it to them. They couldn't believe it. I didn't smoke. At one time we used to get fifty fags in a tin a week. I used my cigarettes for playing cards, I wasn't worried.

I just thought that it was because we had treated them as equals and wouldn't take any money for the beer. They were beginning to have problems in the States and they just thought we were treating them decently and that was our reward.

Ivan Williams

We were there about three months before we had a bath. There was no encouragement to stand out in the cold and wash yourself down so we were not the cleanest of people but that applied to everyone. There were no facilities for having a bath back at command post either. I only got a bath because I drew my own name out of a hat for two days leave at a leave camp at Inchon, so I spent most of that leave in the shower! I don't think I ever washed any of my clothes. We just didn't take much off, you took the parkas off but nothing else. We'd sleep in our clothes for two reasons, one was that you didn't know what was going to happen next as you were always on a semi-alert and secondly because it kept you warm. The front line was never quiet, there was always fire going one way or the other, and it was rarely dark because the Commonwealth Division continually put up star shells to illuminate no-man's-land. It was a strange environment. It was even too cold for rats or any other animals, nothing moved except us. I'm sure there was lots of wildlife in the summer, but they either hibernated in the winter or froze to death. I stayed there for about five months into the summer when it got appreciably warmer. We then dispensed of the winter clothing.

Ken Hawthorne

I used to have to go out sometimes with infantry patrols for various different reasons, sometimes where they thought there might be booby traps. I didn't know that much about booby traps. We had mine detectors like they have now, but they weren't much use to us, so we didn't use them, as there had been so much shelling and so much shrapnel. You'd be going along sweeping with the detector and it would go off, a piece of shrapnel, then another piece of shrapnel, then another sound and another piece of shrapnel and then you think you've got another piece of shrapnel and you haven't, it's a mine! So we didn't use them at all, it was that bad.

We didn't actually arm the mines, the officers did that, we just put them in the patterns and put cones on and then later the officer would come along and pull the pin. We marked everything on paper and which pattern they had been set to. The trouble was that they used to put some mines with trip wires on them but then the vegetation grew up around the trip wires. I never had to do it but some had to go and disarm a minefield with trip wires and that was dangerous. Although they said you had to put two pound pressure on the wire, I wouldn't like to. I used to get very frightened. Although you get used to it, I must admit I was frightened at the very beginning and especially when you're losing lads. When is it going to be my turn? you wondered.

I was working on minefields a lot in the summer, and I was given a day off and it was a lovely day and I knew from my camp that you could see

355 and that was a lovely feature, so I thought I'd go for a walk and see how much of it I could see from near the top of our camp. And as I approached I could see what I thought were loads and loads of white stones on the very top. And as I got nearer I realised they were bones, loads of them, and as I got closer I saw that they were indeed bones. There were shoes and all sorts, all scattered all over the place, skulls and so on all over. I found a little slit trench that had been there a long time. I looked down and there were two American dog tags, I picked them up and brought them back and gave them to our officer. I wish I could remember their names but they were Italian sounding. Obviously they had been in this slit trench and had been overrun by the Chinese. God knows by how many Chinese but they had managed to shoot them all until they were overpowered. There was little bits of uniform, shoes here and there. That must have been a terrible disaster on top of that hill.

Brian Hough

I have said that most people who went to Korea would remember the smell of Pusan, and the rats, but there was a third thing you would remember – the weather. Our first winter, 1952–53, we were more or less prepared for it. The Americans supplied most of the heavy winter clothing but in the first year of the Korean war, that winter, our men really suffered. The Argylls, Sutherland Highlanders and the Middlesex were sent from Hong Kong in September 1950 and were the first British infantry there. It's not an exaggeration but during January 1953 when we were there the temperature never rose above -38°F. That was as warm as it got, -38°F. And that really is cold. I often wonder how we survived it.

For clothes we had normal British issue underpants and vests, shirt, uniform, trousers, but in addition to that we were issued flannel long johns and on top of that the Americans introduced a fleecy lined pair of trousers to put on over the long johns and then the British issue. On top we had the normal vest, plus a string vest, plus a shirt, plus a jumper that tied up around the neck. We had two pairs of mittens. The Americans issued us with a parka; they're common now but at that time I'd never seen one. It was a wonderful thing, it really was. There were pockets for ammunition, and a tail hanging down that you press under here, a big wire framed hood so that you could adjust it to suit your field of vision. We had knitted caps as well. The cold was indescribable. We had standing patrols which were awful – most of the time nothing happened but you were out patrolling in the cold and mainly at night. You'd be in front of your own company's positions and in no-man's-land and all you did was sit there all damn night and wait for something to happen. In the winter it was awful. You couldn't move because the Chinese would hear or see you. And every so often you had to release all the moving parts on your weapons to stop them from freezing up, otherwise they wouldn't work and if the Chinese suddenly appeared, you wouldn't be able to do anything. They'd be frozen. And the trucks, if they were going to be stationary for anything like fifteen minutes or more they'd drain the radiators cos they'd freeze. It was unbelievable. And what they did for warmth in the hutch – damn dangerous thing – we had metal containers and we'd feed it with a rubber tube and a jerrycan of diesel and it would drip and we'd have a hotplate or a stove. We had quite a few accidents caused by that I'll tell you.

In fact there was a lad who used to live in the same street as myself and his mother worked in the canteen at the same factory as my father worked and she received a telegram saying Norman had been wounded. But what had happened was that he had been burnt; the heater had been knocked over and it had spread and poor Norman had been burnt all down the side of his face. He was taken to hospital in Japan and was away for six weeks or so. He came back and had only been back a day or so when he got wounded and lost an eye.

Terry Moore

I don't remember ever seeing any rats. I saw them on sale in the Chinese markets in the little towns. They were a cooked delicacy. But I never saw them running wild, they had more sense than to come out in the cold. All the fleas and bugs came from the straw we slept in during the winter. In the summer when the weather was warmer, you could get into the water and wash yourself.

Brian Hough

You just can't describe the winters. It did snow but it was a hard, cold frost more than anything. I don't ever remember having to dig anything out. It was the wind really which came down straight through Manchuria from Siberia. But there was snow. We also got issued with white suits so when we went out on patrol at nights we used to put them on over all the other stuff.

We washed and shaved but I'm sure we didn't do it every day, in fact I know we didn't. There were times when we've brewed up and I've had a cup of tea and I've used the last half of the tea to shave with. It'd be warm so you could have a quick shave. They introduced a system every three weeks or so and you'd go behind the line – 3 or 4 miles – and there was a mobile shower unit. But we'd only shower once every three weeks. There were no toilets in the trenches. There were connecting trenches all over the place so you'd travel through these connectible trenches to the reverse slopes of the hill and there were toilets dug out there. You didn't hang about too long cos of the cold and in the summer cos of the spiders. To be honest most times we just did it where we were stood. Behind the lines they had pipes so that was a bit better.

Summers were quite mild – in fact it could be quite warm, not like Hong Kong or India but it could be beautiful. Korea is a beautiful country – hills wherever you look. I thought it was a lovely country, I really did. I was in my element because, as a kid, I used to go out camping up in the hills around Hayfield in Derbyshire. It was surprising how quickly the Korean countryside could change from the winter to the mild spring and then the summer. It was a complete contrast, so dramatic. I've got photographs after the ceasefire in 1953 and we're all stripped to the waist.

We didn't really have much contact with the Americans. Well not when we were in the front line although it has to be said that they fed us. When we were in the front line we used to get twenty-four-hour ration packs brought up. Korean porters used to bring it up these hills with great frames on their back, piled high. How they managed it I don't know. I really felt for them. They'd bring it up and in these twenty-four-hour packs there'd be various tins – bacon and beans, sausage and beans, always beans somewhere, tins of soup that were self-igniting. It had a tube and a wick and you could warm the soup up, always a piece of cake or some biscuits and twenty cigarettes. When I was first in Korea I didn't smoke so I used to give them away. Chesterfield, Lucky Strike, Camel – all the American brands of cigarettes. We'd get those and then at weekends we would get a tin of fifty Senior Service from the British. In the end I couldn't give them away so I started smoking them myself. But in terms of individual contact with the Americans, we didn't have any.

Eric Peters

The winters were terrible, how can you describe the cold? Bitter, very cold. There was a Manchester lad who had a moustache and one morning it was frozen and it just came off in his hands. If you carried a jerry-can of water, by the time you got back it was frozen. It was unbelievable. There were no toilets. I had two showers in all the time I was there. In the summer we had a bath in the river. We never had a change of clothes at all, same kit day in, day out. You had a haversack which might have one change but as that had been used, well you couldn't wash things because they would never dry. You just lived in the same clothes all the time, day and night, week after week.

The food was okay, we were on Yankee rations, hamburgers and so on. We used to get twenty Lucky Strike cigarettes a day from the Yanks with your food and got another twenty a day for when you were up the hills. But of course they couldn't get them up there, so when you got down you'd be given 200 fags, but you couldn't use them so you'd end up throwing them away. You'd be getting twenty a day, then another twenty and those who didn't smoke gave their cigarettes away as well. You had far too many, you couldn't smoke that many. We had American rations from day one as we didn't have a cook, so we just had American rations.

Jim Houghton

When we first went it was summer and we only had combat trousers and jacket. You had two shirts, one in your pack, one you wore. You'd be carrying all your things in your backpack so you couldn't have too much. There were no fat fellas in the infantry, so the trousers were all the same size, you just wrapped them around you and it was the same with shirts. Every so often you would hand a shirt in and get another one.

We'd change our clothes about once a month, just one spare shirt and one spare pair of socks. At odd times you might be able to wash a few things. When it became winter we had different clothing, really good clothing, lined parka coats, well-protected American stuff, this was winter 1951. It was really good with ear flaps as well and you needed it, living in the hills. There were no fires.

When the King died they took us off this hill and we had to stand there, each section at a time, and they made us sing 'God Save the Queen,' not King. An officer said, 'You've sworn allegiance to the Queen now.' The snow was over the top of my boots and there was a cold, bitter wind. Now I remember that because it had started snowing four days before Christmas and the snow was still there when the King died and that was in the February! In the summers, however, it could be very hot and dry although there were wet spells as well and you'd get soaked.

Ken Hawthorne

We often got entertainment behind the line and we got in lorries and went down. Some American entertainers came – Bob Hope was one – and we went to see Frankie Howerd[18] as well and some girl singer. Anyway, coming back in the lorry we were all falling asleep when suddenly one of the lads' guns went off and it had put a hole in the side of the lorry just by one lad's face. He was asleep at the time but he just opens his eyes and he says, 'You stupid fucker,' and then went back

---

18   Frankie Howerd (1917–92), English comedian and comic actor.

to sleep again. I thought to myself, it just didn't seem to bother him. Astonishing. You had to have a rifle and ammunition with you all the time but you weren't supposed to have one up the spout, as we called it. So I don't know how that had happened.

Another time, when we were being shelled we jumped into a trench. One of the shells landed very close and frightened the life out of the three of us. It was so close it must have been on top of us. And one said, 'Fucking hell,' and the little fellow in the corner says, 'I hope they do cos that's where I'm going.' Humour at a time like that, I couldn't get over that.

Bill Hurst

The trenches were just dug out of the earth and in the bottom they used to put duckboards because if it rained it would be full of water and if you had the duckboards it would help keep your feet dry, as the water would lie underneath them. It was important to keep your feet dry. Then you would walk along it, twisting around, here and there. In the trenches there were dugouts at the back of you. So if there was shelling you would go in there. The shells would come down and if you were lucky they didn't hit you. But they were well built, they had wooden beams in and they would be filled with soil and then sandbags and then more soil so if anything happened it just made a hole on the top. It was mostly 60mm mortars coming down on us. The trench would be about 5–6ft deep, but there were also parts where you could stand and see over the trench. There was something dug into the wall of the trench so that you could stand on it and look over and fire. So it was a good 6ft in depth. Some were not as deep because there was rock and they would fetch the engineers out to help dig them. The main work of digging the trenches was done by the engineers and sometimes the soldiers themselves. If a mortar had fallen and caused damage then they would have to be dug out again and the front line soldiers tended to do that. The line of trenches also had a G ped, this was further back from the trenches where the jeeps could come with all the things we needed, it was also a kind of gathering area. If the company commander needed to talk to the men they would all go to the G ped. And that's where you would get your briefing. But you still had OPs left in the trenches, keeping an eye on things, to see if anything was happening. Instead of everybody being in the front line all the time, the OPs would be there with their binoculars always watching for something. We'd likely be back in our hutches, cleaning our rifles or whatever. We used to do two hours on, four hours off, something like that. If they thought nothing was happening, then they might only have two OPs on. There'd be just a couple of you watching at the front line to see what's happening. Our living quarters, which were called hutches, were a little further back. They were just dug out in the trench, they had a bit of a cover and that's where we slept all night and lived. But on the front line you'd be there, on duty watching, listening for any kind of sound. There'd be wild animals out there who would rattle the wires, you'd hear it and you'd ask for flares and they would go up and light the whole area so you could see.

Terry Moore

The simple things in life were literally simple. It was an ordeal dropping your trousers if you wanted a crap and there were no public toilets about. At one stage you couldn't dig your own toilet, which you did when the ground was soft. You would normally dig a big trench then put a tree branch across it and sit on it. And when everything was frozen you just did it anywhere in the snow and just covered it up, though obviously away from the area where you lived. I can remember with great amusement one officer who came from Southport. We had come to a position which had previously been occupied and he was wandering around and he said, oh here's a good position for a Bren gun and he jumped into the trench which turned out to be a shit trench and he was in about a foot of piss and turds.

The food came up every day – god bless the quartermasters – we had American tinned rations and Tommy cookers. Tommy cookers were little round tins and you took the lid off with petroleum jelly in it and you just light it and it burns. You could also get a couple of bricks around it, put your mess tin on and it warmed all your food. When we got American rations there was always great delight because they contained what we felt was better food than British army rations and it was more varied food and also came with twenty Lucky Strike cigarettes each time. Have you ever heard the expression a soldiers breakfast? A cup of tea and a Woodbine. But we didn't get Woodbines.

With what time I had we would plan ahead, do a reccie, plot exit routes. We got a bottle of beer every week, Japanese beer, and I had to ident for it on a Friday or Saturday and it came up every Monday morning. So if I had idented for my platoon on the Saturday, for say twenty-eight men, and then by the Monday we had reinforcements, so that there were more than twenty-eight men, starting with the senior officers we did without. So I would do without. One day I was doing the rounds and the men – god bless them – a scouser, it would have to be a scouser. I jumped into the trench when I was doing my rounds, he said, 'Ay sir, saw you never got any ale today, so I've saved yer a bit of mine.' Aren't people wonderful. First of all was the fact that he had noticed it. So he had saved me some of his beer. Bless him, he survived the war.

I had this small book of Shakespeare sonnets. It wasn't mine, it belonged to Lieutenant Max Nicols who was captured and he was into poetry. I thought he had been killed, all the reports suggested he had been killed, and I got this with his effects and kept it with me, and strangely I opened it at the sonnet which began, 'No longer mourn for me when I am dead'. Now isn't that strange?

When the weather got better we dug slit trenches, that's what we called them, it was just a hole in the ground about 7ft long and 2ft wide and about 5ft deep, and either end in the base there was a sump so that any water would drain away. You'd have a hill and dig these trenches, with a machine gun positioned in the lower ones so that people couldn't come up. And then there would be guns in the rear ones in case they attacked from the rear. And then you had the shit trench at the rear as well. And we would live in our trenches and sleep in them at night.

At night we had a stand-to because the Chinese never attacked in the daylight as we had better firearms and we could see them, so they rarely attacked in the day. At night time we would have a stand-to and everyone would position themselves in the event of action. You would stand-to as the light fell and you would stay there – there'd be two to a trench – one awake, one asleep. We would do this for months on end. You were short on sleep but you got used to it: sleep and wake, sleep and wake. Usually two hours on two hours off. But if anything happened everyone was awake. And always cold, cold, cold. In a sense the cold reduced the fighting as the Chinese didn't come out in the bitter cold. No change of clothes. I never changed my clothes or underwear for six months. We swam in the lake once and then washed our thing in the summer when the weather was warmer. And that was the only time we washed.

Ivan Williams

It was extremely cold. They wrap you up in all this gear. Above the waist we had a string vest, army shirt, an action man jersey, a fur-lined nylon coat and a fur-lined parka so you were like a Michelin man, and although it was warm it was very restrictive in the movement. Below the waist we had long johns, battledress trousers and, again, separate layers of nylon trousers, and all this was tucked into boots. It was extremely cold but I think the concentration kept you awake and kept you going. Two hours wasn't long, you could do two hours. It never went dark on the front line.

We stayed in the same area as the AP but the bunker was maybe a hundred yards further back. Once we were there we would sleep mostly. Or if it was in the daytime we'd just sit inside. The other thing is that everything was very Heath Robinson. We were living in these holes in the ground. Some bright spark came up with an idea on how to keep these holes warm. There was an ammunition box with holes knocked in it with a pickaxe and then a tube feeding petrol into the box and set on fire. The boxes got white hot. But of course they were lethal as outside you had a jerrycan full of petrol which was just feeding in by gravity, and above it we had two or three shell boxes joined together to make a chimney. As you can imagine it wasn't the safest thing but it did keep it warm. We had lights with wicks in, fifty cigarette tins with paraffin in them in the dugouts.

Terry Moore

The cold was the real enemy. Oh, it was so cold. We lost men with frostbite, the Americans had men frozen to death. I was slightly more fortunate as I was more tolerant than many to the cold but lots of people unfortunately were not. I often wondered to myself how the poor black American soldiers coped with the cold as I had a feeling – rightly or wrongly – that they might not be as used to the cold as some of us were.

Ken Hawthorne

Another time after laying some minefields they decided to take the tanks, centurion tanks, which were quite new, and take them in broad light across the valley and run over any Chinese they could find. It seemed to go well until on the way back, when going through our minefield they set off a mine and disabled the tank. I don't know what had happened as we only planted anti-personnel mines, and this one was a much bigger mine. Anyhow the Chinese were shelling it like mad but the crew had managed to get out. The gun in the tank had a stabiliser on it which was still a military secret at the time. It meant that the centurion could go over rough ground and the gun would stay still and stabilised. The military authorities were obviously worried that the Chinese would come out in the night and have a look at it. So they said that six of us would have to go into the minefield and sort the wires because they wanted someone eventually be able to go out and retrieve the tank. Now that was hairy because we had to get out early, so an officer took us to the top of the hill on our front line and looked down on the tank. It was being shelled like mad. It was still broad daylight but just going dark. Don't worry he said, that's our shells. He had arranged a time so that we could get down before it got dark. Going down there in broad daylight with the Chinese knowing it was there and shelling we thought we wouldn't have a chance of getting back. So off we went down. But there was no trouble at all. We put the wire back. The barrage lifted as prearranged just before we got there. It was a big worry over nothing. They managed later to get it back with a big tank puller.

We didn't have any aerial bombardment at all, we used to take our turn on the hilltop above our camp with a Bren gun just in case but never saw anything. What we did see was our Brens pummelling the Chinese in broad light and that must have been horrific for the poor Chinese underneath and there was a magnificent display of napalm going off on the hills. Half the time they weren't there, they didn't man their lines like we did, they got out. The infantry would attack a hill and there would be nobody on it when they got there. The napalm was dropped by American planes operating from carriers.

Then one day I went with a truck driver up to a field, by 355, where we were laying our mines and there was a little section of that 355 where the Chinese could see everything coming and going. We laid our mines and on the way back we got mortared and he really put his foot down. There was only the two of us going on this road although when I say roads they were actually tracks which we had covered with stones. That was hairy as well but we got away with it.

Ivan Williams

Was I frightened? Well, you got used to it. Early on we had a stand-to and I was lying in a trench with a Sten gun. I was frightened but mainly because I didn't know what was happening. I had no idea which way the Chinese might be coming but as it happened nothing happened. In a way also the job was quite intense, you had to think a lot to get the best results, we were alert all the time so we got used to it all. You could tell where a mortar would land 500 yards in front or 500 yards behind. The Chinese had Bofor guns at the line and then behind them they had mortars which could shoot 3 to 4 miles, and further behind that were the 25-pounders with a range of 5 or 6 miles. The war was fought with Second World War weapons. Our Bofors shot from behind us and it went over our heads. The phone rang one day and I picked it up and a cultured voice said, 'Sorry old chap, fin off.' That meant the fin had come off and it might land anywhere. So you'd lie on the bottom of the hole until it had gone, hoping it wasn't going to land on you!

4. NEWS FROM HOME

'One by one all these lads would get a Dear John letter.'

INTRODUCTION

THERE'S NOTHING QUITE like news from home to cheer you up. Or, as in some cases, to leave you in the depths of despair. Most of the letters brought good news: reports of family events, gossip about friends, even the occasional football results, although they often seemed to be a month or so out of date. But at least it kept people in some contact with what was happening back in Britain. And if there was bad family news, it was sometimes kept from those serving abroad. When Eric Peters lost his brother in an accident back home, his father decided not to tell him, thinking, naturally, that he had enough worries without being further upset by the news of his brother's death.

Many soldiers received what became known as 'Dear John' letters. These were letters from loved ones telling them that they had found a new boyfriend or fallen out of love and no longer wanted to go out with them. It led to soldiers feeling despair, neglect and loneliness. Yet it was inevitable that any young woman away from their boyfriend for so long would, in time, find someone else. But there were some women who continued to write even though they had changed their minds and moved on. Ken Hawthorne's girlfriend waited to tell him and was there to meet him when he returned home rather than post him an upsetting 'Dear John' letter.

Ivan Williams was especially lucky. He found a pen pal who wrote regularly to him. Then, when he returned home, they agreed to meet up. Love soon blossomed; they married and enjoyed many happy years together. As he says, he had a lot to thank Korea for.

Writing letters home was a task hugely encouraged by the army. It helped focus the mind, gave the men something to do and allowed them to vent their emotions with loved ones. They would look forward to the mail being delivered and when it did arrive was a major event. The men would retreat into their hutchies or sit outside and for a brief moment renew their contact with home.

Newspapers seem to have been few and far between. Perhaps it was expensive to send them, or maybe parents thought their sons wouldn't be interested in local news. Parcels were scarce as well. Anyhow, what could one send? There were enough shortages back home and sending food was pointless as it would probably be stale by the time it arrived. Books may have been sent to officers, but the ordinary soldier wasn't much interested in reading literature. And of course daily newspapers were not ideal for posting, although where there was a weekly edition it was more likely to be sent. The paper would be passed around and after a while became ripped, creased and generally looked well-read. Roy Cox remembers one of the soldiers receiving the *Eagle* comic every week. The others took the mickey out of him calling him a 'sissy' but once he'd read it the comic would be passed around all the soldiers.

As a consequence of a lack of news those serving knew almost nothing of what was going on in Britain. They were told of the King's death in February 1952 because they were all obliged to immediately pledge their loyalty to the new Queen. But apart from that they knew little of general elections, sporting events, the latest movies, or pop records. They were living in a cocoon, oblivious to events elsewhere.

And yet the army postal service remained vital. Soldiers needed to know that they weren't forgotten and that they were in the forefront of

1 Burial at sea.

2 Crew members of HMS *Cockade*.

3 HMS *Cockade* refuelling at sea.

4 Returning home parade.

5 Eric Peters enjoys some R & R.

6 George Stirland on parade.

7 HMS *Cockade* makes its way through ice packs close to the Korean coast.

8 A view from the bridge of HMS *Cockade*.

9 Summer brought some sun and the chance of fun aboard HMS *Cockade*.

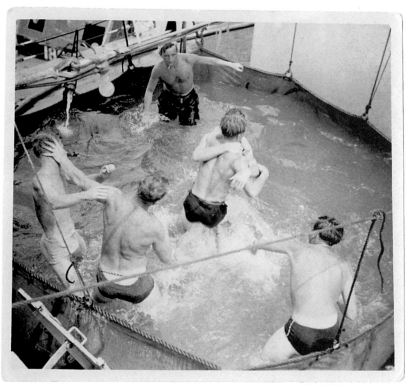

10 North Korean leader Kim Il Sung was not a popular man.

Mr. Moneybags is in Florida this Christmas.

Where are you?   In Korea!
You risk your life, Big Business rakes in the dough.

11 'You risk your life, Big Business rakes in the dough!' Chinese propaganda leaflet.

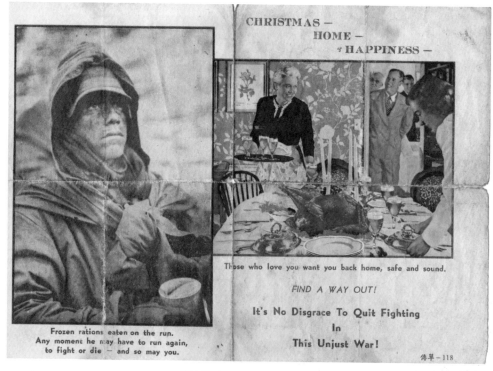

CHRISTMAS —
HOME —
HAPPINESS —

Those who love you want you back home, safe and sound.

FIND A WAY OUT!

It's No Disgrace To Quit Fighting
In
This Unjust War!

Frozen rations eaten on the run.
Any moment he may have to run again,
to fight or die — and so may you.

傳單—118

12 Chinese propaganda leaflets.

13 Bill Fox's Prisoner of War
medal.

14 Eric Peters was a regular who served in India and Palestine before Korea.

15 A service to commemorate the dead.

16 A young Eric Peters in uniform.

17 Ken Hawthorne showing off his shooting skills.

18 Ken Hawthorne at ease.

19 Ken Hawthorne and mining team ready for another mission.

20 Ken Hawthorne outside the cookhouse.

21 Ken Hawthorne laying mines.

22 Always time for a sing-along, though only in the summer.

23 Ken Hawthorne alongside a minefield.

24 Ken Hawthorne, at the ready.

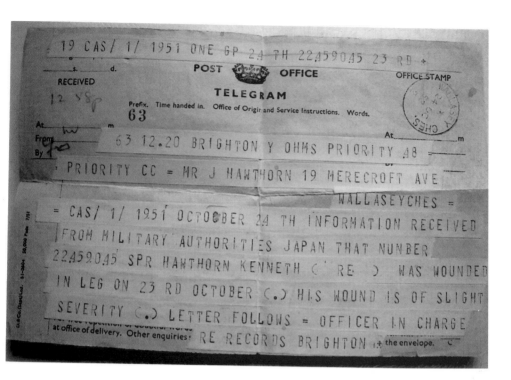

25 Telegram informing Ken Hawthorne's parents that he had been wounded in action.

26 Tree-felling.

27 Winter approaches; Ken Hawthorne and colleague.

28 Troops make for the front.

29 One of the hutches, heavily sandbagged for protection.

30 South Korean helper, Kim.

31 American Globemaster, Seoul Airport.

32 Bill Hurst outside a hutchie.

33 Ken Hawthorne, mine layer.

34 Roy Cox, signaller.

35 Time for a cuppa: Terry Moore and colleagues take a break.

36 Terry Moore, who was wounded at the Battle of the Imjin River.

37 Pusan cemetery already showing the great numbers of dead.

38 Bill Fox, who was a prisoner of war for two and a half years.

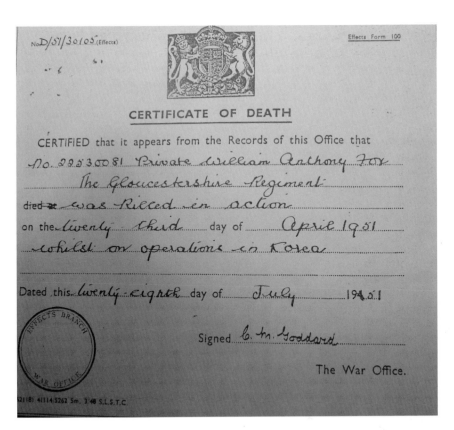

39 Death certificate issued for Bill Fox. The authorities had no idea that he was a prisoner of war.

40 Liverpudlian Jim Lucock still has shrapnel in his legs.

41 Geoff Holland outside his hutch.

42 Wireless operator Geoff Holland, known as 'Dutch' to everyone.

43 Mancunian Brian Hough and his fighting colleagues.

44 Geoff Holland guards his hutch, gun at the ready.

45 Manchester-born Brian
Hough retains vivid memories
of gangs of orphaned children
roaming the countryside.

46 The trash had to go somewhere, so Korean civilians were given the job of digging large trenches.

47 Winter, and the snow, arrives.

48 Breakfast in the hutch.

49 The *Empire Orwell*, one of many troopships that carried the soldiers to Hong Kong.

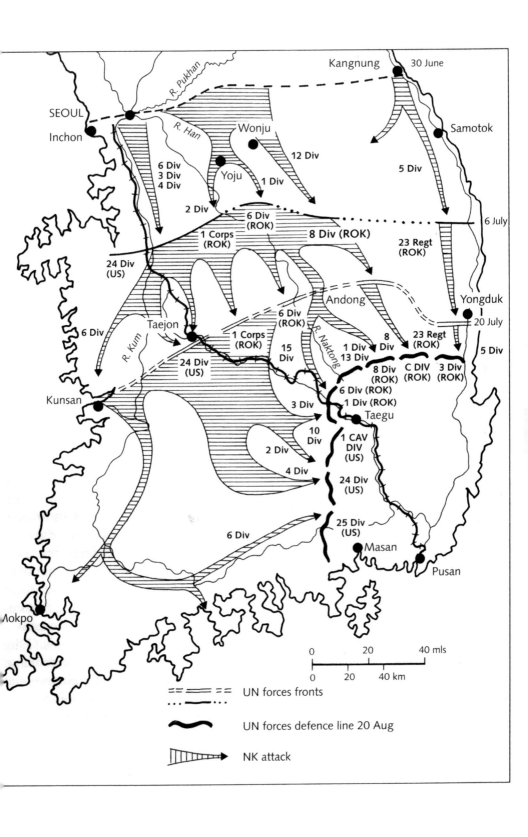

R. Pukhan

Kangnung · 30 June

SEOUL

Inchon

R. Han

Wonju

Yoju

Samotok

6 Div
3 Div
4 Div

12 Div

5 Div

1 Div

2 Div

6 Div
(ROK)

6 July

1 Corps
(ROK)

8 Div (ROK)

23 Regt
(ROK)

24 Div
(US)

Andong

Yongduk

6 Div

R. Kum

Taejon

6 Div
(ROK)

R. Naktong

1 Div
13 Div

8
Div

23 Regt
(ROK)

20 July

5 Div

1 Corps
(ROK)

15
Div

8 Div
(ROK)

C DIV
(ROK)

3 Div
(ROK)

24 Div
(US)

Kunsan

3 Div

6 Div (ROK)

1 Div (ROK)

Taegu

10
Div

1 CAV
DIV
(US)

2 Div

4 Div

24 Div
(US)

25 Div
(US)

6 Div

Masan

Pusan

Mokpo

0   20   40 mls

0   20   40 km

== == == == ==   UN forces fronts

· · · · · · · · · ·

━━━━━   UN forces defence line 20 Aug

▷▷▷▷▷▷▷▶   NK attack

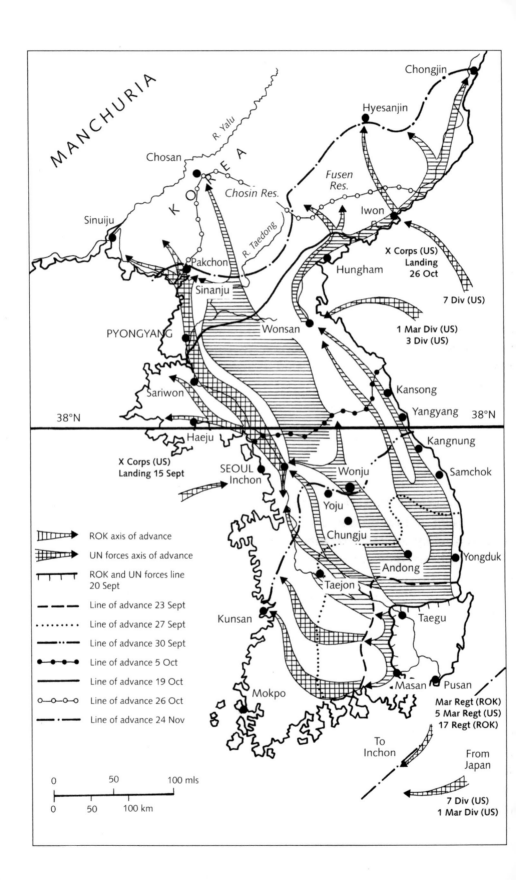

their family's thoughts or their loved one's passions. The service operated against all odds having to locate soldiers and get letters to them as soon as they could. It was no mean feat.

Jim Lucock

I used to get letters from my mother and two aunts, but that was all, but I would write letters back home almost every day. It was all free, the army was very generous. I had my twenty-first birthday out there in the line. My platoon commander was a Mr Williams, a really nice man. Well these birthday cards came one day and he said, 'When's your birthday?' and I said, 'Today, sir.' He said, 'How old are you?' and I said, '21 today.' I was a corporal by then and was due to take a patrol out that night. I went down for the briefing and he said you're not going on the patrol tonight corporal. I said I wanted to do it but he said no, no, someone else was doing it. When I got back to the hutch there were two crates of ale, sixteen bottles in each crate, waiting for me. And it was from the platoon commander and he says, 'Now enjoy yourself.'

The next morning I was in bed and the platoon sergeant – horrible little man – came around and started telling me to get out of bed. I was still drunk. And then Mr Williams, the platoon commander, came along and said, 'Hey, leave him alone, I've given him permission to stay there. Leave him until he comes round.' I was in there for about twenty-four hours, on my own, happy. Later on we had a reunion of the King's Vets and I inquired how Mr Williams was. He'd gone back early to go back to university at Oxford. I was told that he had died shortly afterwards; he'd had a massive heart attack and died. I was sad to hear that.

Brian Hough

There was no restriction on letters. I wrote home and got letters from my mum quite regularly. Yes, we did write them but I can't remember how they were collected; somebody must have come along and taken them off us and we did receive mail. My mum always sent me the Saturday night *Manchester Evening Chronicle*, the 'Pink Un' with all the football results. By the time I got it, it was, of course, about a month out of date. We also had this arrangement where a Christmas greeting would be delivered to your parents or whoever you wanted on Christmas morning. So, I went along with this and wrote out my greeting. Then on Christmas Day the message, via a telegram, was delivered to my mother. Well, of course, she thought it was bad news, because that was they way they told you that someone had died. The army had never thought that one through. She'd opened the front door and the telegraph boy was there. My mother was in a bit of a mess all day. I don't think she ever forgave me for that!

Bill Hurst

I wasn't one for writing; my mother wrote to my company commander saying that she had not heard from her son for so many months and I had to go on CO's orders and he said, 'We've had a letter from your mother and she says you've not been writing home, why's that?' I said, 'Well I've nothing to say, sir,' and he said, 'Well you're writing tonight and I want it on my desk in the morning.' I wasn't in the front line at the time, I was in reserve. So I took the letter next morning and gave it him. He read it and just laughed. 'Is that all you've got to say: Dear Mam, I hope you are okay as it leaves me, Bill.' He just shook his head. I said, 'Well what do you expect, I can't say I'm getting shot at, bombed on. I don't want them to worry.' But, yes, you'd get letters from your parent or girlfriends or like. There was plenty of Dear John letters come back though!

We didn't get any newspapers however; the only newsletter we got was the Kings newsletter and we'd get that every so often. I knew nothing about what was going on in Britain, no football results, nothing and of course they didn't know what was going with us either. The only news they got was on the Pathé news in the picture house. It wasn't like today. You'd maybe see a journalist coming to interview people but you never got your parents ringing up saying, I saw you on the television last night or anything like that.

Roy Cox

Lofty Taylor used to get the *Eagle* sent to him from his mum. It was a comic and we used to take the mickey out of him, what you getting that for, we'd say, you still a child? But I tell you what, everybody used to read it, it would get passed around everywhere. My sister used to write to me, I got a letter from my father about once a year, he was not a letter writer at all, but my sister wrote regularly. My mum had died when I was about three. I used to write home to my sister as well, more than to anyone else. I would write to her while I was looking after the wireless set and telephone lines. She was very good to me. I never got newspapers or magazines or anything like that. I don't think we knew of anything going on in Britain and I don't think we cared. I remember when the King died because the officers wore black arm bands. But we knew of nothing else, no football results, cricket scores, nobody was interested anyway.

Terry Moore

The mail was very good; it came every week. My mother wrote about once a month and my father would sign the letter. Yes, mail came regularly and it was a blessing. There was an Irishman, who shall be nameless, who every month received letters from home and there was nothing in it apart from an addressed envelope. He couldn't read or write so he would put the addressed envelope back into the post and they would know that he was well. He just could not read or write and that was how they communicated. I was able to write home. Because of the way the war was, with no fixed lines, you had time and you wrote home. I don't ever recall getting newspapers or books though.

Ivan Williams

Any news from home was good. They call it the forgotten war and it really was, we felt forgotten and anything from home was good. The great unsung heroes of any war are the postal service. I was getting letters from the UK to the front line within a week. They were airmailed to Japan but the fact that they could find the unit and then find you on the front line in less than a week was astonishing. There was a post collection as well a couple of times a week so that you could write home. You had a lot of time to do nothing so I wrote quite a lot of letters. In fact I had a pen pal. One of the fellas I was with, his sister had friends and she persuaded them all to write to us in Hong Kong and they carried on writing to us in Korea.

Any news from home was nice. I of course had never met the lady I was writing to – but I eventually married her! She died more than two years ago. And that's the photo she sent me while I was in Korea. And she was my pen pal. I only met her when I came home. We got on very well and eventually, four years later, we got married. She was from London, from West Ham. So, I have a lot to thank Korea for as I had a lovely, happy marriage. I wouldn't have met my wife otherwise.

Eric Peters

I never wrote home much, didn't have paper, pens, you also didn't have time. You had to get stuff off company stores. I lost a brother while I was out there, killed on his twenty-first birthday, digging a big trench with an excavator in Neston. I didn't hear until a couple of months after. My dad was to blame for that. He said, 'He's got enough on his plate out there, wait until he comes home.' It was in the local papers but I never got that one. I used to get the *Birkenhead News* sent and the *Neston Advertiser*. I had an officer whose mother lived in Neston and he passed his onto me. I was a football fan but never heard any football news, nothing like that. We did in Hong Kong, but not in Korea.

Ken Hawthorne

I was single when I went. I had a girlfriend but I left her behind and you expect her to wait for you and she expects she'll wait, but one by one all these lads would get a Dear John letter, I didn't get one but she met me when I got off the boat, she was there with mum and dad, and she said, 'I'm very sorry but I didn't want to tell you while you were away but I have been going out with an American!' I wasn't very keen on the Americans, I must admit. It didn't really worry me to be honest. I'd done a year in hell but I was alive and I was young.

5. THE CASUALTIES OF WAR

'No matter who died in that war, it was some mother's son.'

INTRODUCTION

DEATH IS AN inevitability of war. And yet it is possible for many soldiers to experience war without coming into any direct contact with death or serious casualties. Indeed, there are some interviewees in this book who did not personally know anyone who died. But mostly all the interviewees knew someone. In some instances they stood alongside a colleague as they took a hit. And that was when the real horror of war struck home.

In all 1,078 British soldiers died during the conflict, many of them national servicemen. The Battle of the Imjin River alone in April 1951 involving the Glosters accounted for more than 200 wounded or killed. But high as these figures are, they are exceeded by American losses which mounted to 37,000 during the course of the war. The Chinese and North Koreans are estimated to have lost as many as 1.5 million men and the South Koreans a further 1 million.

Almost all of those interviewed confessed to feeling frightened at times. A few just got on with it and tried not to think too much about the chaos that was going on around them. But even for those the tragedy of war really hit home and was felt when one of their colleagues was badly wounded or killed. Then it was a different matter. Even today some do not wish to recall death too vividly and many of those interviewed shed tears as they recounted incidents when friends had been killed. But most were ready to admit, that yes, they had been frightened.

Although death might not have been such an everyday occurrence, injuries and wounds certainly happened on a regular basis. At least three of those interviewed in this book suffered shrapnel wounds and had to be treated in hospital. Both Ken Hawthorne and Jim Lucock still have the shrapnel in their legs to prove it!

The fear could be so oppressive that some deserted and somehow managed to get to Pusan where they were able to stowaway on a boat bound for Japan. But this happened rarely. Mostly they got caught, served some time in a gaol and were then returned to the front line. It was also the case, as is related here, that some conscripts refused to go to Korea when they were given their orders. Instead they fought their cases through the local MPs. They were not always successful. As the figures show there were thousands of deserters. Some had disappeared on the run before they were called up and were wandering the streets of Britain, whilst others tried to escape from Korea itself. The latter was far more difficult as you had to make your way across a country where not only did you not know the language, but you stuck out like the proverbial sore thumb. And even if you could make it to Pusan, getting a boat anywhere was another matter. Few succeeded.

Jim Grundy, who had worked in a funeral parlour with the Co-op before the war, found himself given the gruesome task of finding and bringing bodies back for burial. He wasn't too pleased to begin with, eagerly wanting to be fighting in the front line, but soon discovered that it was an important and necessary job. As he says, you always had to remember that 'it was some mother's son'. Today he devotes considerable time to keeping records of the British dead and visiting the cemetery at Busan (formerly Pusan) in South Korea.

Not surprisingly there were breakdowns. Geoff Holland had to talk one soldier out of suicide, others knew of fellow soldiers who were on the brink. Brian Hough's platoon sergeant, a man who had been through the Second World War, could take it no longer and suffered a breakdown. In the 1950s, a breakdown in the theatre of war would have been frowned upon by the military authorities but today, thankfully, such problems are dealt with seriously and with some humanity. It was the stress of war; the constant bombardment, the cold, inadequate clothing, poor equipment, the fear that you might be the next to get hit or even captured by the Chinese. It was enough to test any man's inner resolve.

Inevitably in the intensity of battle there were deaths by friendly fire. The most brutal was probably when three American P-51 Mustang planes napalmed British troops at Hill 282, killing a number of soldiers from the Argylls and severely burning many others. One soldier, Pat Quinn, witnessed the tragedy. Some interviewees also spoke of other accidental attacks on British soldiers by American planes dropping napalm bombs. There are also hints of atrocities carried out by UN forces, although few of these have ever been officially investigated.

It should come as no surprise that many of the soldiers interviewed in this book regularly return to Korea to pay their respects at the UN cemetery and at the National Memorial Arboretum in Staffordshire where the Korean dead are also remembered. This is the reality of war.

Bill Fox

In January 1951 it was back to it. We were told the Chinese had poured into North Korea in huge numbers so we had formed a line close to the 38th Parallel to defend our position. They were expecting up to a million refugees coming through. The planes had spotted them. The refugees; I'd never seen anything like it in my life. Back home I'd seen films of refugees in the Second World War but this was something else. It was a thick line of people; no young men, all young kids, women, carrying all their belongings, some oxen but mostly the refugees were carrying everything themselves and it was the bitterest winter imaginable; flurries of snow, biting winds. I don't know whether the Chinese had pushed them into the south or they were just coming, escaping from the Chinese.

Our orders were to destroy all the houses, burn them, get the people out. We threw petrol on the houses and burnt everything. And with their thatched roofs and some petrol they went up in no time. They had to pick some of us to go and make sure that this column of refugees kept together and kept moving. They had to keep moving in such a way that women with babies couldn't cope and they had to dump the babies, they just couldn't keep up if they were carrying them. It was such a long way to go, they couldn't survive, no food for them, the mothers couldn't look after their babies, so they passed them on to older women who were down in the gully where the stream was and they were drowning them. These older Korean women were either throwing them into the river or breaking the ice and putting them under it and into the icy cold water. They'd be dead in no time. I was watching from the hillside. You wouldn't believe it. We were told not to interfere, it was up to them, it was their country, their decision. I believe all the young men had been captured and made to join the North Korean army. And if they didn't join it was a bullet in the head. I saw terrible sights. Terrible.

Jim Lucock

There were times when it was frightening because I had three fellas underneath me. There are people who are extremely cool under pressure, but they are exceptional. I was just an ordinary national serviceman and I didn't want to die. I never thought I would die but I got blown up in a minefield.

In Charlie Company we used to send NCOs with so many men out to do patrols on the front of the Hook. It was all underground, passageways, sleeping quarters, we'd go over the top and go down and you could hear the Chinese digging, so consequently the corporal would stay there and the lance corporal would go down with one man and he would listen and if they got attacked we used to have a sweep patrol, go over the top, get them and get them in. That was frightening. I used to be frightened, really frightened. The Chinese just used to leave any of their dead soldiers out there and would just put lime all over them. One night I was out there and I dived into this ditch and it was full of bodies that had been lying there, putrefying. It was awful; it was on my face, on my body, the stench. Now that was frightening. I was taken away and washed down straight away but that was very, very frightening. Horrible. The reason we went into this minefield was that at the bottom of the Hook the Chinese had all these great caverns where they put their troops in and the planes couldn't get at them. The Chinese were great diggers. So our job in Charlie Company was to do an attack and blow these big caves up. The engineers were there and a senior officer.

At twelve o'clock that night we all lined up and started going down, very, very quietly. The two engineers with us were going to lay the explosives and a lad named Robinson was in front and he said, 'Hey corp, I think I've stood on a mine,' and I said, 'Nah I don't think so.' He was going home the next day, he was a married man. 'No,' he said, 'I think I have.' I said, 'No.' I said, 'You hang on there and we'll keep going forward.' So we went forward, not very far and somebody said, 'Nah it's not a bloody mine, stop acting the goat.' So he took his foot off and it was. Not only that but it was connected up. He was killed instantly. All I remember – fireworks for years afterwards I hated them – I used to get this terrible taste of gunpowder. The lad behind me – I had been in the same class in Dingle Vale as his brother – and he hadn't been with us very long and this was just after Coronation Day – he was killed as well. And Tommy, a corporal with me, said he couldn't see, he was blind. It was chaos. I know somebody carried me out. I was there a couple of hours. I was unconscious but I came to and I was just numb, totally numb. Somebody stood on me and I gave him a mouthful. It was the company commander, Major Dines. He said, 'Who's that?' and I said, 'Corporal Lucock.' He said, 'Are you all right?' and I said, 'I can't move but I'm all right.' The next minute a medic came up and he said, 'I'll just give you an injection,' and I said, 'I don't want more injections.' After a while they started to evacuate us. Eventually they blew one cave up but by then the Chinese were aware that something was up. Mr Williams won the military cross that night but there were other fellas who should have done. The Kingsmen should have got something for their gallantry. They carried me back and I was put into this Canadian forward dressing station. I was in there a while. They reckoned I had thirty-six different pieces of shrapnel in me. I've still got some shrapnel left here in my leg. I tried for years to get a war pension but they wouldn't have it. Funnily enough I've been having problems this last few months and they thought I had cancer – fortunately I haven't – but I had to have a scan. When I came out of the scanner the nurses said, 'We have a problem, you seem to have all sorts of metal in you.' I told them, 'Yes I know. I was in the Korean war.' And they looked at me and I said, 'You've never heard of it,' and they shook their heads. I tell you what I said, 'You go and ask your grandad.' So after all these years I've still got it in me. And the pension's board at Blackpool still refuse to accept this.

Anyhow, I was eventually taken back to a Canadian hospital and I was in there for about six weeks. Then I went back to Inchon for rest and recuperation. It was just tents, no patrols, no guard duties. Someone brought a football round so I had a game of football but I was spotted, so next morning I was sent back to the front line!

Ken Hawthorne

We worked on the roads getting them back together after the winter, but as the weather got better we started laying minefields. It was very hairy and one particular night, we got the night off now and again, and instead of us the other team went out and were working on the minefield where we had left off and a friend of mine got killed. I'm not sure what happened but it seems he set his own mine off. There were a lot of accidents like that in the minefield. He didn't die there and then but the Americans whipped the casualties back in small helicopters which had a box like a coffin either side and took them back to the hospitals. He died in the helicopter.

Pat Quinn

Hill 282 was supposed to be a surprise for the North Koreans but it was more of a surprise for the Argylls who were ordered to take it. When the hill was taken the Argylls found themselves under fire from another hill and without fire support. That was until the UN planes returned and blasted their own positions instead of the enemy! I've never seen anything as bad, even as a fireman.

By 23 September 1950, we had crossed the Naktong River in the breakout from the Pusan perimeter. A few days earlier the American Marines had landed at Inchon further north and were driving towards Seoul. Now the Argylls were facing a strongly held North Korean position called Hill 282 on the military maps. We were told that the attack was to be a surprise with no artillery softening up or pre-aerial bombardment to give the enemy a rude awaking.

'B' Company was chosen to lead the assault with 'C' Company hard on their heels. The hill was steep and covered with scrub, loose rocks and fir trees. The North Koreans were not used to being attacked at 5 a.m. and the leading Argylls were able to get within 50 yards before making their charge. Recovering quickly from the initial shock, the North Koreans opened up with everything they had and killed the leading platoon commanders, among others.

It was at this stage that we went into a classic copybook Highlander charge, yelling like banshees, and used our rifles and bayonets to clear the North Korean positions. It was too much for the North Koreans and those who were left alive left the scene. We had taken Hill 282.

There was no rest for us, however. Hill 388 on which the North Koreans were well positioned overlooked Hill 282 from the side of the saddle. They started to shell us and we were soon pinned down. Urgent calls were made for artillery support, but there was none to be had. Some nameless Napoleon far behind the lines had ordered the gunners elsewhere and left us high and dry with no fire support. Our second in command, Major Kenny Muir, led a party of stretcher-bearers up the hill to try and evacuate some of the wounded. Instead he found himself taking command of what was now a desperate defence. Major Muir asked for an air strike on the North Korean reserves that could be seen moving up to the left of our position. After getting confirmation that an air strike was on its way, the major made sure that our positions were clearly marked from the air by using crimson and yellow recognition panels.

Shortly after 12 noon three American P-51 Mustang aircraft appeared. We all cheered at the sight of these aircraft feeling that the odds were now in our favour. Our cheers soon turned to horror as the American aircraft ignored our recognition panels and swept down on our positions with all guns blazing killing many Argylls. The aircraft then circled once and came back in for another run. This time they dropped deadly napalm bombs on us. As this death by friendly fire was taking place, a number of Argylls were climbing up the hill with much needed ammunition. Among them was Alan Barton of HQ Signals. Later he was to go up again to help bring down the wounded and dead.

The Argylls were shot and barbecued and blasted off our hill. The thirty-five survivors of the American air strike rallied together and, led by Major Muir, we managed to reoccupy the still burning hill. Sadly Major Muir was killed while helping to fire our mortar. His courage was a great help to us and he was later awarded a Victoria Cross for his bravery on that day.

With all our ammunition all gone and scarcely a man still unwounded, it was time to leave the hill. The battle-exhausted survivors came down the hill carrying or dragging the wounded. I was so badly wounded that I could not walk and had to be dragged down the hill, but at least I was still alive. The worst part of it all was the napalm. Even as a fireman I have never seen anything like the destruction that stuff does to human skin. I never want to hear of that stuff being used again.

I spent a long time in hospital recovering from my wounds before I returned to the regiment. By then the war had moved on and the United Nation forces had pushed the North Koreans almost to the Yalu River and it looked as though the end of the war was in sight. But on the other side of the Yalu River was Red China.

Attacking in hordes or in small fast-moving groups the Chinese forced the transport bound Americans into retreat, jamming the roads with their seemingly limitless vehicles. Perhaps it was intended as a compliment when an American General asked for the British 27th Brigade as a rear guard for this retreat. The Argylls, the Middlesex, and the Australians had their own opinions. We didn't suffer many causalities during the retreat because unlike the Americans, who were tied to the roads, we moved any-where on our two feet and got there.

Geoff Holland

Was I frightened? Yes, I was frightened every day. One of the lads got wound up and this particular night he took his rifle and went out. I said, 'Where are you going?' and he said, 'Just out.' Then we heard a shot and I went out and he was sat on the hillside. He was a Scottish lad known as Jock, I said, 'What's up Jock?' He said he was fed up and he was crying his eyes out. I said, 'What was the shot?' He said, 'I was trying to commit suicide.' I said, 'you're bloody not'. I sat on that hillside with him for an hour or more. I talked him round. One of the officers came round and wanted to know what was happening. I said, 'It's all right, it was just a shot that went off.' I wasn't going to tell him that he was trying to commit suicide otherwise he'd have been on a charge for not making himself fit for duty. He was alright after but he'd had a Dear John, a letter from his girlfriend to say she didn't want him any more. He wasn't the only one. Loads of lads got them. But he took it to heart. In fact, I went on leave with him to Tokyo. But yes, you do get frightened. You're lying there wondering whether the next one's going to drop on you when they're banging away.

Bill Fox

General MacArthur was a brilliant soldier and when the North Koreans invaded and pushed the South Koreans out of Korea, he landed a force and the Americans poured in and the North Koreans fled northwards, but in doing so they left a lot of soldiers behind and they became a guerilla force, blending in with the locals, so there was a danger of everyone, of all the locals, you didn't know who might be a North Korean or not. Anyhow, we then went up to Suwon, way up north in Korea but still in South Korea and it was a case of getting used to things. We didn't have a camp to go to but we went to this, I think it was a schoolyard or something, and we camped there for a few weeks while we got acclimatised. But we still had to send patrols out. And it was here that a party of guerrillas did ambush a small party of ours. They killed a few men and wounded some as well. That was the first casualties we had and it reminded us that this was dangerous. I recall the two men who were killed being brought back on stretchers, covered up on the stretchers of course, just their boots sticking out of the bottom.

We then went further up north where these Turks had ambushed some North Koreans, or it might have been Chinese, and they took us there to show us the dead enemy. I think it happened a lot with armies to take young soldiers to see dead soldiers in the battlefield. And the older soldiers said to us, 'Look at these Chinese, they're nothing, so be ready with your rifle and have your bayonets ready and blast them; that's how you want to see your enemy.' One of the lads, although he couldn't really say much, reckoned that they had been bayoneted in the stomach and then all laid out. He reckoned they had been alive and they had been prisoners, but you couldn't say anything. It hadn't been done by British or American troops but the Turks and I do believe the Turks would have done something like that. Nothing could be said though, you had to keep it closed, say nothing, but that's what the story was. When you think about it afterwards, the way they were laid out, their guts hanging out and their heads smashed in, it could have been true. Horrible sight but you had to get used to it.

John Hegarty

I will skip the period from November 1949 until June 1950 with the exception of mentioning one trip which took the ship to the port of Ominato in Japan. This was a sheltered deep-water bay which I understood was being considered as a possible operational base for RN ships in the area around Japan. It was surveyed for this purpose and in June of 1950 HMS *Jamaica* was again scheduled to visit Ominato to progress the task.

At this time, there were twenty-two British warships in Far East waters with widespread commitments including the Malayan patrol, the defence of Hong Kong and the Yangtse Estuary patrol.

Whilst in Hong Kong we had cultivated a friendly relationship with the local army garrison and as part of this liaison a party of NCOs had been invited on board for the trip to Japan. It was considered a recreational break from their duties in the New Territories, where the 'Bamboo

Curtain' separated the Colony from Communist China. It comprised men from the Middlesex Regiment and the Royal Artillery.

In early June, *Jamaica* sailed from Hong Kong for Japanese waters on what was planned to be a normal deployment. Whilst on passage we heard the news of a North Korean attack on South Korea. At first it was assumed this incursion was another example of the sabre rattling which frequently occurred on the Korean Peninsula and it would come to little. Within a short time it became apparent this was a major invasion that could change the fragile balance of power between China, Russia and the West. The UN Security Council met in urgent session and, as they say, the rest is history! The Korean War had begun.

Within hours, *Jamaica* and *Black Swan* were dispatched to the east coast of Korea to join USS *Juneau*. Our task was to attack advancing communist troops as they piled south along the coast road. This took our small force to the very border of the 38th Parallel. As we progressed north to the designated area of operations, we saw the first signs of the savagery of what was to come. The sea was calm and we encountered large numbers of floating corpses tied together in pairs. The stench was sickening even from the ship doing about 15 knots through the water. Once in our target area, we commenced bombarding the coastal targets, troops, transport, roads, bridges, rail tracks, etc. In fact, anything of possible use to communist forces was attacked.

It was at dawn on 2 July, the ship was at action stations, and I was in the bridge plot room. Despite having our radar operating, we were surprised to hear the report broadcast from the bridge that a visual sighting of fast-moving surface craft were heading towards our unit. This proved to be six motor torpedo/E-boats, which had approached down the coast out of radar cover. Turning towards *Jamaica* and *Black Swan*, their speed increased and, though hypnotically impressive, they posed a very real threat indeed. 'Alarm Surface Port', I heard the tannoy broadcast. Then followed the well-rehearsed series of orders and responses as the various control stations and guns crews leapt into action. 'Engage' – 'Shoot' – 'Fire!' I was used to the drill, but hell, this was for real! The guns fired, at first with one main salvo that shook the ship to its keel, then the subsequent salvoes that were more sporadic but none the less equally deadly. My plotting team tried to concentrate as we scanned the radar for targets further away. It was vital not to lose control of the overall situation but thankfully the displays were void of any unidentified moving targets.

The visual reports from the bridge continued to come through; 'Target stopped', 'Possible Hit', 'Fire and smoke visible', 'Target sinking', and still the guns continued to fire. Then silence as 'Guns' gave the order to cease firing. The result, five out of six enemy craft destroyed and one MTB grounded ashore and abandoned by the crew. It was an easy matter to direct a few well-aimed rounds to ensure she would not be of further use to the North Koreans.

This proved to be the first action by UN Ships in what was to be a long and bitter war. It was a resounding success for our small force but it emphasised the fact that the North Korean threat was very real.

We continued our task of bombarding the coast road and railway close to YangYang. Our routine was to shell the high points of land overhanging the railway lines and roads by day, bringing down as much debris as possible to block the passage of military convoys. These convoys travelled by night to avoid attack, but when they came across these obstacles, they had to clear the roads manually. This involved the use of lights by the army units and provided an ideal target for *Jamaica* and her small force, waiting, darkened, within gun range of the coast. Occasionally, in the silence of a calm sea, we could hear the shouts and commands of the soldiers ashore as they struggled to clear the debris. The ensuing disruption of supplies to the communists was substantial and from the ship, lying so close offshore, the ammunition and fuel exploding as a result of our gunnery was awesome.

Inevitably, the North Korean forces were sure to take some action to counter our activities. Artillery was moved to defend the road and rail system. On 8 July while *Jamaica*, with *Juneau* and *Black Swan* in company, were bombarding targets on the coastline, the ships came under fire from these shore batteries. *Jamaica* took a direct hit near the base of the mainmast and close to a gun mounting. Sadly, six men were killed. These were the first casualties of the war at sea. Of the dead, five were soldiers of the Middlesex Regiment and the Royal Artillery who had come on board at Hong Kong for what was to be a 'sea cruise'. They had volunteered to act as ammunition numbers at various gun-mountings when required. One seaman was killed and five others were wounded. The ship did not suffer serious material damage but I recall when viewing the carnage from the bridge, our 'Battle Ensign' had been blown away by the blast.

Shortly after, the bodies of those killed were buried at sea with full military honours. It was a sad and sombre occasion. To this day I can vividly recall the six splashes as the dead were committed to the deep.

Jim Lucock

I used to get terrified, yes, very frightened. I didn't like it. I used to go dry especially when you were taking a patrol out. Sometimes we'd have a listening patrol, a bit like they had in the First World War. We used to call it a standing patrol. And if anything was out there, you warned the battalion. There'd be three of us and one of them would always be more tired than you and would want to go to sleep and I'd be saying, 'Hey wake up, wake up, I'm bloody tired an all, you know.'

It was a corporal and second lieutenant's war, the second part of the war. As far as I'm concerned the second lieutenants and corporals did all the work, all the patrols, we had all the duties. I've spoken to fellas since and they've agreed.

I put one fella on a charge and he got fifty-six days for telling lies. What had happened was that a second lieutenant and a sergeant had gone out on a recce and it was rather active that night and they couldn't get any signals back to our HQ, so it was coming back to me, so it was up to us to keep alert to make sure where they were by map references and if they got into any trouble we could then bring the artillery in. They would say, 'Dog fire', and give a map reference number. This fella wanted to go to sleep – arrogant little fella – we moved three times and I left him there. I said we're all tired.

Peter C Le P Jones

Shortly after the UN forces started to move forward we came to a range of hills running each side of the road and the enemy fired on our convoy. Brigadier Coad ordered the Middlesex troops to clear the smaller hill to the right, which they did with great dash.

Argyll 'A' Company took up a position on a smaller hill at the bottom of Hill 282, and as there was insufficient light 'B' and 'C' Companies took 'lying up' positions in front of 'A' Company and bedded down on the ground for the night. I doubt many slept, as this was our first dawn attack and all were naturally very apprehensive of what was expected to happen, wondering whether we would be found wanting and how would we acquit ourselves. The question that ran through my mind, and I am sure the minds of others, was how many 'Gooks' were up there and what was going to happen. Would you be wounded or killed?

It never got better with each attack, but the first, going into the unknown, was the worst – thereafter it was no longer not the unknown, but rather what you had experienced before. Each assault was always a different situation and always full of the unexpected – this was, to put it mildly, somewhat nerve-racking. Just before dawn on a dry day, we were told to prepare ourselves and to leave our heavy gear and blankets where they were and just take our water bottles, weapons and ammunition. A hasty breakfast on cold American 'C' rations – a cardboard box with a black substance between two layers of brown cardboard that burnt very well, with no smoke to heat cans of food delivered daily. Each box consisted of three main meal cans, twenty cigarettes, coffee sachets, coca slab (marvellous), two small cans of fruit salad or similar. We formed up with 'B' Company on the right and 'C' Company on the left. Each company was to climb up through dense fir woods on two separate spurs leading to the top. The command to advance was given at 5.15 a.m., and we moved off, our platoon being in the lead for 'C' Company. Every tree and mound you felt may hold 'Gooks' ready to fire, which was a time of high nervous tension and natural fear. We heard firing from 'B' Company who had pulled ahead of us and had surprised a breakfast party of 'Gooks'. Soon after, we came on unmanned enemy trenches. By now there was a lot of firing and some mortaring all around the area. We arrived at the top and met up with 'B' Company. No 7 Platoon, of 'B' Company, under the command of Lieutenant Jock Edington, was engaging the enemy in a large firefight in the woods to the left, which turned out to be only half of the hill, which was a surprise to us all. This area latterly was found to contain a 'Gook' observation post that was controlling their mortars. Our platoon was told to hold a position immediately below the top ridge as a reserve but we were soon under fire from the enemy who were working their way round the hard pressed No 7 Platoon, who had done sterling work against a numerically superior enemy. The Argylls killed many, but eventually had to retire despite being reinforced by Lieutenant Buchanan's platoon. Both platoon commanders were badly wounded: Lieutenant Buchanan was subsequently killed with others wounded when American planes dropped napalm on us.

Things were getting bad, with a considerable number of wounded and killed when Major Muir arrived with a party, some from the Middlesex Regiment, carrying stretchers loaded with ammunition. They were to try and evacuate the wounded. The Americans had withdrawn their artillery support from us, as they said there were no enemy on the hill. Because of the height of the hill, some 900ft, our 3-inch mortars could not reach the enemy over our position from where they were located. Our Vickers machine guns were with 'A' Company and could not fire over the hill, although they did give covering fire into the woods where the enemy were infiltrating round our left flank.

Without support from artillery or mortars our commanding officer, Lieutenant Colonel Neilson, called in the American Air Force to attack the 'Gooks'. In the middle of our position we laid out our florescent aircraft recognition panels in the correct code for the day – these panels were used to warn planes of the whereabouts of UN troops. We heard the planes, US propeller-driven Mustangs, arrive and hopes ran high, but instead of hitting the 'Gooks' they dropped napalm on us killing some of our wounded and severely burning others. Many had to try and escape the wall of fire by running from the position. Our location was fortunately on a mound and burning petrol and oil went down the gully within 30ft of us – we were singed from the heat. The planes came back machine-gunning our position. There was, naturally, tremendous shock, despair and anger with frantic attempts to get the correct Very light flare to stop them.

The signaller had been killed, so I and another Argyll were desperately trying to find the correct Very light flare, which was in the dead soldier's haversack, as firing this would stop the attack. Finally, we found the correct red flare, and as one of the American Mustangs came in strafing we fired the flare, which he saw. 'A' Company was also being machine-gunned and they were firing Very lights. Major Muir was still on the hill and gathered the few remaining unhurt men, of whom I was one. He led the charge to the crest where one remaining Argyll, Private Watts, with one or two others, was still holding and defending the position – the battalion history says there were only fourteen of us. The enemy was late in taking advantage, but had by this time realised what had happened and came charging up the hill.

I was near Major Muir on his right while he and, I think, his batman manned and fired a 2-inch mortar from Major Muir's hip. They were sitting on the top of the crest in full view of the enemy under heavy machine-gun fire. I was firing at the 'Gooks' as they advanced with all the few Argylls remaining doing the same and we had only two Bren guns left.

Major Muir was leading a charmed life it seemed, but was soon hit by two bursts of machine-gun fire and mortally wounded. He had to be carried off the hill, and died upon reaching the bottom.

As conditions were so bad and casualties so high, the CO gave Major Gordon Ingram, 'B' Company commander, permission to withdraw the remainder of both companies and we moved off firing as we went. The enemy, by this time, had reached the top of the hill and were firing at us. One 'Gook' was after me as he placed a round each side of my head, luckily missing. It must have been my lucky day, as earlier two machine gun bursts came within 12 inches each side of me and I made a very hasty drop into a deserted 'Gook' foxhole, having also escaped the earlier napalm. One Argyll, while trying to retire, was attacked by three 'Gooks' – he bayoneted one and took his Burp gun (Chinese machine gun) and killed the other two, and he then escaped. Almost all were carrying wounded or extra weapons to deny these from the enemy. No doubt due to the severe fighting, the enemy did not pursue us and we reached the bottom of the hill safely.

We returned to 'A' Company's position unbowed, yet sadly a much smaller number than that which had left in the morning, having suffered some 90-plus casualties with 13 dead out of a total of some 180 from the 2 companies assembled that morning. I saw Major Muir's body at the bottom of the hill where he had been left when he died and he later was awarded a posthumous VC.

We were under strength, as we had left Hong Kong with only three companies instead of four but after Hill 282 we were down to just two companies in the battalion until reinforcements eventually arrived. Just before dark I led some of the remaining men to collect blankets and ponchos from where we had left them in the morning at the bottom of the hill. Men who had been carrying stretchers and had been driven down by the flames were starting to drift back to our position.

Some days later we had our packs brought up to us and we were told to take anyone's pack. I walked over and there was my own pack. We had not shaved or washed for several days, so to have one's own pack returned was especially welcome. We heard, rightly or wrongly, that the American pilots, before attacking, had radioed their base to say there were fluorescent panels on the ground in the correct code of the day. Their base said that there were no UN troops on the hill and that the enemy were using captured panels – they ordered them to attack; hence we were hit instead of the enemy. The American pilots visited the wounded in hospital and were most upset about what had been done – the fog of war rears its ugly head again.

After Hill 282 we had a few days break from rushing around, though we were still near the front line when our reinforcements arrived from the UK, quite a few of whom were volunteers from other regiments but keen as mustard to join what they thought was an elite unit. What price the notoriety and press coverage of Hill 282? They soon realised we were just a normal Scottish battalion doing an unpleasant task as best we could.

Around the end of September, our transport caught up with us and once again the advance continued daily until the end of October. We were joined by an Australian battalion and later, New Zealand 25-pounder gunners, Indian Paras, a Field Ambulance unit and Colonel Snow's American unit of 4.2-inch mortars. This Commonwealth 27th Brigade was later joined by two Canadian battalions. Our advances were made in convoys of lorries with tanks, or in set piece assaults with one battalion passing through the other day after day. The Korean Peninsula has large ranges of hills running across it, instead of up and down the peninsula, thus making very hard work of the advance. One battalion would attack one hill range one day and then the other would pass through the next day and so on. We had the Australian battalion supporting us, and they were superb fighters that loved a scrap, and the Canadians partnered the Middlesex.

Ken Hawthorne

I got wounded just before we came home. I didn't know where we were but we were heavily involved in camouflaging the roads. We used to string nets up in front of the roads, any road that was under observation by the Chinese. If a vehicle came along it would throw up dust and then it would get heavily mortared by the Chinese. So we were putting up these nets and we had to work in the early morning when the sun came up and was in the Chinese eyes. We knew that if they saw us they would throw things at us. We had been working for four or five days on this and we were getting fed up with having to get up early and then knocking off early and on the last day we should have packed up and gone but we only had a little more to do, put a few more nets up and we'd be finished. So the officer in charge said, 'What do you want to do, shall we take a vote on it, get it finished or leave it for tomorrow?' So we all decided to carry on. He said, 'I don't want to risk all of us down there so we'll just do three down there.'

We were getting on fine until it was my turn along with two others. We were stringing the nets to the Chinese side of the track and my friend was right up a pole at the time and I was halfway up another. The lad who was passing the nets to us had just gone to get some more bits and pieces when we were spotted and they started to mortar us. I never got down a pole so quickly in my life. Eric, my friend was there with me too. I don't know what happened to Eric but I threw myself down on the ground when I heard them. There was a lull after the first three came in, so I got up and then more started coming in, so I got down again. I was lying on the road close to the bank and then I felt a terrific pain right between my legs at the top of my bottom, then there was no pain at all. When the dust settled and the noise had stopped I looked up and poor Eric was lying in the middle of the road spread-eagled with a hole in his head. I knew that I had caught a piece of shrapnel but couldn't feel it. So I called over to him. We all carried a bandage and syringe with morphine He was still alive and I was feeling quite groggy myself. Nobody came along. The lads at the top didn't dare come down until it had all stopped, so I crawled over and started to put a bandage around his head and tie it around the back of his neck as he was cut there as well.

Just then somebody said, 'Come on let's drag him out.' I looked up and it was a chap from the signals who had seen what was happening and had come down to help me. So between us we dragged Eric to the top of the hill and our lads then came half way down and took over. I said to this lad, 'Where did you come from?' and he said, 'I was just testing the telephone cables and I saw what had happened.' That was very brave of him to come down as he didn't know the barrage had stopped. We got Eric on a stretcher and the officer said, 'Thank goodness you're all right,' and I said, 'Actually I'm not.' I showed him my leg and ankle. There was blood all over my trousers and I was bleeding quite a lot, so they shoved me on a stretcher as well and I went in an ambulance back to the field hospital. I went into the operating theatre, I don't know if it was the Indian or Norwegian hospital. When I came round a surgeon came to see me and I asked him if the shrapnel was very big and he said, 'No, but it is in very deep and we don't want to take it out.' He said, 'We don't think it'll give you any trouble. It might even work out some time on its own.' So it's been there ever since and I've never felt it. He reckons it had got underneath the coccyx. How lucky was I there? I wasn't at the hospital long, they shipped me on an ambulance train down to Seoul. The train was full of Americans with arms hanging off and screaming all the way down there, obviously come from a big battle somewhere. As we pulled into the station in Seoul – I hadn't seen any women for a long time – I heard two female American voices and they were saying there's an English lad on here somewhere, and I thought, my god they're going to ask me where I got wounded. They took me in an ambulance to the American hospital and as I went in there was a fellow standing in the hallway giving out Purple Heart medals to every soldier as they came in. He gave me mine and then took it back off us and said, 'You're a Limey, you cant have one.' I wasn't there half an hour when the British ambulance came and took me to the British and Commonwealth hospital and I was there for about a week. And then they sent me back to the front line. It hadn't damaged anything.

I didn't know what had happened to Eric and couldn't get in touch with him. Then about ten years ago I went to a reunion at Chatham and I was asking people and telling someone about Eric and they said, 'Do you know where he lived?' and I said, 'Yes, he was always writing home to a place near Brighton.' So they said, 'Why don't you just look him up in a telephone directory?' I hadn't thought of doing that. You know the war was over for me. So when I came home I went to the library and looked him up, and sure enough his name was in there, so I rang up. A woman answered and she said you've got the wrong one, it's my brother or cousin or someone and she gave me his number. So I rang him and I told him who I was and started having a chat and he said, 'I'll have to stop you there. I can't remember anything.' He said, 'I don't remember a thing until I was in the hospital in Japan. I can't remember anything that happened before that, all the childhood and my days in Korea, I can't remember anything that happened before. All I know is that I have a feeling I was somewhere I shouldn't have been.' I said, 'Well, are you OK?' and he said, 'Yes, I had a good neurosurgeon who put a plate in my forehead.' That was it. I couldn't take it any further could I?

Brian Hough

The first casualty I ever saw was again after I had been out on patrol. It was mostly night patrol work. We'd come back and we were sat not doing anything in particular and the breakfast chorus started. One landed near us and we went down. When it had stopped we got up and somebody said, 'George has been hurt.' He was a Welsh lad from Bargoed in South Wales. When we got to him he had obviously lost an eye, one side of his face was a mess. So we did what we could and the medics came and took him away. We never saw him again. But I did meet up with him many years later at a reception at St James's Palace with Prince Charles and he came up to me and said, 'It's Hughie, are you brewing up?' And yes, he had lost an eye.

Geoff Holland

I do still think about it a lot. When some people say how badly done to they are, they'd think how badly done to if they'd fought in a war. One I particularly remember: an attack came in, it was sporadic, we'd taken potshots at one another, mortar bombs and then it would quieten down and nothing. I think this attack was the Chinese spring offensive and they called for the mortars. This particular night somebody must have been on the radio but the rest of us we were just doing nothing but carrying bombs and giving them to put down the chute. The barrel of the mortar was red hot. It was boom, boom, boom and the noise was horrendous. The sky was lit up, there were Chinese flares and our flares and it just seemed to go on forever. When you think about it you're frightened, but then when you get into it you just forget to be frightened. I don't know how to put it. But that particular night I'll never forget. It was like bonfire night. The sky was just so lit up and all these bangers only they were real bangers.

Peter C Le P Jones

The brigade was moved by air and road to north of Seoul. I was lucky to fly and we were loaded on to American Skymaster planes. The American loadmaster handed us each a parachute, showed us how to wear it and simply said if the plane gets hit jump out and say 1,000, 2,000, 3,000 and then pull the ripcord. This was greeted with usual Jock remarks that are unprintable, false bravado, and with some prayers that we would not have to try this urgent way to earth. Luckily all went well and we landed safely.

The brigade moved forward and crossed the 38th Parallel after the Americans had had a vicious battle to capture it. Rumours abounded and many said that the Argylls and Middlesex would be sent back to Hong Kong for Christmas. We were all very poorly equipped, having come from Hong Kong in tropical clothing, having been intended as a stopgap until the much-heralded 29th Brigade arrived from the UK. This of course turned out to be false and both brigades remained in Korea.

After various moves forward heading north, the battalion 'spearheading' entered Sariwon, the North Korean's Aldershot. 'A' Company led the way and had a good firefight, assisted by Sherman tanks, and soon had the enemy on the run. I remember advancing with 'C' Company, in the usual freezing conditions, through the so-called high street with men each side of the road. We got out to the far end of the town and waited while the Australians moved through us. Next we were told to move back to the south side of the town. As we moved south on each side of the street, other men were found to be moving north in the centre of the street.

To our horror we realised that these were North Koreans, but for a while everyone kept very quiet and moved along very much on the alert. The Koreans thought that we were Russians arriving to help them and even gave our mortar platoon officer, Robin Fairrie, a Korean comfort girl in his jeep. We heard it was an American tank commander when being asked if he was Russian who said, 'Hell no, we are Americans'. All hell broke loose for a few seconds and then strangely we went on passing each other, they in the centre of the road and us each side of the road. The Koreans went north to be met by the Australians who killed many of them – one Korean had a full magazine (thirty rounds of .303 Bren gun ammunition) in him and still was only just stopped but lived for a long time.

We moved back into a secured area for the night and then continued the advance in the morning through the Aussies who had had a great shooting match the evening before. The Koreans, who had passed through, were retreating north and had no idea the UN was ahead of them in the town.

In the morning, we met the CO, Lieutenant Colonel Neilson, returning from a recce they had been on the night before when they too had driven through, in their Bren gun carriers, the same troops that we had met in the town. They were also thought to be Russians and very carefully reached the end of the enemy column and then hid themselves until the morning.

Riding on tanks, we continued our advance and soon reached Pyongyang where we were one of the first units through, and here we came across a Korean armed convoy that had been blasted apart by the American Air Force. There were vehicles, mobile anti-aircraft guns, armoured vehicles, tanks and bodies everywhere. The tank we were on was in the lead and simply pushed aside everything or ran it over, as the order was not to stop. Best not to look at what we and the following tanks had done, especially to the bodies.

At Yong-Yu, the American Airborne had been dropped three days before and had a big battle. When we entered there were snipers everywhere, so we were ordered to burn the town, which we did very efficiently, but as soon as it was well alight we were told to put it out because the artillery gun limbers could not get through. When you are told to burn down a town it first causes some concern that you should do such a thing, then you wonder how to start it. The houses were mainly made of wood and a match to the ceiling straw had amazing results.

We headed for the MacArthur Line (named after the commander-in-chief, General MacArthur), a point beyond which the UN was not expected to proceed but did. There was to be some considerable fighting and advancing before the brigade eventually reached Chongju where the advance stopped. The Americans moved through in front and we could clearly see the hills alongside the Yalu River. Ahead lay China's border with North Korea.

Within twenty-four hours the Chinese had entered the war. The brigade was asked to move forward and hold a position while other forces moved back. At one stage the battalion was some 25 miles in front of all other UN forces. Eventually, the Americans sent us enough tanks to move the whole battalion out. We travelled south over hard-gained ground and saw much evidence of the hasty retreat by the Americans who had left masses of equipment, machine guns, artillery, etc., where it had been sited. This was later captured and turned on the UN forces, along with huge quantities of stores at Pyongyang that had been only partially destroyed. We did not catch up with other UN forces for a long time.

It was very demoralising to keep retreating, but we did. One night was spent across the river south of Seoul before the bridges were blown and the whole town was on fire from end to end. The UN retreated south of the 38th Parallel and then dug in. General Matthew Ridgway took over command when General Walton Walker was killed in a jeep crash in December 1950. Ridgway was made of sterner stuff and ordered all commanders to have plans for advance and not retreat – he later became Supreme Commander of UN Forces when General Douglas MacArthur was relieved of his duties by President Truman in April 1951.

We eventually moved forward until we reached Daffodil, 3,000ft up on the 38th Parallel. This was at the height of the winter and we occupied an old American, and later Chinese position, at the top of a long ridge on a hill. I remember bedding down for the night close to what I thought was a pile of logs covered in snow. In the morning I noticed a hand sticking out and rather than logs these were all frozen bodies and there were many piles of them amounting to many hundreds of bodies.

Due to the heavy snow and frost we did not know that we were in an American minefield. There were tripwires all over the ground, but fortunately these were held firm by the extreme cold thereby not going off, except for one that did explode when a fire was lit and the ground thawed out – luckily there were no causalities. This alerted us but it was impossible to find the location of the other mines due to the heavy snow and frost.

Fires were forbidden, so we had to stay where we were. I climbed up some rocks that were along a footpath we used daily and held onto a branch of a tree to help myself up. It was later found when the thaw set in that another South Korean unit had soldiers killed at this point as there was a wire attached to the tree and a land mine. We had spent days in the middle of this minefield and except for one case had got away with it.

Jim Houghton

I was in 'Z' Company at the battle for Hill 217. The battle was on 5 October, but we set off on the 4th to go to it and went about midday. We were taken there by Major General Wilson. He had been in Dunkirk. He was company major at the time and he took us on this zig-zag route so that we couldn't be seen, it was three times as far as you would normally go. Well, we got to this place on a ridge the night before. It was about 100 yards from Hill 217. Every company had a Korean interpreter attached to them who spoke good English. We also had these Korean labourers with these frames to carry our equipment. The next morning they knocked us up at quarter to five, and it was getting daylight. This lad – Kim was his name, they were all called Kim – and he got us kitted up with guns and ammunition and he said, 'Good luck Jim'. He knew everyone's name. We went up that hill most of the day, got to the top ridge and just before we got there, there were deep trenches all around. I was told, 'Check that doorway Houghton.' So we kicked the door open and threw a grenade in. Nothing there, so he said all right. We went in and it was a big room inside, and at the back overlooking the river there was a piece, a slit, about 18 inches square with a bush in front. They could put a gun there or they could just sit and watch. You could see for miles and that was the reason they wanted that hill. They reckoned if you were sat on the top of this hill you could see to the south side of the Imjin River. Anyrate, nothing was there luckily enough, so we got out and we were on the ridge then. Everything was coming at us, you name it. Anyhow, this sergeant was next to me and the next minute the sergeant was sat up to shoot and I was shooting across him, he had seen something. Then he took one shot in the stomach and went down. I said to my mate the sergeant's out. Anyrate, they got to him. He died the following day. I thought he was dead then, to be honest. He came from Newcastle and his widow got the military cross for him. I always remember that. When we finally got back to our night positions we were about half a mile back and the next morning Major Wilson took our photos. He called us out and lined us all up. As we lined up I couldn't believe it, I suddenly realised how many men we had left, half the company had gone. In those days you had these box cameras but he had an American one with all these gadgets on it. I never saw him again until long after I left the army. It was 2001 and there was a service at Newcastle cathedral and I went up there. I spoke to him and said, 'Do you mind me asking, I remember you taking our photo, we were all lined up.' He said, 'Yes,' and he's still got that camera and I asked if I could have a copy of the photo. But I never did get it. A lot of the fellas on the photo were later killed. Sixteen died, 94 were wounded and 3 were taken prisoners. A lot of those killed were my pals, including my own sergeant.

We took Hill 217 and then we handed it over to the Canadians. The Chinese got driven off and we took one or two prisoners. Six weeks later the Chinese took it back, they wanted it for the winter and, as I say, they could see all the way back to the Imjin River. They're still up there, nobody's taken it since and nobody else has been up there.

After we'd handed it over we didn't do any more major assaults, we just did patrols. We were doing some fighting but it was winding down. Its difficult to take a hill because the enemy is always looking down on you, so it's very difficult. They throw grenades at you, throw anything at you and their grenades went off with a real bang. After that no, we had no major battles. I joined up with the Leicesters on 29 November after the Canadians had lost it. They said, 'Stand-to, we're pulling out in an hour.' There were lorries there, we piled into them and we drove all night, and I said to my mate, 'We're back at 217.' The trucks had gone and that afternoon they decided to attack it again; the Chinese must have been watching us all day. They were sending mortars down on us all the time. We got halfway and then pulled back. No one has ever been back.

George Stirland

We were called to defend some islands. At night when the carrier didn't have planes flying, sometimes two cruisers would leave and would go inshore so that the Chinese couldn't take any of the islands. They wanted to take them. We got a call one night as there were all these junks trying to get on the islands, so we went and were shooting them up and down. One of our lads got hit on the aft gun and it killed him instantly. Luckily it didn't explode or it would have killed a lot more, it just hit him and he got killed instantly. We carried on with the action, took him to the sickbay, then cruised off and the next morning we buried him at sea. He was called Mick Skelton. He was just a bit younger than me, but like me he came from the *Ganges*. That was the only fatality we had.

Most ships had some fatalities if they got a bit too close inshore, these Bofor type guns could reach us. Normally we could bombard them from 5 or 6 miles. We were close in and one round came in and he was killed.

That was our first action and it made us realise that this was no joke, this was serious. Funnily enough, after that we actually didn't see a lot of action. There isn't that much action with the carriers as it was just protection work. You were just guarding them, going up and down, zig-zagging. At night if we had to go in between the islands we'd fire star shells every fifteen minutes and light everything up in order see if anyone was coming across. We never had Chinese or Russian planes coming over.

Roy Cox

We got up to the company that was being shelled when they grabbed hold of me and tried to push me into a dugout. But there was a dead Chinese solider in there and I said, 'I'm not getting in there.' Anyhow the sergeant grabbed hold of me and said, 'Hey, get in there. The dugout had a window this big, and they pulled me through it. Anyhow, I was all right even though there were mortar bombs going off all over the place. One bloke there was shaking like a leaf. The sergeant gets hold of him and shakes him and says nothing's going to hurt you. Huh, I thought, there's mortar bombs going off all over the place! Anyway, he was taken away and I never saw him again. I think there was a couple of them like that, nearly always national servicemen. There were a few couldn't take it. I remember my father talking about shell shock in the First World War. But I'm not sure if these lads were suffering from shell shock.

Brian Hough

Yes, I was afraid of the action, of course. For me the worst part was the constant shelling. You'd come in after a night's patrol and you'd be cleaning your weapons, maybe preparing a brew and then the Chinese would start shelling, mortar shells, and it would be constant, almost constant. It stopped at times, of course, and there were quieter times but once it started it went on and on. You very quickly got to identify whether it's coming in or going out, there's a different sound. We'd hear one and say, 'Oh that's all right, it's one of ours.' Then we'd hear another and say, 'Hey that's Chinese, get your head down.' You just didn't know where it was going to land. That was the worst part to me. And if you were out on patrol and you engaged with the Chinese, that was frightening. But it happened so quickly. Usually you didn't have time to think but afterwards you'd be a bit shaky. But one of the things was that you didn't want to show it to your mates, did you? Yes, it was difficult; there was fear there, of course. Sadly, there were one or two who did get affected, not least my platoon sergeant. He served in the Second World War and he was one of the few human beings in my life who I have disliked. We had an unwritten rule between us; he hated me and I hated him. But the poor man within a month of being in Korea had gone to pieces. He was sat in the bottom of a trench and we didn't see him again until we left Korea and went to Hong Kong. The poor man had gone to pieces.

Roy Cox

Before we left for Korea I was told I was going to be in 'A' echelon. Now 'A' echelon was at the back. Other blokes were going to be with 'B' Company, including Frank Holden, who was married with three kids. Frank was a mate and a typical yokel lad. Put a bit of straw in his mouth and he was the ideal yokel. He had a beautiful wife as well. Now I wanted to swap places with him so that he could stay at the back but Frank wouldn't have any of it, he was very proud. I said to the sergeant, 'You should swap me, he's got a wife,' and the sergeant told me to mind my own business, it was his decision, not mine. So Frank went up the front line.

I remember the incident very vividly. 'B' Company had taken the roof off their dugout. I'm not sure why, but I think it was to deepen the dugout. It was something I would never have done. Anyhow, a shell landed in it and killed the major, plus two signallers, one of whom was Frank Holden. This always upsets me because if that sergeant had let me go instead, then Frank would still be alive today with his three kids. It was so sad. They all got blown to bits, another of the blokes who died was married as well. We were losing signallers all the time. The Ministry of War had said there must be 10 per cent signallers, so they need a national service corps of signallers.

One of these blokes, Jones, he got hit in the chest and they took him back down and he died three days later. This was all in the same incident; he was married as well with a daughter. Then they sent a chap up there to try and sort things and he came back shaking, saying, 'There's blood all over the place, I can't take it.' I said to the sergeant, 'If you ask the CO if he'll release me, then I'll go up there.' Anyway, the CO did release me and I went up there and it was awful. The place smelt and I remember sitting down listening to the wireless set and looking up at the ceiling and the logs that were resting on what was the grass and it was all red, and I thought to myself, bloody hell they must have red grass in Korea. It wasn't until a couple of days later that I realised it was blood. The sergeant major had actually gone in there as well, found bits of bodies, put them together, wrapped them in a blanket and sent them back down. They came down on the carrier and one of these dead blokes was the younger brother of the carrier driver. That bloke went a bit funny and we were actually going to send him home because that's what you did if you had a brother in the same regiment who was killed, they sent you home straightaway. Anyway, he wouldn't go. A while later when I was with 'B' Company we had an attack come in and the lad I joined the army with, Ronnie Cridland, the only other regular, got shot in the leg and somehow he got tangled up in the barbed wire and they had to leave him. I wasn't allowed to leave the wireless set and go to help him. He bled to death, an artery had been severed by some shell or shrapnel. At least fifty out of our regiment got killed while I was over there, though some were just attached to our regiment.

Bill Hurst

A good friend of mine got shot, a Welsh lad. We was on the forward positions and the officer said, 'We want fresh wire putting out, barbed wire on the bottom.' We said, 'It's on the forward positions, what about them over there?' And he said, 'They won't see you.' In the morning the mist was sometimes so thick you couldn't see anything. 'Get down there, get the wire strung out as quick and you can and get back up.' Yes, but that mist lifts really quickly. Anyhow, they all go down there putting the wire up, watching this mist, and all of a sudden, whoosh its gone. And as soon as it had gone, boom, boom, boom. The mortars started coming over. And one of the lads, Davies his name was, nice lad, he just fell down. They got hold of him and got him into the trench. He was moaning but they couldn't find anything wrong with him. At the time they took me to the hospital as well because I had a high fever and a temperature of 103, so they said, 'You'd better go with him.' They put us on a jeep on a stretcher and took us to the hospital. They got us in and they gave me an injection, bathes me, put me in bed and I said, 'How's the lad going on?' Dags we used to call him, Dags Davies. And they said, 'He's dead.' I said, 'What do you mean he's dead! We couldn't find anything wrong with him.' What had happened was that some shrapnel of the mortar bombs – a piece like a needle – had gone straight into his brains in his head. One of the medics had put his hand in his hair and cut his finger, the shrapnel had gone right into his brain and that's what killed him. Only 19, a nice lad. So sad, it shook everybody up.

Brian Hough

I was in a couple of patrols that clashed with the North Koreans and the Chinese but everything happened so quickly that sometimes I'm not sure that we knew what we were doing. There's one patrol that sticks in my mind. There were three of us – a lad who had joined up with me and one of the Koreans that was with us. We had catcombs, they were called catcombs – young Koreans – each battalion had a number of Koreans with them, maybe four or five to a company and they lived and worked alongside us. They were given British army uniforms and British ranks and the likes.

We were on patrol and it had been raining for two or three days. It was awful – there were paddy fields everywhere in these valleys and after a couple of days we were ankle deep in mud. We must have walked into this trap because the first thing we knew there was the most almighty crash of guns and fire and this young Korean lad went down and died. My mate Jack was hit as well. Jack got hit and he went down. I thought he was dead. You don't have any vision of time so I don't know how long we were exchanging fire. Anyhow the firing eventually died down and Jack was probably 20, 30 yards from the group and from where the firing had first started. Somebody said, 'Jack's moving.' Well I thought he was dead because it was dark. But yes, he was moving, so we said we'd better get him back. So two lads went out, one called Wilf Rawlinson and the other was Stan Jackson and they dragged him back. But what a mess. The whole of the bottom of his back had been shot away and he was in and out of consciousness. We got him back to our lines and they took him off and that was the last I saw of him. I really thought he had died.

Years later I was a bus driver, must be twenty years later, and a guy got on my bus and he said, 'Hughie, hello fancy seeing you. What a coincidence. I was talking to a mate of yours the other week, Jack Goulding.' Well I got a bit angry with him and said, 'Hey, don't take the piss.' Cos I thought Jack was dead. I really did. But he said, 'No, he didn't die, he's living in Langley.' Anyhow, eventually I met up with Jack and, yes, he had survived. He died in 2002 and he had got married the day before going to Korea, and every day for fifty years his wife had to clean his wounds. For fifty years she did that, day in, day out. The wound had never healed in his spine and he had constant abscesses. And his wife Veronica had cleaned the wounds every day, such love. When the guns stop firing it doesn't mean the agony and pain stops. It doesn't. It's things like that that stick in your mind.

Bill Hurst

A few of our soldiers went missing. We have three or four in the King's who have no grave. They were never found. Nobody knows what happened to them.

John Smith

The RMPs keep things moving, it's not just sitting on a station like Euston. We all got on well together, working together. I saw all these fellas with black faces. I said, 'Who are you?' They were mining engineers, laying mines all their faces had been blacked up. Then out come the wounded and the driver of one of the jeep ambulances with four stretchers in. And the driver says, 'Corporal there's someone here wants to speak to you.' I look in the back and someone says, 'Hiya Smudger.' 'Blimey,' I said. 'I can't talk now the driver will have to go on.' I can't talk to wounded men, they need attention. It was a lad called George and he was from Glasgow and we had been on leave together once. I felt a bit guilty chasing him but we're talking about lives here. Years later when I was a young policeman in Liverpool, there used to be a restaurant coffee shop in town called Reeces. I'm standing outside Reeces – this is after the war – and suddenly there's George and he was on leave. We shook hands and I said, 'I'm sorry I couldn't talk to you then in Korea.' And he says, 'I thought at the time you were a right so and so, but when I got to the hospital and I was with other wounded soldiers, they said don't you realise why he wouldn't talk to you, because he had wounded soldiers in the back of an ambulance who needed attention.'

Terry Moore

The Battle of the Imjin River lasted three days. It was a Chinese attack at the Imjin River. They wanted to cross the river and they wanted to make for Seoul. They were coming from the north and the traditional entry route into Seoul over thousands of years was via the west flank which was our left-hand side. The British brigade were put there in view of it being the traditional entry route and we were told to stand and fight. And we did stand and fight, everyone else disappeared. There was this intense danger of us being surrounded, which eventually we were. The Ulster Rifles were originally on the eastern side on the right-hand flank, in reserve, and were soon deployed to the other side because the Chinese were trying to flank that way. The Gloucester's were duly over-run, they weren't quite overrun but they were forced back and forced back. When the eventual order came to get out, we got out, but the Gloucester's – bless them – couldn't and that's where I was hurt, coming out on the last day. They got some British tanks to come up. I was the last out and we were taking our wounded down the hill to where there were some tanks coming through. We loaded a few wounded out, and coming down that hill a Chinese mortar bomb landed near me and blew me up, knocked me over, knocked me out. I split my head. The lads thought I had been hit in the head because I was unconscious but in fact I had hit my head on some rocks on the ground as I was blown. It did both my eardrums. I now have a war pension because of that. I got a 46p a week increase the other week for my deafness! One eardrum has gone but the other has mended itself. Although it's still on the blink as I speak. On the way down, some Chinese in a bit of a copse fired on us. But we fired back and just drove through. I was conscious by then. And then we went behind the lines where they unloaded the injured. We were dead tired. The 8th Hussars took us off the tanks and when we woke up the next day we were on the ground asleep on blankets. We hadn't slept for three days; I went back to an American hospital. I then reported back to my battalion. By then I could hear slightly. We were sure officers had been killed in that action and they just needed officers so I went back.

I was hauled onto the back of this tank and brought down the road, unconscious, by the 8th Hussars. We knew that the Gloucester's had been under more constant attack. But we were not aware of the full extent of casualties. We knew they had been threatened for days and that the Americans had left. As it transpired we had slightly more killed and wounded but they had masses of them taken as prisoner of war. We assumed it was Chinese who had napalmed them. You don't really find out until later.

Bill Hurst

We were in the Red Cross tent near the Imjin River where the hospital was. The Americans had built a new bridge over the river. We were all in our tents, and the Americans, can you believe, bombed the bridge. You wouldn't believe it! We were sat there and we had to get out of our beds and race out and get into the ditches. They'd got the bridge mixed up with another one. And they bombed the bridge that we were virtually on. There were big holes in the bridge. Fortunately it didn't kill anyone but it could so easily have killed all of us in the hospital tents.

Terry Moore

At a later stage when we were advancing north we had to go and hold a small hill above a crossing of a small river, a stone built crossing, which they thought they might need for tanks and transport and didn't want it blown. There were some villages above it across the river which were occupied by the Chinese at a night-time to do their cooking. Eventually, when the action started, this area was mortared. One night I was awakened by some men coming up the hill. It was four men with a huge water pitcher carrying it between them up this steep hill. I don't know who they were. I had them covered. It turned out they were men from the village, ordinary Koreans who were bringing us some water. Later the village was hit and I went down and discovered that there were three wounded civilians and one of them turned out to be one of these men who had been bringing us water. As he was being taken out on a stretcher his wife ran after him and gave him his rosary beads. So, there was quite a number of Christians there. I know that there was a German Jesuit monastery up in the hills, and the bulk of these people – nuns, white men had been killed. I think it was the North Koreans who had done it. On balance the Chinese were slightly more humane I feel. You walked these track roads which were not tarmacked and they were full of dead people hundreds of them just lying on the side of the road, dead.

When we had enemy casualties on the slopes the British soldier would go out and give them water and ciggies. These were the people who had been trying to kill us the night before. They, like British soldiers, would have photos in their top left hand pockets of their family, girlfriend. They all had that just like the British soldier.

Jim Grundy

When we got to Korea we got taken up to Daegu and while we were there we had these examination people come round to see what you were fit to do. Now obviously I wasn't fit enough to go into the front line so I was transferred to the King's Own Scottish Borders after they had been badly hit – the first battalion. They asked me what was my work before I joined the army and I said my last job was training to be a mortician with the Co–op in Eccles. 'Oh,' they said, 'you're just the man we want.' So after a couple of days this major comes round from the Royal Army Medical Corps and he said, 'I've got a nice little job for you, Mr Grundy, nice and easy.' So he took me into this hospital, into this mortuary, and there were two or three soldiers, dead bodies there and he said, 'These have just come in. Look at the state of them. Now I want you to do something for me, try and clean them up a little bit until they are manageable for us.' There was no coolers to keep the bodies in. They had been dead a month or more, so you can imagine how terrible it was. So I did it and he says, 'Just the job. Now you're going on the Recovery Programme.' On the Recovery Programme there were three teams – British, Australian and New Zealanders – and in each team five men. Four picked the bodies up and one had the radio on his back. So that's how I started working in Korea, on the Recovery Team.

What we did was, we went to as near the front as they dared send us. Let's just say we were in a paddy field and we would know the names of the soldiers missing. But the North Koreans would switch the dog tags, put one on the other, switch the watches, switch the pay books. When we got them down to Pusan there was no dental records as we could check, so they were buried as unknown soldier of the British army. I must have buried thirty to forty men in that cemetery in Pusan. If we just picked up one body in that area then obviously they couldn't switch the dog tags so we could safely say it was that person. But if there were two or three of them and they were badly decomposed we could do nothing about it. Every now and then we would take the train and take the bodies back to Pusan. And we'd take them to the hospital in Pusan and they would examine the bodies there and the doctors might say, no there's no identification, so they would be buried in graves of unknown soldiers, some were North Koreans we found, some were South Koreans, Australians, New Zealanders, Filipinos. And there were many civilians; men women and children, we picked up. But we didn't deal with them. If we found civilians we left them to one side But the Australians and New Zealanders we brought down to Pusan to the cemetery. We didn't send any bodies home.

Only the Americans and Filipinos sent bodies home. All the British soldiers were buried at Pusan.

I saw hundreds of bodies. I can guarantee that I buried at least fifty in the cemetery itself. There were 200 soldiers there on permanent burial detail because we had to go back up to Imjin. I never saw any actual action, but I heard it. But it takes all sorts to fight a war, from the back to the front to make things run smoothly. At the time I felt like I was cheating on these front line soldiers who were doing the fighting. But I found later that my work was very, very important. I was used to dead bodies having worked in the Co-op at Eccles but they had coolers. Over there, there were none, so sometimes we could just pick up a body and it would just fall to bits. Sometimes it was just a skeleton. I would say that of all the bodies I found we were lucky if we identified ten or twelve of them. Just to give you an example. They'd found a body in the North and it has been handed over. Now you have to be 98 per cent sure before you give a body a name. Now, I might know who he was, the chap who asked the questions knew who he was. But when they found him – two of them had been found in the same area – and they could tell that the bodies had been tampered with – one was Australian and one British. The British lad was the last one buried in that cemetery as unknown soldier, British army, in his own big plot there.

We only worked in the daylight. Now the North Koreans or Chinese when they sent their team out to look for bodies – there's only five in a party – so if you went out looking for bodies they'd fire over your head. So you'd put your hands up, you have the Red Cross flag, so you'd put that up. Sometimes they'd let you go and pick the bodies up, sometimes you'd have to wait for another day. But they knew who you were cos there was only five of you. If there was six or seven of you they'd just shoot at you.

In the evening, after the work, you'd get yourself cleaned up and go to the NAAFI, have a couple of beers.

Bill Hurst

We had one lad at our barracks back in England at Ashton barracks and he didn't want to go to Korea. He saw his MP, his JP and everyone else and in the end he didn't go. And all the lads called him a coward for not going but it was his principle. He was the only one of forty-six lads who didn't go. We had a few deserters but they always got caught. We had one lad who finished up in Singapore from Korea. They'd get down the docks, get a boat. When they got him they sent him back and put him in clink. There were a few jumped off the boat. They'd catch them, put them in clink and they'd be back.

Jim Grundy

What worried us more than anything – and I've always said this – no matter who died in that war, it was some mother's son And when we fetched three bodies in and we knew that they were not going to have any names, it used to get to me at times. I don't know whether it was the training at the Co-op funeral parlour in Eccles or what, but it never really made me not want to do the job. It made me want to try and do better. The soldiers died doing their duty and my duty was to clean them up the best I could and try and identify them. My worry now is the children we found who had been shot by the North Koreans or Chinese or froze to death; old men and women. Now that's upsetting. And even now I wake up in that bedroom sometimes in the middle of winter sweating – not about the soldiers, the soldiers don't bother me – it was the civilians that gets to me and you'll find that if you go to see Brian Hough – he found that many children in Korea. You mention children to him and the tears will roll down his cheek. And that's why he works with children now. He devotes himself to that. That's what turned Brian, so you try and teach children, tell them what happened.

Jim Houghton

One night we were up there, it was September 1951 and it was warm and we were in the tent at the back of the front line and the Chinese are attacking us so there's a stand-to. Fortunately we always slept with our trousers and boots on. There's some Aussies nearby and all hell is let loose. It went on through to daylight with flares going off everywhere. This massive Aussie must have been sleeping in his tent as he had no shirt on and the Chinese were trying to get over the wire and he was knocking them off, he was calling them mongrels. This went on for over two hours and we could see them, they just kept on coming, their commissars would blow a whistle and they would start coming, they had to choice, they kept coming and they were all being shot down. Next day we were 50 per cent on stand-to. We could hear the Chinese shipping the dead and wounded out. All the ammunition was spent. We were using Enfield .303 rifles and Bren guns. They were fine at that time although you wouldn't use them today. You couldn't complain about the weapons, but clothing, now that was a bit different.

Jim Grundy

I was very naïve, I knew nothing of what was happening in Korea, I was only 19 years old. I'd hear all these lads who were reservists saying, 'Let's get over there, let's get stuck into them.' And you'd be thinking, 'Oh aye, lets get over there.' They be saying, 'Oh yes, this is good this.' But once you stepped off onto that landing you didn't know where you was. It was a funny sensation and I never lost that until I left Korea. I could never trust anybody. The South Korean soldiers were trustworthy enough but you never really knew if they were South Korean or North. Sometimes you'd have North Koreans in South Korean uniform. We came across very few Chinese, I'd say three or four, but if we found North Korean or Chinese bodies we'd dig them up and carry them to the side and as we were walking away we'd wave to them and point, that meant that they were theirs. But they'd leave them there for months sometimes, though in the end they'd take them. They may take them straight away but sometimes they'd leave them there for weeks, even months. But there was nothing we could do about that. But if it was our lads they were dealt with swiftly and we'd do the best we could.

The weather was four times as cold as you get here but in the summer it was four times as hot. So in winter although digging was very hard it was easier because there wasn't any smell. But in summer when the gas bubbles were coming up the smell was horrible, just unbelievable and sometimes even today I can still smell it on my hands when it's hot. It's something that will never leave me. And then children I saw who had been shot or frozen to death has never gone out of my head. It's something I just can't get rid of. But I don't let it get to me too much. They were there and I couldn't bury them, I could do nothing to help them, I couldn't put them in a decent place. That always worried me, that, and does to this day. Could I have done a little bit more, could I have done this or that to help them. So when I came back from Korea I was determined to work part time at the cemetery, voluntary. As I say, I now have 200 to 300 photos of British soldiers who died in Korea.

Now there's only one lad left from my team. He took it badly after the war, he won't talk about the war. I can talk about it but there's others who won't talk about it.

John Smith

Was I ever frightened? Sometimes. I had to stand in this place, on my own and I was told that someone had been standing and been killed on the same spot and that his ghost haunted the place! You did see people praying.

We had a house boy who was with us most of the time, used to follow us around. He did a good job for us. I always remember having to go somewhere in the jeep one day, about 30 miles away, and the boy wanted to come with us. I said why, and he said his mother lived there, so I took him with us to see his mum and dad and he was so made up, over the moon he was. He'd been with the army for months and months, he was only a young lad, maybe 12 or so, helping out.

Jim Grundy

The only way you could find bodies in the summer was by the gas bubbles in the rice fields. The gas bubbles used to come up through the mud.

Then we knew there as a body there. But in winter, of course, there was nothing. We used to have a stick which we put down and if it hit anything solid you had an idea there might be something there. We'd dig it up but there'd probably be nothing there at all. But the callousness always sticks with me, the way they treated the bodies. There was no explanation for it whatsoever. But any body we found we always treated with the deepest of respect.

I spent my whole time with the Recovery Programme but I had a little spell of six weeks in Hong Kong at the end of 1952. With the work that we were doing, it got to one or two of the lads, so they gave us this break in Hong Kong. Then we had to go back and start again until three weeks before the end of the war. Then I got posted to Japan.

When we were in the NAAFI of an evening, People would ask, did you find anybody here, did you find anybody there, but you didn't tell them or discuss it. So you'd have a game of darts or cards, just to pass the evening away. But we always had that smell on us. There were no showers, just once a month the Red Cross used to come up with portable showers and you could have a shower. That was the only way you could get rid of the smell. Sometimes people wouldn't come near you because of the smell. You'd have a good wash down, scrub down with soap and water, but you still smelled and people wouldn't come near you. It was your clothes that smelled of dead bodies. We were on duty seven days a week.

Sometimes you'd go out three or four days and there'd be nothing, nothing at all. But you would wait on the radio and the radio would say someone's been killed in this area so you'd go to that area if it was in your patch. Sometimes it could be every day but even if you found the bodies and it was going dark you had to leave it. If you'd dug them up, the North Koreans would come and put them back in again in the night, but if there was more than one body you could guarantee they would take the dog tags, watches and the rest.

I was never frightened, no. Others had it twenty-four hours a day, gunfire down their ears. I heard it but I was never on top of it like they were. We went on the second advance up and we followed them up. By then a lot had been dead three or four months. You'd dig them up and then two of you would pick them up and a leg would fall off or a head would fall off so you'd put them on the back of a wagon and go and pick the rest up and put it all in a black bag, take it to Daegu, the big American camp, where you'd put it in a black bag and put it on the train and take it to Pusan, though it wasn't always me who took them on the train.

John Hegarty

HMS *Jamaica* continued operations on the east coast of Korea, and US and UK units were soon joined by ships from Australia, New Zealand and other Commonwealth countries. European countries also took part and ultimately produced the largest international naval force since the Second World War.

Sasebo in Japan was the main base for logistics and shore leave. It was a small port with little to offer ashore. US facilities included a club, but Royal Navy personnel were restricted by the draconian fiscal rules prevailing at that time which did not allow UK personnel to exchange sterling for US dollars. The next phase for *Jamaica* was to switch operations to the west coast of Korea and ultimately to the Inchon landings. Immediately before September 1950, the North Korean forces, supported by the Chinese Red Army, had forced UN land forces back to a perimeter around the port of Pusan. It was a desperate situation and required a bold initiative to release this stranglehold. General MacArthur decided to take such an initiative with an amphibious landing at the port of Inchon. It was a difficult task, but if successful would outflank North Korean forces at a stroke and could change the course of the whole campaign.

The Inchon operation would take many hours to describe, but suffice to say *Jamaica* participated in the bombardment before the landing and covered the operation throughout. However, one daring action, prior to the affair, remains in my memory. The evening before the landing, four US destroyers sailed up to the port of Inchon in confined waters with no cover and little room to manoeuvre; their purpose was to draw enemy fire in order that an assessment could be made of likely resistance when the landing craft went in next day. They proceeded in formation, flags flying and guns manned. The inevitable response came from the defences ashore as the ships drew fire from the shore batteries. It seemed like an age to those of us awaiting their return, but eventually all four reappeared, still in proud formation, but perhaps their upper works not quite so shipshape as before. We learnt subsequently one of the destroyer's COs had been killed and many others too, but the likely strength of resistance was assessed and it surely went a long way in ensuring a successful assault next day.

The day following the landing, together with other ships, *Jamaica* was at anchor in the approaches to Inchon. Nearby was the HQ ship, USS *Mt McKinley*, with General Douglas MacArthur on board. All appeared to have gone well ashore, but nevertheless, in accordance with usual Royal Navy practice, the ship went to dawn action stations as the first signs of light appeared on the horizon. From long experience over war years, this was the time of maximum threat from attack. Being landlocked, our radars were not effective. Just as it got light, over the tannoy system came the report, 'Alarm Aircraft Starboard', and then followed the usual commands for the guns to stand-to. An aircraft was sighted and was reported over the broadcast system. Those of us below decks could understand what was happening. We heard the thump of two explosions and the broadcast reported, 'Two bombs have been dropped astern of the *Mt McKinley*'. Again the broadcast – 'Aircraft turning towards'. Immediately, those guns sighted were trained on the approaching aircraft. There was a desperate urgency throughout the ship to hear our guns respond, but the Captain, calmly but with complete assurance, ordered the guns not to fire but to track the target as it closed in on the ship. Then, when near enough to read the insignia on its fuselage, the order came – 'Fire'. *Jamaica* shook from stem to stern as every gun free to engage fired and the unfortunate pilot, together with his aircraft, disintegrated in a flash and disappeared into the water. A second aircraft was sighted and again engaged, this time it veered away from us as it saw the first aircraft explode, but the guns were successful and, although not quite so dramatic, the aircraft was last seen losing height and subsequently crashed as it crossed the estuary. Later reports indicated the aircraft had strafed the ship causing some casualties and one sailor, Boy Seaman Ron Godsall, was fatally wounded.

6. PRISONERS OF WAR

'One medal, that's all we got, one medal.'

INTRODUCTION

TO BE TAKEN prisoner by the Chinese was the worst fear of any soldier. If it happened then they knew that torture and brainwashing were very likely and perhaps an even worse outcome. Their fears were more than justified.

But there was another problem, as Bill Fox outlines. It was the continual anxiety of never knowing when you would be released. If, as he says, you had been convicted of a crime you would know precisely what your sentence was. It might be six months, a year, five years or whatever, but as a prisoner of war you had no idea how long you would be held. The war could come to an end tomorrow and you might be released, but equally it might be a year, three years, ten years, who knows. In the case of Bill Fox, he was a prisoner for two and a half years and had no idea as to when he might be released until he knew that a ceasefire had been signed. The army had warned their soldiers that there would be brainwashing and indeed there was. There were constant lectures, although in Bill Fox's case he actually found some of it quite interesting and educational.

Some Americans were actually convinced by what they heard and remained behind in North Korea or China after the war ended. One British soldier remained, although he returned to Britain in 1960.

Bill Fox's story is an astonishing one, full of heroism and hardship. Fortunately he survived to tell the tale whereas many did not. And even among those who did survive few wanted to recall their time of imprisonment. Most former POWs were left with deep scars and disturbing memories that they preferred to keep to themselves.

Bill Fox also had no idea whether anyone in the army or at home had any idea as to his whereabouts. As it happened they didn't, and the army had assumed that he had been killed in action. They had no means of knowing otherwise and his family was duly sent a telegram, informing them of his death. How many other soldiers' families must have received similar telegrams. There was even a letter sent on behalf of the United Nations Command.

It began, 'Dear Mr Fox' (with no mention of Mrs Fox). 'The untimely death of your son, William, has been a tragic loss,' before concluding that, 'I have faith that his devotion to duty, in defence of all that we and the free peoples of the world hold most dear, has helped us on the long, hard road by which alone we may expect some day to reach a just, an honourable and an enduring peace.' It was signed by Lieutenant General Ridgway of the US Army.

At that stage in the war there was no agreement about prisoners and the Red Cross was helpless in being able to ascertain any information. The Chinese simply said that they had taken 1,000 prisoners, or whatever. There were just numbers with no names, regiments or nationalities being revealed.

And, of course, there was torture, although in the case of Bill Fox's experience it tended only to happen if you committed some misdemeanour such as trying to escape, or if you hit a North Korean or Chinese soldier. In other camps torture was far more widespread and undoubtedly resulted in the deaths of soldiers.

As he was being marched to his camp, Bill Fox had an image of a Second World War prisoner-of-war camp where he would be greeted by some high-ranking British officer sitting on a bunk bed smoking his pipe and welcoming him with a few words of advice. That image turned out to be as far from the truth as possible. Conditions at the camp could barely have been worse, plus there was the freezing weather, and unlike being on the front line there was no extra clothing to combat the winters. Many have said that the Korean prisoner-of-war camps were far worse than the renowned Japanese camps of the Second World War.

Precise figures on the numbers taken prisoner are impossible to come by. Records were never kept but research carried out since the war[19] suggests that just over 1,000 British servicemen, the bulk of them from the army, were taken prisoner. Of these, seventy-one are known to have died with a further eleven presumed to have died in the camps. Most of the British prisoners were from the Glosters following the Battle of the Imjin River. Some 600 were taken prisoner, with 200 wounded or killed in the battle. The total numbers of American prisoners during the war was far higher, estimated to be around 7,245. Of these, 2,806 died in the camps. When an agreement was finally reached in 1953, 4,418 American servicemen were released with twenty-one refusing repatriation, instead choosing to go to China.

Terry Moore

Some of my soldiers were killed and one was captured. The enemy never reported your casualties to you in the way that we had previously experienced, so you didn't know if people had been killed in action. You knew they were missing but didn't know if they were dead or prisoners. And it was eighteen months before the Red Cross were able to find out that some men were still alive. They had been presumed missing in action and a lot had been presumed dead but one or two appeared alive after the Red Cross had got into the camps. He later told me that in the camps he became cook so that he would have more access to food than the rest.

---

19   For detailed information on prisoners, see Anthony Farrar-Hockley, *The British Part in the Korean War Vol. II*. This is further explored in Phillip D. Chinnery, *Korean Atrocity*.

John Smith

Mostly I was working with convoys, going across the bridges. There was a phone either side on the bridge and we would inform them. Your priority is the ammunition. We did patrol areas. At one time I picked up a regiment and I had to take them up to the line. We were also looking after prisoners at times but generally we would hand them over to the Americans. I remember seeing this prisoner, I was 20, and he was only a kid. They called them the Chinese volunteer force; that was a load of rubbish. No way would he have volunteered. I said to him, I asked the interpreter, 'How old is he?' '15.' 'Ask him if he volunteered.' He said, 'No, he worked on a farm in China and they came around,' like they did, many years ago in our country and just press-ganged them into the army, back of a wagon. I was stuck with him for a couple of days but he was no harm. I took my mess tins down to get some food. I said to the mess hand, 'One for the prisoner and one for me.' And he said, 'You're not having one for the prisoner.' I said, 'You've got to feed him.' In the end they said OK. What it was, a lot of men had memories from the Second World War and we hadn't been treated well had we? But he knew me and said OK. I kept him for a while then the Americans came to pick him up. I gave him to the Americans and he starts speaking to me in Chinese. He spoke to me, again through the interpreter. He wanted to tell me how happy he was to be taken prisoner by the British. Can you believe! There's probably some old guy in China remembering this. Some of them were in a hell of a state. We never really saw the prisoner-of-war camps as they were at the rear. There was trouble at one point in a camp and some of our fellas had to go down to help. There had been an uprising. But I was up with the brigade and never went.

Roy Cox

We only had three of our people taken prisoner. When they attacked Hill 227 they took some of our blokes prisoner. When they took them prisoner, they waved them to go down the hill thinking that the other Chinese were down there but they weren't so the lads escaped. I did talk some years later to one of the Glosters who had been taken prisoner. I don't know how long he'd been a prisoner, but it made us feel sick what he told us. He was telling us about the conditions inside the camp. They got bugger all to eat, they got cabbage water, stuff that wasn't fit to eat, stuff stewed in water. One bloke said he was made to stand outside in the freezing cold without his clothes on. When they got him back inside he was suffering from hypothermia. They had to put blankets around him and rub him until he came to. One of them said that they all had worms at that particular camp. Some camps were worse than others, though of course they were all bad.

Ted Beckerley

Although the weather got better, the food remained much the same. Now and again we had a real luxury of rice and once we had a small hard loaf of bread per man. The loaves were absolutely laced throughout with weevils, like caraway seeds, but they were dead and we were so hungry that we ate those loaves. Because our diet was so monotonous and lacking in vitamins some of our chaps suffered from 'burning feet' a terrible burning sensation that made it almost impossible to put your feet on the ground. I believe it was a form of Beriberi, which was the liquid swelling of limbs and body that some suffered. To prevent this, and hopefully to increase our supply of vitamins, we began to boil and eat a non–flowering weed that was prolific in the camp. It was not unpleasant to eat – something like spinach. It was green and there was nothing else to eat. However, Charlie Adams and I both started to swell. Within a few days we were both like Michelin men when naked. When we lay down the fluid spread evenly and we just looked swollen with faces like a full moon. But when we stood up the change was dramatic. The fluid drained from our upper body and our faces became ordinary but not the legs, feet, arms and hands. The hands swelled and the fingers were like sausages. Charlie just kept getting thinner. He had developed a nasty cough and occasionally coughed up blood. It looked pretty certain he had TB and the Beriberi had been masking the symptoms. In peacetime, Charlie's job had been as a gardener at the local TB sanatorium and he had worked there for four years. Knowing Charlie, he had probably helped out in a lot of other ways in addition to his main duty. Charlie got worse and worse and was desperately thin. His face became that of a skeleton with huge staring eyes. He still prayed constantly and had such a longing to be home with his wife, Hazel, and their two children. Eventually, the time came when he had to be taken to hospital early in July. Four of our chaps came with a stretcher and he was taken away. I had dysentery and was pretty weak so I was unable to be one of the four who took him. I walked out with them as far as the gate (the hospital was outside the camp) and said goodbye. Charlie was still holding on to his prayer book. He died a few days later in the early hours of the morning. According to an American orderly who was with him, Charlie cried out to Hazel just before he died. Her name was the last word he uttered.

Bill Fox

We were on the main line by the Imjin River for, I think, it was about three weeks. We were well dug in, we were so well dug in. The army didn't build its dugouts on top of a hill as you would be silhouetted, so they built them below the top so that you've got ground behind you and can't be so easily seen. I was there for three weeks and we were loaded up with so much ammunition; hand grenades, magazines for the Bren gun. What do we need all this for, we thought? Little did we know we didn't even have enough. We had loads. We had loads of food up there as well in case things started and they were unable to get food up to us.

During those three weeks you'd look over the river and it all looked so peaceful. Now and then you'd see an old Korean farmer working in the fields in the far distance but we didn't bother shooting. But we did do patrols over there. We rowed over on boats and into North Korea but every time we went over there was a strange feeling. It was quiet, dead quiet. There didn't seem to be any birds or animals around, it was dead quiet and it shouldn't be that quiet. The young ones were as scared as us, we couldn't see any sign of anything. But you had a feeling that there were all these eyes on you. You felt that there were thousands of Chinese spying on you from the distance and if you go too far they'll pounce on you like a fly getting too near a spider's web. We were always glad to be heading back to the line; we never stayed too long.

Towards the end of April we got reports that the Chinese had mustered up a huge army and would attack at any time. We had observers and we had spotter planes out there and spies over there and the likes, but the army had a view that they would attack but they didn't know when. But at least we knew we'd get an early warning when they came over the river. And true enough they expected them this night. We could hear them coming over and we heard the bugle call. Then you hear it coming a bit nearer. Oh my god, it got frightening. You could hear our officers shouting, 'Don't shoot until we can see them.' Then they started throwing up flares. And you could see them. We were blasting away and they were coming in waves. In their first attack they had stick grenades and were throwing them. They're not as powerful as our hand grenades but still enough to kill you. And they had machine guns that would blast you. They were 100 yards away but we were well dug in. We blasted them, shooting them. One fella came running up, almost on top of us throwing grenades, we gave them everything we'd got, and then they retreated a bit. 'I think I got him,' I said. He was stuck against the privet. Some of the lads weren't sure I'd got him, so I gave it him again and he was still stuck there. 'I'm sure I've got him,' I said. 'I'll go down in the morning and check it.'

But I never got the chance because no sooner had they retreated than another wave of Chinese came. That's how they do it, wave after wave. Had they got their tactics better they could have overrun us straightaway. At the end of the battle we were exhausted and the orders came to withdraw. Unfortunately, we were right in the front but we didn't get them orders. My mate Derek Ball was with us – three of us together. A machine gunner had got our range and all the bullets were whizzing round us. Derek got a bullet in the head, might have been two, there was that much blood. He was right next to me, shoulder to shoulder. He dropped onto the floor, I never had a chance to pick him up or anything, he was dead. I tried to feel his pulse but there was nothing. It was too dangerous. When the heavy machine guns are firing you'd know the Chinese weren't on top of you because they'd get hit by their own machine-gun fire. When the firing stops, that's when you know they are advancing and you have time. That was Derek Ball, from Colchester. To this day I remember him, his accent, everything about him. I'll never forget.

Eventually the three of us pulled out, but no one was there, all the others had already pulled out. Then we started being shelled by mortar fire. To this day I think it was our own fire. This was our chance to escape, get down the bottom of the hill, so we crawled out of our holes and crawled down the hill using the gully to the bottom where we saw a big hole we could dive in. I'd got cut on barbed wire and had shrapnel and I was bleeding but I managed to stop the bleeding. There was just the two of us and we stopped in this gully whispering, saying, we'll stop here until nightfall and then we'll creep out, get to the bottom of the hills, go along the gullies and make our way south. But we decided we'll go tonight when it's dark and nobody's about. We didn't know that by then our lines were well back. We thought it might only be a mile. We had no food or water either so we knew we had to make a break for it that night because we wouldn't survive with no food or supplies and wouldn't have the strength to get away. So we waited and kept quiet.

Some time later I could feel something coming, on the ground above us, and sure enough, oh my god! I saw this face appear, a Chinese soldier, he looked down at us. Oh my god, I jumped up. I put my hands up. There were no John Wayne ideas of grabbing him and chinning him and wrestling the rifle off him. Oh no, my hands were way up, straightaway! By then this Chinese was fumbling for his gun. Luckily he didn't have a gun in his hand as he probably would have shot us there and then. But we got our hands up pretty quickly and then all of a sudden the place was surrounded by Chinese. There were dozens of them, all jeering at us. I suppose they were happy they'd got two prisoners of war. They searched us all over to make sure we had nothing on us, then they took us further down to the very bottom of the hill where it flattened out a bit and there, down below, was rows and rows of dead Chinese soldiers, rows of them. They must have been brought down from the side of the hill after the battle and laid out ready for burial or whatever. Rows of them. I thought they'd taken us down to show us that we were going to get the same – a bullet in the back of the head. All sorts of thoughts start coming into your head.

They took us into a sort of wood of heavy bushes and small trees full of Chinese soldiers. Normally the Americans would have napalmed all these woods and if they had done they would have gone up in a great blaze and have killed loads of Chinese. But for some reason they hadn't.

Anyway, they started to bury us in the ground. I thought they were going to bury us alive at first. There were about six soldiers with us but there was no way of escaping. They were all staring at us, probably never seen a white man before and I don't know whether they knew we were English, American or what. They gave us a little water out of a bottle. One of them came to me with a British army water bottle and pointed to it and started making gestures for me to smell it. I knew what it was. It was rum cos some of the lads used to save it in their water bottles and have a piss up once a month or keep it for when the weather was freezing cold at night. He wanted me to drink it in case it was some kind of poison but I knew what it was, so I put it to my mouth and had a good quick swig of it. He, of course, then realised and pulled it away from me. But I did get a good swig of it, it made my day. Anyway, they weren't too bad these Chinese, they weren't too bad at all. There was one who I surmised was the platoon leader of about fifty men and he was trying to talk to me in sign language, saying he was married, had kids and so on. And he asked me if I was married and I was trying to make the sign of the Union Jack in the dirt. He seemed nice and friendly but he was still guarding you. He didn't put handcuffs on us or anything like that – he didn't need to. There were plenty of guards there and, anyhow, you weren't fit enough to do much. I was beginning to get weary from not having food or water to drink. Then for a few weeks, at least I think it was a few weeks, cos we had no idea about time, we were with the same group of Chinese. We had to follow them up and down.

One day a couple of Chinese came along on horseback. They looked like a couple of generals and were flanked by lots of other soldiers and guards, all smarter looking than the mob we was with. Lots of conversation went on, yabber, yabber, yabber, and we got a feeling they were saying goodbye to us and wishing us well. They had been friendly but now we had these new guards with fixed bayonets and much tougher looking. They didn't need to speak your language, if they wanted you to move they made you move. I was never the hero type so I just got on with it. You get used to the bullying types.

We were taken to a village nearby where there was about twenty other prisoners of war including a British army officer. He only had one eye, he had a patch over it. It was a mixed bunch – Turks and a Filipino who was a tankman. We were there a few weeks and there was an English-speaking guard who looked like a villain and talked like a villain. He was calling us, 'Running dogs of war, American imperialists', and so on; 'You are invaders, you shouldn't be in our country, you're going to die, you should be shot on sight, you swines!' Really bitter he was.

The food was a sort of dry milk, and if you wanted, you could mix some water with it. You only got one drink of water a day. There was no other food and when you went to the toilet it was just a watery crap, like dysentery. We were only let out of the hut to go and have a piss in the gully. Forget about toilets, toilet paper and things like that. Then I noticed one day when I went for a wee, there was body lice on my hair. 'Oh my god!' I thought, 'what's that?' Then I found out that everyone in the hut had it. And it wasn't long before it was all over my body. It was terrible. A terrible, degrading thing. They grow quite big and you could get them between your fingers and crack them. And when you take your inner garments off you can see the all eggs along the seams of your clothes. Loads of these little white eggs and they formed in no time at all into body louse. You are covered with them. It was not only degrading being a prisoner but having this as well made it doubly degrading.

Now the thing was that you never knew how long you'd be a prisoner. It wasn't like you'd committed some crime and been sent to Strangeways prison for six months or whatever. Here you don't know how long you're going to be in for or even if you'll ever get out. You just don't know in that kind of war because you're not a prisoner of war until you're registered. The Germans and Japanese used to register their prisoners of war fairly quickly. People back home would then know they were prisoners of war. You felt a lot safer then. The Chinese might say they were holding 1,000 prisoners but you wouldn't know who because they didn't register prisoners in the early days of the war. And you knew, because common sense would tell you, that they could put a bullet in the back of your head any time they wanted to and nobody would ever know. It was a terrible feeling. Already when you're sick you fall asleep and then you wake up and think, am I still a prisoner? Then you'd feel the cold air on your face and you'd look round and think, 'Oh my god.' The only peace you got was when you were asleep. But during the day you wouldn't know what was going to happen to you. And consequently you're not in a mood to be friendly to your fellow prisoners, you're not in a mood to be friendly, ask them where they come from, America, or wherever. You don't want to talk, you feel sick and depressed. You see in war films prisoners chatting, I'll look after you buddy, and so on, and there's pleasant music in the background and they all die gloriously. Well, let me tell you, it's not like that in real life, not when you're a prisoner like that. You're feeling sick and you are sick. Inwardly and outwardly you are dirty as well, you haven't shaved, people are growing beards, you've got stubble everywhere over your face and neck, you're grubby everywhere, your socks, clothes, you don't get a change of clothes or socks. You can't wash your socks or put them on the line.

I think we were held in this village for about three weeks, but again it was impossible to know because you just lost track of time, you didn't know what day it was, you didn't have a calendar to tick off the days or weeks, but I guess it was about three weeks. And then they said, 'You're going up north.' By then there was more prisoners coming in and that was sickening because the more who came in, the more you thought that the Chinese were winning. They were mainly Americans coming in. Eventually, we had a speech from this prison guard telling us we were going to a prison camp where we would be educated in the ways of communism. We were going to be brainwashed although we didn't know about such things then. Eventually there was enough in the line to form a column of prisoners so they started marching us northwards, we had to cross the Imjin River where it was very shallow but there was no stopping, drying your clothes and socks, you just had to keep marching and much of it was at night to avoid American planes. We might stop somewhere and they'd put us up in a barn or something. We had to keep going on the march; it wasn't a forced march, just a slow march, but you couldn't stop, you just had to keep going. We knew we were going north but would we ever be seen again, might we end up with a bullet in the back of the head? Some were very sick but they had to keep going. I could hardly walk myself because the cuts on my legs had dried up and were painful.

Near the end of the march I could barely walk. It took us an age before we got to the prisoner-of-war camps, it was probably about six weeks. I was hoping that when we got there, the camp would have huts like you see in Second World War films where there would be a British army officer smoking a pipe, welcoming us and saying, 'Now men, I want you to do this,' and you'd get a haircut and a shave and proper food and Red Cross parcels. I thought it won't be too bad if we get things like that.

Sometimes they'd march us through small villages and the North Koreans would be lined up to throw stones at us. I honestly think they were ordered to do so because I don't think the Koreans are the type of people to throw stones at others. I tried to put on my saddest mournful face, like I was begging, 'Don't throw those rocks at me.' They would kill you, some of them bloody rocks, some of them would lob the stones at you so that you could see them coming and dodge out of the way.

One particular day, we stopped for a rest and this particular North Korean officer who was us a bit different from the others was trying to speak to me, going on about American planes and saying, 'MacArthur, MacArthur,' but I couldn't understand and I was saying, 'Yeah, yeah, yeah,' and he whacked me with his stick. I should have been saying, 'No, no, no, I agree with you.' He whacked me with his stick, I was knocked to the ground and almost knocked out. One of the Chinese guards stopped him and ordered him away and they helped pick me up.

Anyhow, eventually we got to the prison camp but it was nowhere near like what I was hoping it would be. It was terrible. I looked at all the prisoners, mainly Americans there, but they'd been there some months before us and they looked terrible. And the death rate was terrible among them. People dying regularly and they got their mates to carry them out with two bamboo poles and a straw matting in between and they'd carry them to a pit and dump them and then come back for more. It was terrible. There was unimaginable, terrible conditions, all the soldiers looked terrible. Our first thought was that the Americans couldn't take it as we can but there was more to it than that. They'd had the winter there as well, that awful first winter, and they looked dreadful. Looking back I don't think I would have lasted twelve months there, especially having to go through a winter like that and it would have been our second winter there, not in those conditions. The food was terrible, the conditions were terrible, everything was terrible.

I remember seeing films years later about prison life and one was a really tough American prison, but how many of them survived compared to that prison in North Korea? The American military have said that their worst loss of life among those taken prisoner of war was in the Chinese and North Korean camps in the Korean War, far more than in the Japanese War. Now that's surprising because they always say how bad it was in the Japanese prisons, but it was nowhere near as bad as Korea, according to the Americans, anyrate. And I could believe it. When they came home as prisoners of war, the Japanese had been given medals galore but we just got one medal. That's all we got, one medal. We were there for three years as well, none of the others were, they only did one winter. By the time those who came after twelve months, the line had stabilised, there was no going backwards and then forwards all the time, no digging, no refugees to worry about. Some feel very bitter about it, there were no celebrations when we came home. We got a great welcome from our own soldiers, it was wonderful, but from the army officials nothing. When we were released back to the British army camps the reception was marvellous but nothing from the government or when we got back home.

I was held prisoner for two and a half years. So I had nigh on three years in Korea. I stopped in this camp the whole time. We never knew how close we were to the Yalu River until we were released and when we were released these wagons came to pick us up, open back troop vans, and they took us along the Yalu River to a railroad that had been built. We thought it had been destroyed but it had been rebuilt and we were put on a train to take us south. We didn't go all the way, we had to get out where a bridge had been destroyed, go down the gully up the other side and onto another train to take us south to Panmunjom on the border with the demarcation line.

We were released when the peace talks came to a success. It was a ceasefire that all firing would stop. We knew that talks were going on, the camp commandant told us from time to time. When we first went there to the camp it was terrible and I don't think we could have survived another winter in those conditions and I don't think the Americans could either but once the peace talks started and we were told about these peace talks – though they told us in a very low key way – we were so happy to hear that, it was like winning the lottery, and once the talks had started, conditions in the camp improved dramatically. And by the time of the end we were being treated like human beings.

The toilet facilities were nil, you had to go outside to this huge pit, about the size of this room with planks across, you can imagine the flies and rats all around there. But the toilet facilities improved later as we built them. We had engineers. The farmers used to come out and take all the shit away to use on their paddy fields. You can't begin to imagine the smell. We got paper to wipe our backsides, that was a luxury. Before that you just had to use your hands and then wipe them in the dirt or on leaves.

The food also improved once the talks were under way. And eventually news filtered home. We were given a pencil and paper and had to write our names and addresses on it and hand it to the Chinese guards. When we wrote letters home we were told that we had to tell people that the Chinese were lovely people and that they treated us well otherwise they'd rip your letter up. We had to say 'Dear Mum and Dad, I am a prisoner of war but the Chinese are treating us well. We'll be glad when this war is over, don't worry about me.' My parents thought I was dead. They got a letter off the United Nations, signed by General Ridgway of the US Army telling them that I had died on duty. That was dated 11 May 1951.

Later there was a certificate from the Ministry of War telling them that I was dead and I have a copy of it here:

No 22530081 Private William Anthony Fox, the Gloucestershire regiment, was killed in action on the 23rd day of April 1951 whilst on operations, dated 28th day of July 1951.

You can imagine what my mother went through and, of course, all the other mothers. Not only that but they made another cock-up. Another fellow called Fox had been wounded and taken to military hospital and they got us mixed up and had sent a telegram to my mother saying that your son is safe, he is wounded and is here in hospital. But it was my dad who noticed in the second telegram cos he had served in the

Second World War that the number was wrong and was not my number. My mother refused to believe that I was dead cos they knew the military could make a cock-up.

They all thought I was dead. When she heard from me, my mother went down to the recruiting office in Manchester to tell them and she told them I was a prisoner of war. They didn't know anything. What had happened was the Chinese had sent the letter through eastern Europe, via Moscow first, and they then posted it as international mail and an ordinary postman took that letter to our house. My family thought I was dead! My sister always tells the tale about how she went down one morning and saw this letter. She was screaming, 'It's from Bill, it's from Bill.' My dad come down, 'What!' They were crying and everything. At first my dad said it might be an old letter that's been delayed. But no, he's a prisoner of war. Jesus. Big celebrations and everything. They didn't know until this letter comes in the letterbox. So they then had to go and notify the army in Manchester. I'm not certain how long this was after I'd been captured as I was still in the camp and had no concept of time whatsoever and I didn't know about any of this until I came back. But it would have been months. But my mother always said that she believed I was still alive.

Other mothers were the same. I had to go and see one mother and her son was an officer who lived in Sale, not that far from me. She'd had a 'killed in action' telegram as well and she believed he was still alive. I went to see her a few times but in fact I found out that he was dead. Very sad.

Eventually I got a letter from home from my mum. You feel a lot better then and everyone else was getting letters as well. Not regular, we only got a few but at least you knew that they knew that you were a prisoner. You also felt safer being registered as a prisoner of war. The food improved as well as the toilet facilities. The engineers were able to make reasonable toilets by building proper planks and they were put over a river where there was running water. It was a lot cleaner and healthier. There were probably up to a thousand of us being held prisoner by then, and in the wintertime we were sleeping in huts and they had a heating system. Everything improved once the talks were under way and in the second winter we got clothes. Before that we had been in our tatty old clothes that we had been captured in. But we got this thick padded uniform.

You didn't get tortured for doing nothing but you would get tortured if you committed a crime. You'd get tied up and you could see the marks on the arms where they tied you on a rope on a beam so that you were on your tiptoes and they'd leave you for hours. The worst form of torture was not being beaten with a rubber stick but being put in the pit. They would put you in a hole in the ground and put a lid over you and leave you there to the beetles, worms everything. They'd give you some food and water just to keep you alive cos they didn't want to lose too many. They'd do that to people who tried to escape and had been recaptured. Jim Clarkson, he tried to escape and was recaptured and tortured. He was never the same after that; he was a changed man. He's dead now.

They also started brainwashing us. In the summertime we were able to take our clothes off and boil them and start to get rid of all the body louse, it was such a terrible thing and could cause typhoid. We had some new clothes as well, it was unbelievable as we were able get rid of all those old clothes, finally get rid of the body louse. Every now and then we would get news of the peace talks. They would tell us that they were stalling and we'd get depressed again. Then they'd be on again and some progress was being made and we'd feel more cheerful. Then it was bad again and we'd be depressed again. There was only one item holding up the peace talks and, believe it or not, it was the prisoner of war question. Why should that be a problem, we thought, why not just release them all? But it was a problem. There was a serious problem at the end of the war. I believe that when the Russians were advancing it became more complicated. There were different nationalities. The Chinese wanted all their captured soldiers handing back whereas the Americans only wanted to hand back those who wanted to be handed back. Plenty didn't. There were thousands of Chiang Kai-shek[20] supporters and the Americans were not going to hand them over to the Chinese. Most of them willingly wanted to join up with Chiang Kai-shek and they weren't going to hand them over to Communist China. And it was the same with the Russians because they had Poles fighting for

---

20   Chiang Kai-shek (1887–1975). Ruthless Chinese nationalist leader who was ousted
      by Mao Tse Tung and the Chinese Communist Party in 1949. He fled to Taiwan
      where he continued to oppose Mao's communist rule in China.

them as well. So it all became very complicated. We handed people, like the Poles, to the Russians and they were sent to camps. It wasn't good.

When the peace talks started, everything improved. We got a lot of brainwashing. But we did other things as well. We had to gather up wood for the winter every other day. We'd march up to the hills to gather the wood. We had no officers, no sergeants in our camp. We put a play on once, near the end, it was very amateurish. We had other social activities, some used to catch these big dragonflies, some would be writing letters home; they'd hand them in but only so many went. We played cards and we had chess boards and eventually we got barbers. I had all my hair shaved off to help get rid of the louse. We had one fellow who said he had nits and he said that the body louse got rid of his nits.

They brought in well-educated English-speaking Chinese who could speak decent English; many of them were university educated. Their knowledge was impressive and they even had an astonishing knowledge of Manchester. They started to say this – they weren't like the guards, they would come and chat amongst you. They would say we want to educate you before you get released and once the peace talks have been successful you'll be sent home. They told the Americans that they were already brainwashed. We had French soldiers in the camp as well and they told them that the French had got rid of their royalty and that they admired them for that. We admire the ordinary down-to-earth American people because they fought against the yolk of British imperialism in a war of Independence. But, they said that American business – financiers and industrialists – had grown rich and fat off the poor and that their wealth should have been shared with the poor. And they said that Britain was the same. But they said, 'We want to tell you the history of the people of the world. We want to tell you from the very beginning if you'll only listen,' and they told us about history from the Ice Age.

I listened intently to the education. He was telling us about how industry began and he was quoting Karl Marx and he said, 'Don't read Karl Marx because it's too complicated,' but he told us all about it and what it meant. He said that Marx had a friend called Friedrich Engels who was another founder of the Communist movement and that he had lived in one of the big industrial cities in England called Manchester. And

I thought, 'What's he talking about, Manchester that where I come from?' And he told us how Engels had studied the poor working conditions of the people and he wrote about it. And when he talked about the press he mentioned the *Manchester Guardian*. I'd never heard of it as we only used to get the local paper, and how Manchester had slum conditions and some of the worst slums imaginable. They told us how we should share the wealth that we had created. Some thought about becoming communists and about eight or nine Americans stayed behind after the war and, I think, one of the British became a communist as well. I didn't, although some of it I liked. I wanted to get home as quickly as possible.

7. WELCOME HOME!

'Half a crown, a cheese sandwich and a train ticket.'

INTRODUCTION

ONE OF THE greatest tragedies of the Korean War is that nobody at home seemed to care about the war, or that British servicemen were out there fighting. Close family cared, of course, but friends, employers, working colleagues, seemed barely to have been touched by the war. And when they returned nobody asked much about what they had been doing, what it was like or how they had been treated. Perhaps it was the same after the Second World War, and certainly it was true after the First World War. There were many frightening memories and many soldiers themselves had no wish to talk about the war. Even today, in compiling this book, I came across those who simply did not want to talk about it. Possibly they have never spoken about it, even to their closest family members, but instead have preferred to block it off, put it aside, get on with life. Some memories are too painful to recall.

In 1950, Britain was still in a post-war situation. The Second World War was only five years gone when the Korean conflict began. Soldiers returning from a war were hardly unique. Their fathers, uncles, brothers had fought for an even longer period in the Second World War in difficult conditions and with higher fatalities. They may have come home to a hero's welcome, but they didn't dwell on it or recount it in any detail.

Many veterans were surprised at the lack of coverage in the media and papers back home. Some have been to local libraries and scoured the newspapers for reports from Korea only to find that there was little or no news coming from there. As a result they have wondered why. Was it a conspiracy to keep the appalling events out of the public eye, a government cover-up of sorts, or what? Certainly the government would have done all it could to hide bad news, particularly of high fatalities and particularly where there were large numbers of fatalities among young national servicemen. The reason, however, is probably a lot simpler. Coverage in the media was certainly limited. Television was still in its infancy and did not really 'take off' until the Coronation in 1953, and by then a ceasefire in Korea was about to come into operation. Plus there was only one channel. There was the occasional Pathé news coverage at the cinema, but only if there was something to show. By 1951, the war had ground to a stalemate and although there was constant bombardment of enemy positions there was little to show in the way of 'pictures' that could in any way be described as interesting or news. Genuine news from Korea was limited. It was the same with the newspapers. The cost of sending journalists to Korea was expensive and, given the limited amount of 'action', made it even less worthwhile. News is about events and if events are not happening then there will be no coverage. Hence, there were fewer reports in the papers after 1951. Korea was some distance away and bringing pictures back home or even news reports was not that simple. Stories and pictures would often arrive days after the event had taken place, so it needed to be an important event for it to ever make the front pages or indeed any page of a newspaper.

What is also surprising is that few of the soldiers on national service seemed to be counting down the days when they would be sent home and demobbed. Perhaps in the heat of battle such considerations were irrelevant. Nonetheless, for more than one soldier, news that they were going home came as a surprise, especially as it was immediate.

The voyage home was far different from their outgoing trip. It was more relaxed with less drilling and presented an opportunity to acclimatise to the normality of nights and days without the constant barrage of guns. At least one interviewee here recognised that this was an important period of recuperation from all that had gone before, allowing him to adjust.

And when they rolled into port, usually Liverpool or Southampton, there was no fanfare. At most there might be a handful of relatives, if they lived nearby, hopeful that a son, husband, brother might be on this particular ship. Often the family had no inkling that a son was due home and certainly little idea which ship or when and where it might dock. Many had left to the sound of American bands playing a farewell. But there were no bands, no streamers, no government ministers, no high-ranking officers to welcome them back to Britain or to say a 'thank you' for all their painful endeavours. There was simply nothing. A troopship slipping quietly into port on the tide, soldiers disembarking down the gangplank with their bags on their shoulders, perhaps to be greeted by a relative. For most of the soldiers there wasn't even a relative. Some had expected to take a train straight home but instead when they looked at their orders they were told to take a train to Woolwich, Formby, Colchester or some other military camp where they would be officially demobbed after a short period of time. And even at that camp there was little sympathy. Arrangements were often haphazard and in more than one instance the arrival of soldiers took the military by surprise. Some were allowed to take a train home for a short period of leave almost immediately; others had to wait a few more weeks for their leave and often for little or no apparent reason. Not even the army seemed very grateful. Again, there were no thanks, parades or letters of appreciation. When, and if, they did receive medals they came by post in a small cardboard container.

When they did eventually get home, it was only their families who seemed to be genuinely pleased or understanding of the pain they had been through. Friends were often indifferent, former work colleagues even more so. Nobody wanted to talk to them about the war, about what they had seen, what it was like. Perhaps some had grown indifferent. After all, many soldiers had returned from war only a few years earlier, in 1945 and 1946, and after a brief interlude had got on with their lives.

Other conscripts had served around the world, returning home to the same lack of fanfare and interest. The attitude seemed to be, why should the soldiers of Korea expect anything different? Perhaps people had wanted to put war behind them and not think too much about conflict. If so, that was understandable.

Post-traumatic stress had never been heard of, or at least it had never been recognised. And yet it is quite clear from these interviews that some of the returning soldiers were to suffer from traumas for a number of years. Sadly, there was little or no support from the army and the ex-national servicemen were left to get on with it, sometimes unable to recognise that their symptoms might have something to do with the experiences they had suffered in Korea. Death, fear, the appalling cold and even the constant noise of gunfire.

Many had left a grey Britain still deep in recovery from the Second World War with rationing, bombed sites, rubble and an economy still on its knees. But by the time they returned, Britain was beginning to emerge from the gloom. By 1953 there was a new monarch and a new government and the shop windows were beginning to fill with the new white consumer goods that were flooding in from America. Washing machines, electric irons and even televisions were now part of the new consumer culture that was sweeping through Britain. Many of the soldiers and servicemen were returning home to a very different country.

Some of the servicemen who went to Korea genuinely enjoyed the experience. They found a camaraderie which never existed in Civvy Street and one or two even thought of signing up as regulars. But once they were home and back in the groove of everyday life, the moment had passed. Most of the soldiers were just glad to be back home and able to get on with their lives. They soon found work; the economy was booming and there were plenty of jobs to be had. Some employers generously welcomed them back to their old jobs. In more recent years many of them have become involved in the Korean Veterans Association and have been back to South Korea visiting the graves. They all found it a unique experience to see Korea again and to pay homage at the cemetery to all those who lost their lives. It also came as a revelation after all the devastation that they left behind to see South Korea as a major industrial nation.

More soldiers died in Korea than in any conflict since the Second World War and more ordinary servicemen served their country. And yet, sixty years on, there has still been little gratitude shown to the soldiers. Today, the Korean War is, as so many of the interviewees in this book called it, 'the forgotten war'. While the Falklands, Afghanistan and other recent conflicts are remembered, Korea remains largely forgotten. Many of those who have returned to Korea have remarked on how grateful the Korean people are for their role in the war. 'They all wanted to shake our hands and thank us,' says one veteran, adding that, 'To see Korea as it is now, seemed to make our hardship worthwhile.'

Jim Houghton

We were only given £1 going out but I did have more coming back. I hadn't been paid while I was out there so I was due some money. I asked for £40 and I got it. When I got to Pusan I was in rags. I had lost my kitbag as well – I don't know where that went – so I got a new British uniform, new boots, socks and, everything and they gave us £7 for the boat coming home and to buy presents or whatever. Well, I had this £40 as well, though I didn't tell them that. I came home with a watch for my mother, a watch for myself, and bought a few presents and spent most of this money. I got home and two nights before we docked at Southampton we were playing bingo and I won 15 shillings and that's all I had when I left the ship. I'd spent it all. They then gave us a fiver when we docked to get back home. They said they couldn't give us all the money they owed us but they'd send it on. Anyhow, a short time later I got a cheque for £130 and that was a lot of money in 1952. I did quite well out of it, I suppose.

Jim Grundy

When I got back home I got no help whatsoever from the army. Everything I do now at the cemetery is voluntary. I collect photographs of the soldiers and we have a hall of remembrance there and I go two or three times a year and make sure all the photographs are the same size and in order. I don't feel bitter in any way, like I've said before, every soldier we found, whether he be North Korean, South Korean, Chinese, Australian or whatever, they are somebody's son and we treated their bodies just the same as we treated ours. I've never had any bitterness. The North Koreans were very callous, very callous with the bodies. They'd just dig a hole and throw them in.

Jim Houghton

I stayed until the beginning of May 1952 and then they sent me home because it was a four-week trip on the ship in those days. And I got back here in June 1952 and was demobbed in the July. They owed me that much time and money that I was back in work still getting paid by the army. I had all this leave due but had no time to take it so they had to pay me thirty days pay on top of my ordinary money.

Jim Lucock

I got off the boat, the *Lancashire*, at the pierhead in Liverpool. There was about twenty of us and I was the corporal in charge. I was walking through the customs and this fella said, 'Empty your bags.' I said, 'Everyone else has gone through and I'm saying to you that you *ask* me, you don't tell me.' He looked at me like, and where have you been doing your national service. I hadn't washed anything for six weeks, it was all manky and all I had was an extra 200 cigs. I said I've been out there in the Far East in Korea. Anyhow, his boss came along, told him to pack all my things away and let me through.

All the lads were giving us some stick, yelling and so on and then they all started singing the 'King's are coming up the hill boys.' They sing it at Liverpool on the Kop now though with different words. It used to be the Duke of Wellington's song but the King's then adopted it.

After that we all went to the barracks at Formby and then after a couple of hours they told us to go on embarkation leave. We got ration books given and some money and eventually they told us we had to do our TA. I was put in the Liverpool Scottish Regiment.

I always thought that the war had been a terrible waste of time, a terrible place to have been but having been back to South Korea, I said to Margaret, my wife, that I now felt different about it all. I've seen a country with children well fed, people well educated, well dressed and they were most humble to me, always wanting to shake your hand. They were so generous and really nice. I've seen films of North Korea since and it's pretty grim. If that's made them people in South Korea happy then I accept that my time there was worthwhile.

Bill Hurst

Nobody ever asked me about Korea from coming home to being demobbed. I went to a dance in town one night and got into a fight. I had my uniform on. These two lads were saying, 'Why've you got this uniform on.' I said, 'I've just come out of the army. I haven't got anything else to wear yet.' This girl had invited me to this dance and of course I had just gone in my uniform. These cocky lads are saying, 'What's the ribbons for?' I said, 'Fighting.' 'What do ya mean fightin'?' 'Piss off, go away.'

I said, 'I was in Korea.' 'What? What's Korea, where's that?'

They'd never heard of it. Nobody had. So they had a go at me.

I can't say as I felt bitter about it all but some did. I don't know why. I think some were bitter just because they had been away from home. But I enjoyed it. We came from Collyhurst and lived in a two–up two–down, gaslights, cold water. When I went to Ashton barracks there was electric lights, hot water, a shower, it was luxury. I enjoyed army life. I wish I had stopped in. But my brother had been called up and he was off to Hong Kong. We passed each other in the Med. My parents said come home. But I didn't want to. I was going to sign on but I told the army I'd go home first and then sign on later. But it never happened. I got home and never went back. I wish I had.

Jim Grundy

When I got home nobody wanted to know, nobody wanted to talk about it. I never talked to my family about it or to anyone. You'd go to work and they'd say, 'Where've you been?' and you'd say, 'I've been to Korea,' and they'd say, 'Oh aye,' and they never ask you how things were or anything like that. But because of what you had done, you did get a job, they'd take pity on you and give you a job. I was very lucky I did get work when I came out of the forces.

When I joined the Vets I would come across modern day senior officers and they would say, 'Oh that police action in Korea, I've heard about that.' They didn't know what had happened. Now I'm lecturing at schools and the kids are very interested in what went on. It's wonderful to be able to speak about it. I tell the students everything, I don't hold back. They don't know how many civilian died, over a million and a quarter. The children don't believe it. More civilians died than soldiers.

There are still 7,000 Americans missing, don't know where they got to, there's no Americans buried in Korea, they took them all back home. They lost 34,000 in all. We lost 1,100. All British casualties were accounted for. There's only one lad left from my team. He took it badly after the war, he won't talk about the war. I can talk about it but there's others who won't talk about it.

I stayed in the army for six and a half years and left in 1956. I was discharged on the boat coming home. I should have had a week's disembarkation leave but didn't get it. I went to live in Leicester for a few months, then came back to Manchester, met my wife, married and stayed here.

Geoff Holland

When I got back home there was no sympathy. They say it was called the forgotten war, and they didn't think of you. When we sailed out of Pusan coming home, there was a big American band sending us on our way and they were playing, 'So long, its been good to know you!' That was great. But when we sailed into Southampton there was nothing. Nobody.

A few lads whose mothers and fathers lived close by turned up to see them in but apart from that, nothing.

We then had to go back to Woolwich. We got off the ship and they put us on the train. I had two kitbags, one had stuff that I had acquired. A bloke come round and he said, 'Is that your own?' and I said, 'Yes.' He said, 'When you get to Woolwich they'll take it off you.' He says, 'Take my word, take your kitbag and put it in the left luggage office.' There were three of us and we all did the same. When we got to Woolwich, before you got into the barracks, they stood you on the square and you had to empty all your kitbags. It was like customs. I was in charge of this group. I was the NCO in charge and this customs-like lad came and asked what we had and he said, 'You can't have much from where you've been.' But some had pearls, and I had about 1,000 cigarettes. After we got to Woolwich and they'd taken all our kit they said, 'You're going on leave tomorrow.' Great. I went for my leave pass and he said, 'You're an NCO, you'll have to stay behind, all NCOs have to do a weekend guard at Woolwich.' Anyhow, all we NCOs marched in to see the RSM and we said we want to hand our tapes in. He laughed, 'Get out!' He wouldn't accept it so we had to stand guard over absolutely nothing. I had to guard a square in the middle of Woolwich, nothing happening. The treatment we got was appalling. I got my fortnight's leave after that. Then I had to go back to get my formal discharge.

I had family back in Manchester – mother, father, two brothers and a sister. They were glad to see me back. My father had been in the army during the war. My mates had booked me a holiday to the Isle of Man. I remember getting a letter off them asking me if I wanted to go. So it was only a few weeks after we got back and we went to the Isle of Man. None of them had fought in Korea.

I don't recall ever having nightmares or anything like that. I was in Korea eight months. But I'm glad I did it. I'm proud to have done it. In fact I have a letter from the president of South Korea. Today, the Koreans are appreciative but I don't think the British people are. It's a sad story, you tell the Americans and they don't realise we served in Korea. Typical Yanks.

Brian Daly

The war may not have seemed worth it in terms of the loss of life but the Koreans were liberated. I went back in 2008 to Korea on a revisit organised by the Korean Vets. We got a discount, so about four of us went from our branch. We stayed there and went back to all these places as a remembrance. We stayed in Seoul and travelled from there. It was quite an experience after all those years.

Eric Peters

I didn't leave until August, September 1952, though I thought I should have left earlier. I came home on the *Empire Halladale* straight to Liverpool. But nobody was there to meet me as I had to go straight up to Stirling. I was up there for a month and then got leave and came down to see the parents, first time in three and a half years. Things had changed, the town had changed, people had changed. The elder brother was in the merchant navy and he was home and he had cash and he'd treat me, give me some money, buy the drinks. A few mates had got married while I was away. A lot of people, of course, didn't even know where Korea was. When I went there nobody had a clue where it was, even the officers. The lads here never wanted to talk about what had happened, they never even mentioned it. They had their own worries. I enjoyed my army service apart from that sergeant major. I left the army in November 1952 after I came back from Stirling. I went to work for the Atomic Energy Authority at Capenhurst. I became a welder, it was a new thing then. I really took to it and worked there until the plant had been built. The Koreans really appreciated what we did for them but not here, it's the forgotten war.

George Stirland

When I got home people didn't know about anything about Korea or the war, nobody knew. When we went to the Far East, I'd heard of Hong

Kong but not Korea. We never really saw Korea, we never landed there. I came home to Southampton on another trooper. We sailors were the last off, we had a hammock, big kitbag and a case. I'll never forget, we got to London in the rush hour. You can imagine going down the underground not really knowing where we were going, trying to get on the tube to get to Euston to get the train home.

People didn't want to know what we'd been doing. When I left in the August, my girlfriend was expecting so we got married, and my eldest son was born in the December. I was 21. I came home and he was two years old and he had never seen me. It was very difficult. He didn't know who this bloke was in uniform. We were living with her mother; we had the front room in her house. I had twelve weeks' leave, I didn't know what I was going to do. I went back, down to Devonport and I was upgraded and went to Portsmouth to do my training. I liked it but didn't like the theory and I failed that so I went back and picked another ship up. I was glad cos I was told that if I had passed I would have been out in the Far East for another couple of years. If you were in the UK you got Easter, Christmas, summer leave but if you were anywhere else you didn't. I finally left the navy in January 1958. My wife was ill and it was recommended I come out, otherwise I would have stayed in.

Ivan Williams

I left Korea because my two years' national service was up and I had to be back demobbed by the time my two years was up. I didn't even know I was going home until the morning I left. I reported into the command centre and the officer said, 'You're going home,' and I said, 'What do you mean?' He said, 'I hope you're not arguing, get on that truck.' I didn't even have much time to say goodbye to the lads. We were taken by truck to our HQ and then to Seoul on a train with wooden seats, and then to Pusan where the boat was already in. The next one must have been too late, there was a boat about every four weeks. It was the same boat as I went out on, the *Empire Fowey*. It was one of the better troopships and as we had been to Korea we were excused all duties on the boat. It was a good thing because we were all very jumpy and it gave us four weeks to cool off, if you like. I feel very sorry for the troops in Afghanistan who get on a plane for ten hours and the next day they're on the streets. It must be difficult for them.

The boat brought us back to Southampton and then we went to Woolwich to be processed. I then went to a camp at High Leigh in Cheshire, which is now a housing estate, to be demobbed. It was not a good place to be demobbed as it is a training camp. The tradition was that when a new intake arrived the previous intake attacked them and you can imagine we were in no mood to be amused. We travelled with rifles and then, as the first of these approached, my mate hit him over the head with his rifle. That stopped them in their tracks and then they saw we were wearing military medal ribbons so they said we'd better not and they ran. Never heard no more! We hadn't had any leave and we still had three weeks to do. I'd inherited a stripe while I was out in Korea. I was promoted and it came in handy on the boat. One of the lads, a scouser, said, 'I'm over the wall if we don't get any leave,' so I was appointed to go see one of the officers. I had to ask permission off the sergeant major and he didn't like that at all. Nobody asked to see officers. But I saw the officer and he said, 'I'll check the records, come and see me in the morning.' By morning he'd given everybody two weeks' leave which suited us. So when we went back we only had a few days to do.

I was then put into the TA for three and a half years so I kept my kit. You had to do three annual camps and so many weekends, so you came home with all your kit, though no firearms, of course. I was posted to the Bolton artillery because it was a survey regiment.

If you said to people that you had been to Korea, they'd say, 'Where?' It really was a forgotten war. People didn't know so many were involved, and I don't think wanted to know. There was very little press coverage apparently in this country. So the reaction to us was nil. I don't think they were appreciative; in fact I'm sure they weren't. They didn't buy me a pint in the pub or anything like that. The people at home were glad to see me and I was glad to be back and I met Sylvia and met all her friends. We had about a week at Woolwich and we used to go out every night. But I don't think people cared. It's a terrible thing to say. If it's not in the press, people don't know.

When I got home, I got a job in a construction company mainly because of my experience as a surveyor. I spent most of my life in the construction business.

Terry Moore

Some call it a stalemate; I don't know if it was quite a case of fighting each other to a halt. I think both sides realised it was useless, that it was so futile. So it stopped. They just decided it was useless, seen the killing. Had they been able to sweep down into Seoul again the Chinese might have been encouraged but they couldn't do it this time, so decided to call a halt and talk. The war just died.

For us, the government said no soldier could spend two winters there so the Royal Ulster Rifles, who had been first in, were first out. The regulars went into Hong Kong and a handful of us reservists stayed on the boat and came home. That was in early 1952.

I don't think people were interested when I got home. My parents were at the quayside to greet the ship when it came into Liverpool. When I got to the custom shed my mother was there with my sister and she rushed into the shed, saying, 'I know you haven't eaten much,' and thrust some sandwiches into my hand. Nobody I knew from work, or about, had been out there fighting.

Today when I think about it, and although I am glad I survived it, I'm grateful for having met so many nice people. I don't feel an evil or bitterness. People are just different, not better or worse. I was glad when it stopped but I don't know if it was worthwhile. I only think about it occasionally. But it is the forgotten war. You try and find a mention about it. You have the Falklands, which they call the great post-war conflict, but it's not. I just know that I met a lot of nice people, some died, but that's war for you.

Jim Daly

I left the Imjin in 1954 and went back to Pusan to the transit camp in September 1954. Then on the 17 September 1954, we left there to go to Pusan docks where we boarded the *Empire Fowey*. We sailed from Pusan back to Britain, stopping in Kowloon, Singapore, Colombo, Aden, Port Said and then onto Southampton. Then it was back to Woking, then some leave and then back to Woking, and I was finally demobbed on 4 November 1954. And then it was back to Salford.

Brian Hough

When we got back there was no support. No one was interested. I got good support from my dad. I hit the bottle for a while after I was demobbed. I hated my job as a sheet metal worker, I hated it. I had a row with the boss and told him to stick it. I walked out and for a while I was not a very nice person. I did not accept that at the time. My dad – I've never known him go to a public house on his own – but I was coming home every night loaded. My mother was worried. So I suppose it did affect me.

The reception we got? Well, here's a story. We left Korea and went back to Hong Kong for demob and we left the battalion in the New Territories and we left Hong Kong in December 1953 and arrived in Southampton in the early New Year. Korean war heroes – all the ribbons up. The ship docked on the Friday and let those living south of London off. The rest of us going north had to stop until the following day. We went up to an officer's table with all the gear, packs on our back, rifles, and he gave us half a crown, a cheese sandwich and a rail ticket for Manchester. And that was it. They took us off the ship and into some huge sheds at Southampton and the customs man came along. We were all lined up and he asked us if we had anything to declare. We said no. They put us on the train and then it was up to us. We changed trains in London. When we got there we had a couple of hours to spare. Most of us went into a pub and the half crown went there, we'd eaten the cheese sandwich and we arrived in Manchester at about five o'clock on the Saturday afternoon. My dad had been checking and the ship wasn't supposed to arrive until the Monday morning. They didn't expect me. My mum was sitting in the house sewing some bunting. I think if I'd arrived later and seen the bunting across the street I would have turned and run. Anyhow, that's how we were greeted – half a crown, a cheese sandwich and a train ticket.

Steve Hale

My uncle was changed when he came back. Whatever he'd seen or been involved with, he was very quiet about it. He'd gone very quiet and introspective and had started smoking. Nan was very strict and against smoking and she wouldn't allow it in the house. He talked about it later on but it was a lot later on. Nobody pressurised him to talk about it because they knew he didn't want to and he didn't for quite a while. We got letters off him but they never came on a regular basis because they'd be going all over the place and they took a long time to get here. And they were always on those blue airmail letters that you had to carefully open and then fold out. I used to run downstairs when I heard the postman to see if there was anything from him. And if it was a blue airmail letter then we knew it was from him. Other than that we just got bills like everybody else.

When it was all over we'd had a letter off him to say that his unit was being taken out of the front line and that he was going over to Japan with a few mates out of his unit, because he had some R & R. He said he'd be gone for a couple of weeks and when he was back he'd write and tell us which ship he'd be on. So he went over to Japan and visited Tokyo and I know he visited Hiroshima because he did talk about that when he came back and what he'd seen. He was very keen to go and see that and what this bomb had done to a complete city. He did however talk about Hiroshima when he gone back even though he didn't talk about the war in Korea. He said he couldn't believe the total annihilation of a city by one explosion. He'd taken some photos as well, tiny little black and white pictures and he was trying to explain about that monument, I think it's a church that was left standing. I think it's still there. Anyhow, whether he forgot or whether it got lost we didn't get the next letter to tell us which ship he was coming home on. We found out that the first ship was coming into Liverpool with the King's Regiment soldiers on board, so we got up early one morning about five-ish to get a tram to the pierhead with my mum and my nan. And we waited hours and hours, literally, until the last soldier had come off the ship, then my nan just burst into tears because he obviously wasn't on it. She then went to see somebody immediately after the last soldier had come down the gangplank. And she asked this person if her son was on the ship and he said no, but he might be on the next one and there will be three or four coming in over the next few weeks. So we didn't go down again even though my nan kept tabs on when the ships were coming in. But then there was a knock on the door one night, it was April, either a Thursday or Friday, and I answered the door and there was Peter standing there in his uniform with his kitbag slung over his shoulder. I stood mesmerised for a minute. I of course recognised him but it was just odd that he should arrive home like this with just a knock on the door. My mum was shouting from the kitchen, 'Who is it, who is it?' And I said, 'You're not going to believe this.' She said, 'Don't tell me,' and I said, 'Yes, it's Uncle Peter'. And she just flew out of the kitchen, through the living room and into the hall. My nan was upstairs and she near broke her neck coming down the stairs. The next thing, my dad came home from work because he worked quite long shifts, from seven in the morning to seven at night. He had a bike and we heard him coming in the back with the bike and Mum said, 'Hey, there's someone here for you and it's a big surprise.' And of course it was Peter. Next thing, my dad hadn't had his tea, he jumps back on the bike, goes off and ten minutes later comes back with a crate of brown ale on the back of his bike. Then we knocked on the neighbour's doors and they were invited in and within the hour there was another big party going on to celebrate Peter coming home. The community was like that then. Maybe lives were duller at the time and for someone to have survived that and come home gave them a good excuse to have a good time. My nan was on the piano banging away and everyone was singing. I'd been sent to bed then to try and sleep but what with the excitement of Peter coming home and all this noise going on downstairs I didn't get to sleep for ages.

Next morning when we got up he was delving into his army kitbag bringing all this army washing to give to my mum to do. When he got to the bottom of it he pulled out this brown paper bag and in the bag were two things. A satin bomber jacket with a tiger on the back that he bought for me in Tokyo or in Japan somewhere and a little tin fire engine. Of course, I was straight out in the street with my jacket on and with my fire engine. I'd be about 7 or 8 then. I was everybody's best mate in the street for a while cos of this jacket with the tiger on the back. Of course, I wanted to go to school in it but I wasn't allowed because it would have been ripped off my back by the older guys.

Brian Hough

I got my medal through the post. When we left Korea, they gave us the ribbons to wear but we didn't get the medals. I got home and two, three months later the postman arrived with a couple of boxes, there's your medals. It was a different time. You'd done your bit, now come home, get back to work. My dad spent six years in the army in the Second World War. Four years he was abroad and he was wounded in the Battle of Caen in July 1944 and had a piece of shrapnel still in him. He was demobbed in early 1946 and went to work the following Monday. And that's after six years. You just went back to work. Why should I have complained.

Jim Houghton

I was treated OK when I got home. They asked if we wanted to sign on as regulars. In Korea, two or three did sign on, but once you were back, it was a different matter. You had to sign on for five years then. I'd had enough. The army offered us nothing. All I got was that I had to report to Liverpool, down London Road, just before Lime Street, there was a barracks and I had to do three years in the Territorials. I was still there when Suez started. But I didn't get called up. They sent me a letter wanting to know where did I work, etc. I was married then, I'd bought a house, the wife was pregnant and I had a regular job. Anyrate, three or four days later I got another letter saying to report to the 1st Highland Division in Perth in Scotland. Anyhow, the whole Suez thing blew over quickly so I never went out to Suez

If I hadn't have got a regular job I might have signed on and stayed in. There were good lads in the army, we all got on together. I wasn't bothered about the politics, you just got on with it. The only thing was that there was no money in it. I was earning far more driving than I would have done in the army.

Ken Hawthorne

I was due to come home. When I got out of the hospital and back to camp we had taken over the Hook from the Americans and my friends and lads were down on the Hook. What we did when lads were due to come home, a few weeks before they were due to come home, they never gave them any dangerous work to do, it's not fair they thought for you to cop it in the last few weeks. So I took the liberty of not going with them to the Hook. But then an officer came walking round camp one day and saw me doing nothing. He said, 'What are you doing here?' and I told him. He seemed a nice man he said, 'Well you'll be up there with your fiends on the Hook tomorrow.' I said, 'Well even if I hadn't been wounded I wouldn't be expected to go,' and he said, 'Well, I expect you to go.' I'd never seen him before, I didn't know who he was. I got up next morning, went to see the MO and he had a look at my wound, and he said, 'Stupid devil, I'll give you a sick note.' He just put on it, 'No bending, can you find him a nice light job to do in camp because he's been wounded.' Anyhow, the other guy never came back and I never saw him again.

Brian Hough

I was hospitalised in Japan and I was recovering – November 1952 – and they asked if anyone wanted to go on a coach tour to Hiroshima. It was seven years after the bomb had been dropped and they were starting to rebuild the place. CND[21] wasn't around at that time. What I saw there made more of an impression on me than some of the things I witnessed in Korea. They took us around a UN hospital and he said, 'We're not taking you to see some of the worst cases, but we'll show you some of the people recovering. And this is seven years after.

The bus we were on had about twenty-five of us. We got off the bus and we'd been to several places. And we were on a bridge. We had a Japanese guide and he said that the bomb dropped at 8.15 a.m. on 6 August, people going to work, children going to school, and he said, 'Crossing the bridge at this time was a man and a child.' I wondered how he could possibly know that. He said, 'Just turn around,' and there, burnt into the side of the bridge was a man and a child holding hands. That hurt me, I couldn't imagine it. He told us how people had gone in search of their families and could not recognise them. People also had jumped into the river to get away. They were burning from the heat of the bomb blast. That moved my politics to the left somewhat.

I was aware that the Americans were planning a nuclear attack. I went to Korea after Attlee had lost the election and I was aware that Attlee and President Truman had been trying to pull the reins in on General MacArthur.

People didn't want to know about Korea. Life was grim enough in Britain; there was austerity and rationing, everything was a black and white. If you didn't have anyone there fighting in Korea people didn't want to know. There was no television either. It was a very different world. My daughter has asked me why I didn't object to going into the army but that was the way it was. You could not in those days go out of your door without seeing someone in uniform; that was life, so you didn't object. It was what you had to do.

---

21   CND – Campaign for Nuclear Disarmament began in February 1958.

Ken Hawthorne

I came home in February 1953. We docked at Liverpool and my mum and dad met me. We docked at night and there were only three people on the dock. It was winter and there was mum and dad and somebody else, no band, no fanfare, people didn't know it was going on or didn't want to know. I came off the following morning, got on a train and had to go down south to Chatham where I handed in my uniform and was formally discharged. And that was it apart from having to do TA for three years. Most of my male friends, we were all about the same age, and naturally I found them again. We used to do a lot of ballroom dancing and most were serving their time, we had all gone in the forces at the same time and came out the same time. I was the only one I knew who served in Korea. Nobody wanted to know, it was get back to work, not like it is now with parades and all that. I got a job as a plumber right away. In fact, I was building these houses I'm living in now.

John Smith

Eventually I came home. I had set sail from Liverpool on the *Lancashire* for Hong Kong on 10 August 1949, and came back to Liverpool over three years later on the *Devonshire* and we docked here in Liverpool. It took about six weeks. We stopped at various places. I was in Korea itself for fifteen months. I had been at a lot of places in Korea, I was all over the place. It was good to come back, the family had got a taxi down to the docks. I then had to report to a training depot in Woking after my leave. My family were pleased to see me. Most of my mates were away in the forces doing national service themselves. I met one of my old mates in Hong Kong. There were lots of good things and some good things happened. I met these Australians and they couldn't get their money changed so I helped them and they said you'll hear from us and a while later the phone went and it was the Australians and they said, 'What night can you get off, we want to meet up with you?' So we went down to Kowloon and they said, 'Your night's been arranged, see that motorboat, well it's taking you out to our boat and our skipper is going to entertain you.' So we went out in the boat and they had the mess all arranged. I only realised then that these guys were officers and they entertained us that night, all the food and drink we wanted. So, late on the skipper says, 'I'll bet you're wondering how you're going to get back?' but he says, 'Don't worry, it's all organised.' There was a taxi waiting for us and it was all paid for by the Australians. They were the good times.

We were told that this was a stepping-stone to world domination by communism but I never gave it much thought. But one thing that crossed my mind when it was all over, I thought, good grief when we were in Hong Kong we were the 40th Infantry Division, nine battalions, and when it was all over I thought, what chance did we have, one division, against millions of Chinese? All they had to do was come over in their numbers and we were going to run out of ammunition at some time.

I went to a reunion fifty years later and I've gone to the washroom and this voice says, 'Its big Smudger.' Well it was Georgie Shearer. Fifty years after. I still recognised him after all those years. I saw him every year after that. He was one of the fellas on Hill 282. He was on Hill 282. Imagine how they must have felt. They were asking for air cover and two Mustangs fly over and drop napalm. Friendly fire! Poor George was on that, although he was OK. Lots died though.

I stayed in the army but people weren't grateful. Even now we have stickers, 'Korea, the forgotten war.' I went to a reunion a few years ago and there was a ceremony but no mention of Korea. Ignored, the forgotten war. The 14th Army in Burma, they were the forgotten army as well.

When I came out, I went in the police force. I came out June 1953, just as the war was finishing. But it's not all over, just a ceasefire. I came back and went to barracks in Colchester and was doing various things – I went on the Canvey Island floods helping people, I got promoted with that. They wanted me to stay and offered me another stripe, but I said I was going to join the police force in Liverpool. I'd just met a girl, but he said, 'No problem, we've got married quarters'. I said, 'I don't really want married quarters, they're like a barrack room'. So he said, 'March him out, let him go!'

John Hegarty

Jamaica remained in Korean waters for several more months, ultimately returning to Hong Kong for maintenance. While we were there, it was discovered that the ship required extensive mechanical repairs to her engines and it was decided this could best be completed at a UK dockyard. Some of the ship's company were allocated to other ships before we finally left for the UK, so it was not quite the end of the Korean 'adventure' for them. Fortunately, I remained on board and returned to England with the ship. When we arrived at our home port of Plymouth, the ship had an ecstatic welcome, especially as we were the first major warship to return from the Korean War.

Brian Hough

I am totally opposed to national service. I hear people saying to me that they should bring back national service. Well they shouldn't because we were an army on the cheap. We never got the same pay as regular soldiers. But it's not really about the pay. We got 28 shillings a week, and a regular got 10s 6d extra. That was a lot of money in those days. I sent 10s back to my mum and I only got 18 shillings a week. Apart from that there was no difference between the regulars and national servicemen and there was never any ill feeling between the two. But it was an army on the cheap. I don't think we would have gone into Malaya, Cyprus, Suez and so on if we only had a regular army. We had an army on the cheap, sending men out to all these hotspots in case the cold war might escalate – it was a sort of training ground. Seventy per cent of the men in Korea were national servicemen. That's an awful lot and that's conveniently forgotten. And because of the high number of casualties, they didn't want the public at large to know what was really happening. People just didn't know the extent of casualties among national servicemen. It was kept quiet because it was the national servicemen who were being killed and wounded.

Peter C Le P Jones

My war had been, first in a tropical summer, and then a very severe winter with temperatures of minus 40°F to 50°F. We had slept, eaten, washed, shaved and fought in the open in all these conditions. Tanks and lorries had to keep their engines running twenty-four hours a day, seven days a week or they would freeze solid causing irreparable damage. Hardly believable now, but it was amazing what a human being can put up with when he must. As were many others, I was 21 years old, and some were a lot less. It was wonderful to get back to the warmth of Hong Kong – showers and real beds, which was bliss after sleeping on the ground for all those nine months.

During the campaign I was lucky enough to get seven days leave in Tokyo in the middle of apple blossom time. I did not go to visit Hiroshima as some did, as I had already done this when I was on HMS *Jamaica*.

At the time you thought, 'What the hell am I doing here?' and when you got away with it 'scot-free' you felt it was some experience. I had nightmares for many years after, especially about Hill 282 and other events. It was not all doom and gloom – we had many laughs, great comradeship and on occasions, parties, especially with the New Zealand Maoris making a wicked brew in a bath they had found in a dry paddy field.

The Argylls left Korea at Inchon in April 1951, on board an American troopship, the USS *Montrose*. HMS *Belfast* was there to see us off. The ship, with all the sailors manning the decks, gave us three cheers and their chief engineer, a Scot, stood on a forward 6-inch gun turret in full Scottish regalia playing 'Highland Laddie', 'The Argylls March Past', and 'The Campbells are Coming' on the bagpipes – there were not many dry eyes among those tough Scottish soldiers.

Roy Cox

We left Korea in September 1952 and it was straight home, I think, to Southampton. I remember on the train we were saying, look at all these television aerials, we hadn't seen them before. I got £150 when I got back. They had to put armed guards around the payout desk, it was the biggest payout ever. I still had nine months to do, they sent me off on a month's leave, but after three weeks I got a telegram telling me to come back and report to the School of Infantry for a signal instructors course. I did three months there, then off to Germany where I was training signallers. My time was up then. I would have signed up for longer but it was getting back to the bull of polishing boots, belts and so forth. So, I left. I got a job at the Cowley car works but later became a fireman.

Bill Hurst

When we got back home nobody was bothered, not one bit. I got off the boat in Southampton with twenty-odd lads and we had to find our way on the underground to the station. We got on the train to Manchester and we all got off at Piccadilly station. I think there was twenty-two of us and we all had our kitbags, suitcases and so on. We were all stood there thinking, what are we going to do, we have to go to Ashton barracks? So I got on the phone to Ashton barracks. The sergeant came on the phone. I said, 'Good evening, Kingsman Hurst here.' He said, 'Yeah?' I said, 'There's twenty-two of us here, can you send a truck down for us.' He said, 'What?' I said, 'Send a truck down. We can't all get on a bus. We've got all our kit.' He said, 'Where've you come from?' I said, 'Korea.' He said, 'Korea!' He said, 'Hang on a minute, I'll get the duty officer.' The duty officer came on. I told him the same. He said, 'How many of you are there? I said, 'Twenty-two.' He said, 'Bloody hell.' I said, 'I think we need a three-tonner.' He said, 'I haven't got anything.' So I said, 'Can I make a suggestion, sir? Can we all go home and we'll report Monday morning to the barracks?' 'Good idea that,' he said. 'Be here Monday morning, anytime, doesn't need to be seven o'clock or anything like that.' I put the phone down and turned round to the lads and said, 'You can all go home.' What!!! 'Just make sure you're at Ashton barracks Monday morning.' I said I'd take all their bags, put them in a taxi because I only lived five minutes away in Collyhurst. So they put all the kitbags in the taxi and I went home. I knocked on the door, opened it and started slinging the kitbags up the lobby and all I heard was, 'Who the bleeding hell's that?' It was my dad.

I said, 'It's your son.' My mam said, 'What've you come home for?' Anyhow, they put their arms around me and that. But that was it. Next day I went out but couldn't find any of the lads. So and so had got married, so and so had moved. I'd lost contact with everybody. The girls you went with had all got different fellows!

We went to the barracks on the Monday and they said, 'Hand all your kit in and you can go on leave for seven days, then report here and you'll get demobbed.' After that, I did three years with the TA as a reservist. And that was it. I got no support from the army, but then I never asked for it. I had a couple of weeks off, sorted myself then went to see my old boss and started work again as a coalman.

CONCLUSION

It's now sixty years since the Korean War ground to its inevitable and miserable end. A stalemate had been reached and little or no progress was being made by either side. Instead, they simply manned their trenches and held their positions. It could have gone on much longer in the same way but both sides saw some sense and opted for a ceasefire. No peace treaty has ever been signed and there remains little hope of anything materialising in the near future. Instead, there is an armistice and a fragile peace. Soldiers on either side of the border peer through long-range binoculars into no-man's-land maintaining a watchful eye for any irregularities. And each year the tension is upped by one side or the other, usually the North Koreans, in order to gain some compromise or concession. Nobody really believes that the North Koreans will ever invade but nothing can be left to chance. The consequences of such an invasion would be too catastrophic to imagine.

Many of the soldiers interviewed in this book have returned to South Korea since they served there, some of them on a regular basis, to pay homage to their fallen comrades in the cemetery at Busan. Jim Grundy, whose task during the war was to retrieve the bodies and prepare them for proper burial, now returns to the cemetery three times a year to work voluntarily and to help build up a collection of photographs of all those who died.

But with each passing year there are less of them returning. It's now estimated that fewer than 3,000 of those who served in the conflict are still alive and all of those are now in their eighties. Those who have returned to Korea speak of the country's inherent beauty and the enormous economic progress that has been made. It's barely believable, they say, that sixty years ago there was such a terrifying conflict that left the nation destroyed, with its landscape battered and its people demoralised. But since then, the economy of South Korea has boomed. Seoul has hosted the Olympic Games and the football World Cup and there is political stability. Many of those returning talk of being greeted by South Koreans with open arms, a nation grateful for what they did for them. If there is one thing that has made their time in Korea worthwhile, they say, it is the enthusiasm and gratitude that the Korean people have shown them. Indeed, most of the soldiers feel that the Koreans have shown them a great deal more gratitude than the British.

Across the border, however, North Korea remains a closed nation. Visitor access is almost impossible; the economy is in a perpetual state of crisis, with dictatorship, political prisoners, censorship, oppression and overwhelming poverty. People exist in misery. North Korea is more like George Orwell's *1984* than any nation on earth. North Korea has little or nothing to endear it to the rest of the world. Even Russia and China have grown weary of its belligerence and threat to stability in the area.

There remains a view among the veterans, rightly or wrongly, that they have been ignored. The Second World War, the Falklands and so many other conflicts have all been remembered and commemorated, but the Korean conflict remains largely forgotten. Nobody talks about it, nothing appears in the newspapers or on television. Tell people you are doing a book about British soldiers in the Korean War and they will look askance, not realising that Britain was so involved, or that over a thousand British troops died. It's difficult to know why it has become so forgotten. Perhaps because it was so far away, perhaps because most of those serving were conscripts rather than regular soldiers, perhaps because it came so soon after the Second World War, or possibly because nobody knows the full extent of the hardship so many soldiers suffered.

Even during the time of the conflict there was little recognition or appreciation of what was happening on the other side of the world.

Coming so soon after the end of the Second World War, there was a natural reluctance to talk of war or conflict. People were tired of it and simply wanted to forget. Back in Britain, life was difficult enough as it was without being constantly reminded of it. There was rationing, rebuilding and austerity, but life had to go on and a war thousands of miles away did not affect the vast majority of people and was not the number one item on their agenda. Out of sight, out of mind, seemed to be the general attitude. So, the British people got on with rebuilding their own lives and dwelt little on events on the other side of the world.

The conditions in Korea were about as bad as is possible. The cold winters, particularly the first winter of the conflict in 1950/51, saw freezing temperatures that tested every soldier. Although the winter of 1946/47 in Britain had been appalling, it was nothing compared to the cold experienced in Korea. In that first year provisions and equipment were not of the highest quality. The war was only months old and no one had properly geared up for what was to come. Clothing in particular was poor: the attitude was that if it was cold, just put on another pullover and some long johns. There were no proper winter clothes. The troops even had to acquire parkas from the American army, who were far better equipped for the conditions. Food was also of poor quality, with most of the British troops relying on American or Canadian rations.

The first year of the war was dreadful in many ways, not just because of the horrific cold of that winter, but due to the fighting itself. The Glorious Glosters were all but wiped out at the Battle of the Imjin River, whilst many who did survive were taken prisoner and had to suffer months or years in Chinese prisoner-of-war camps. For many, the war was simply too much. There were suicides, desertions, breakdowns and long-term trauma. Much of it was neglected or ignored by those in charge.

After a year of fighting the war slipped into a stalemate with neither side making any significant advances. As in the First World War, the soldiers dug into their trenches and did their best to hold their positions, occasionally being forced back only to advance once more a few days later but often ending up in the same position. It was a war of attrition.

Talking to the soldiers today, two things stand out: first, the bravery and the fortitude that they showed in facing up to such challenging conditions.

It should be remembered that 70 per cent of those serving in Korea were national servicemen, young conscripts, straight from the shop floor, factories and offices. Only the long-term regulars had experience of fighting in a war. The second is the bitterness that many, though not all, feel about the way they have subsequently been treated. Any other war, they believe, and they would have been honoured and respected. Instead, they returned from Korea to empty quaysides and have, ever since, been all but ignored.

Some of the soldiers witnessed unimaginable sights – babies being deliberately drowned because mothers could not cope as they fled from Chinese and North Korean soldiers. They watched helplessly as their own troops were napalmed by American aeroplanes on Hill 282; they witnessed comrades killed by enemy action while standing next to them; they saw lines of refugees fleeing from the enemy; they spoke with orphaned children roaming in packs, homeless and hungry; and marched down roads littered with civilian corpses. Bill Fox, who was taken prisoner of war for over two years, fought back tears as he described the conditions in the camp. There were disturbing scenes that he still vividly remembers and more than a few others shed tears as they recounted their tales. Jim Grundy can still smell the dead on his hands, while Brian Hough was so upset that he has campaigned ever since to educate young children about the horrors of war.

Once a year the veterans meet at the UK's Centre of Remembrance at the National Memorial Arboretum in Staffordshire to commemorate the lives of those who served in Korea. Many of them also meet at their regular association get-togethers up and down the country in British Legion centres, village halls and clubs. They're a friendly bunch who like nothing more than to tell you what Korea was like. They will invite you into their homes, ply you with tea and biscuits, and entertain you with stories about the cold, Dear John letters and their lives back in Civvy Street. But when it comes to talking about their fallen comrades, the tears begin to well up and roll down their cheeks. Sadly, one by one, the veteran groups are closing down due to lack of numbers. Each November they will parade to their nearest war memorial, smartly marching behind their colours; but it won't be for much longer. Another ten years and there will be only a handful of Korean veterans left; the men who fought in what they all call 'the forgotten war' should never be forgotten themselves.

INDEX

38th Parallel 11–3, 15, 70, 92, 136, 144, 154, 157
Aden 20, 22, 31, 38, 46, 50, 52, 59, 68, 207
Afghanistan 198, 205
Aldershot 23, 36, 155
Americans 9–12, 15, 54–6, 60, 61, 65, 67, 69–71, 73, 81, 83–5, 87–90, 92–8, 101, 106, 107, 114, 116, 118, 119, 125, 133, 139, 141, 142, 148, 152, 154–6, 166, 169, 177, 179, 184, 186–8, 191–3, 201–2, 211–2
Amethyst, HMS 32
Argylls 11, 26, 33–5, 66, 67, 116, 136, 139–41, 147–9, 155, 216
Armistice 13, 15, 219
Army Catering Corps 36
Astoria 50
Atomic bomb 12, 49
Atomic Energy Authority 203
Attlee, Clement 13, 42, 73, 212
Australia 51, 70, 72, 77, 82, 83, 85, 102, 105, 112, 141, 150, 151, 155, 168, 169, 174, 199, 213, 214
Ball, Derek 22, 182, 183
Barton, Alan 141
Beckerley, Ted 180
Belgians 26, 70
Berlin Wall 11
Birkenhead 39, 40, 132
Birkenhead News 132
Black Swan, HMS 144, 145
Blood, Sgt Major 51
Bowerham barracks 23
Britannia Camp 78
British Legion 222
Buchanan, Captain Neil 67, 148
Buckingham Palace 24
Busan 36, 135, 219
Caen, Battle of 210
Campaign for Nuclear Disarmament (CND) 212
Canadians 51, 64, 65, 77, 83, 99, 112, 113, 138, 139, 151, 159, 221
Canvey Island floods 214
Cape Collinson 38
Ceasefire 11, 76, 83, 87, 107, 118, 145, 176, 188, 195, 214, 219
Ceylon 38

Ceylon, HMS 27, 35
Charles, Prince 154
Chatham 45, 102, 153, 213
Chelsea barracks 24
Chiang Kai-shek 191
China Fleet Club 38, 51
China 9–15, 21, 25, 35, 42, 49–51, 54–7, 61, 65, 69–74, 77–9, 83–7, 90, 92–4, 99–102, 104–109, 111, 116–7, 123–6, 134, 136–8, 141, 143–4, 149, 151, 154, 156–7, 159–61, 163, 165–7, 169–71, 147, 176–9, 181–92, 206, 214, 220–2
Christmas 31, 38, 56, 62, 86, 87, 97, 98, 120, 130, 155, 204
Clarkson, Jim 191
Cockade, HMS 71, 75, 76
Colombo 20, 22, 31, 38, 50, 59, 68
Commonwealth Brigade 13, 72
Coronation 138, 195
Cox, Roy 24, 54, 57, 96, 99, 128, 131, 160, 161, 179, 216
Cyprus 215
Daegu 167, 174
Daly, Brian 37, 80, 203
Day, Doris 103
DDT 80
Dempsey, Paddy 73
Devonport 33, 204
Devonshire, HMS 30, 55, 59, 71, 213
Dines, Major 104, 138
Duke of Wellington's Regiment 27, 56, 83
Dunkirk 157
Düsseldorf 25
Eagle 128, 131
Egypt 26, 27
Empire Fowey 31, 46, 204, 207
Empire Halladale 203
Empire Lancashire 36
Empire Orwell 38
Empire Pride 76
Engels, Friedrich 192, 193
Esan 51
Falklands War 9, 198, 206, 220
Filipinos 168, 169, 185
First World War 11, 23, 56, 92, 105, 109, 146, 160, 194, 221
Formby 23, 28, 42, 43, 196, 199

Fort George 34
Fox, Bill 21, 49, 92, 97, 101, 136, 142, 176, 177, 181, 189, 222
French Foreign Legion 24
Ganges 28, 29, 75, 159
George VI 41
Gibraltar 22, 46
Glasgow 10, 35, 165
Glasgow, HMS 29
Globemasters 61, 83
Gloucestershire regiment 13, 21, 93, 134, 178, 180, 189, 221
Godsall, Ron 175
Gooks 57, 66, 67, 111, 147–9
Goulding, Jack 164
Grundy, Jim 36, 95, 135, 167, 168, 170–2, 198, 201, 219, 222
Gurkhas 55
Hale, Steve 18, 28, 208
Happy Valley 40
Hara-Mura 51
Harding, John 35
Harrington barracks 42
Hawthorne, Ken 45, 52, 99, 102, 105, 107, 115, 120, 125, 128, 133, 135, 139, 151, 211, 213
Heath Robinson, William 79, 90, 124
Hegarty, John 32, 143, 174, 215
Higham, Albert 51
Highland Light Infantry 26
Hill 159 64
Hill 217 157–9
Hill 227 179
Hill 282 136–40, 147, 150, 214–6, 222
Hill 325 101
Hill 327 101
Hill 355 64, 78, 79
Hill 388 140
Hiroshima 36, 49, 208, 211, 216
Holden, Frank 161
Holland, Geoff 20, 37, 76, 87, 107, 135, 142, 154, 201
Hong Kong 10, 19, 20, 22, 25, 27, 30–3, 35, 37–8, 42, 47, 50–2, 55–7, 60–2, 66, 68, 71, 74, 76, 77, 85, 86, 100, 116, 118, 132, 143–5, 150, 155, 161, 173, 200, 206, 207, 213–6
Hook, Battle of the 83

Hope, Bob 120
Hough, Brian 40, 44, 81, 86, 103, 109, 116, 118, 129, 153, 160, 163, 170, 207, 210, 211, 215, 222
Houghton, Jim 27, 56, 59, 110, 120, 157, 158, 170, 198, 199, 210
Howerd, Frankie 120
Hurst, Bill 43, 55, 57, 60, 103, 121, 130, 162, 164, 166, 169, 200, 217
Imjin River 13, 56, 70, 76, 80, 102, 106, 158, 165, 166, 169, 181, 186, 207
Imjin, Battle of 134, 165, 178, 221
Imperial War Museum 14
Inchon 12, 48, 54, 62, 66, 73, 79, 84, 114, 139, 140, 174, 175, 216
Irish Guards 33, 34, 103
Jackson, Stan 110, 164
Jamaica, HMS 32, 33, 143–5, 174, 175, 215, 216
Japan 11, 13, 21, 25, 36, 48, 51–2, 60, 61, 71, 79, 80, 83–4, 102, 105, 110, 113, 117, 123, 132, 135, 143, 144, 153, 173, 174, 178, 185, 188, 208, 210–2
Jones, Peter C. Le P. 66, 96, 98, 101, 147, 154, 162, 216
Juneau, USS 144, 145
Karachi 26
Kenton, Stan 81
Khyber Pass 19, 26
King's Regiment 23, 28, 41–3, 56, 83, 103, 209
Kings Shropshire Light Infantry 24
Korea, North 10–4, 21, 65, 67, 73, 77, 92, 111, 134, 136, 137, 139–45, 155, 156, 163, 167–74, 177, 181, 187, 188, 199, 200, 219, 220, 222
Korea, South 10, 12, 15, 28, 66, 95, 111, 134, 135, 142, 144, 157, 168, 171, 197, 199, 200, 202, 219, 220
Korean Veterans Association 7, 197
Kure, Japan 36, 48, 49, 51, 52, 60, 71, 110
Ladysmith barracks 43
Lancashire 23, 36, 44
Lancashire Fusiliers 23
Larkhill 30
Leicestershire Regiment 59
Liverpool 10, 19, 20, 22–4, 27, 258, 33, 34, 40, 42–4, 50, 165, 196, 199, 200, 203, 206, 209, 210, 213, 214
London 10, 27, 95, 132, 204, 207
London, HMS 33
Luckock, Corporal 104
MacArthur, General 12, 13, 21, 73, 92, 142, 156, 157, 174, 175, 187, 212
Malaysia 18, 27, 41
Malta 22
Manchester 10, 21, 22, 34, 36, 37, 40, 41, 43, 44, 83, 119, 190, 192, 193, 201, 202, 207, 217
Manchester Evening Chronicle 130
Manchester Guardian 193
Manchester Regiment 41, 43
Manchuria 12, 73, 118

Mao Tse Tung 12, 191
Maoris 216
Marines 30, 67, 71, 93, 94, 140
Marx, Karl 192
Maryhill barracks 35
MASH 9
Middlesex Regiment 144, 145, 148
Monte Rosa 22
Moore, Terry 39, 68, 98, 117, 122, 125, 131, 165, 167, 178, 206
Moscow 190
Mt McKinley, USS 175
Muir, Major Kenny 140–1, 148–50
Mustangs 136, 140, 148, 149, 214
Napalm 10, 70, 73, 126, 136, 141, 148, 149, 166, 184, 214, 222
National Memorial Arboretum 136, 222
National Service 10, 15, 17, 21, 22, 24, 27, 28, 36, 37, 39, 40, 42, 50, 88, 90, 134, 137, 160, 161, 195, 197, 199, 204, 213, 215, 222
Neilson, Lt Col 148, 155
Neston Advertiser 132
New Brighton 31
New Territories 20, 31, 38, 42, 50, 51, 143, 207
New Zealand/New Zealanders 51, 77, 84, 150, 168, 174, 216
Nicols, Max 123
Nixon, Digger 73
Northumberland Fusiliers 69
Northumberland's 56, 59
Observation Battery 61, 62
Ocean, HMS 27, 33
Olympic games 10, 97, 220
Ominato 143
Oxfordshire and Buckinghamshire Light Infantry 24
Palestine 26
Parachute Regiment 23, 24
Pathe News 130, 195
Peters, Eric 19, 25, 72, 119, 127, 132, 203
Phillips, Major 54
Plymouth 215
Poles 191, 192
Port Said 20, 38, 59, 207
Portsmouth 29, 204
Purple Heart 153
Pusan 12, 36, 48–56, 60, 66, 68, 69, 72, 78, 80, 81, 107, 116, 135, 140, 168, 169, 174, 198, 201, 204, 207
Pyongyang 94, 95, 156
Queen Elizabeth II 41, 65
Queens Own Cameron Highlanders 39
Quinn, Pat 100, 136, 139
Randle, Frank 22
Rawlinson, Wilf 164
Recovery Programme 168, 173
Red Cross 166, 169, 173, 177, 178, 187
Red Sea 22
REME 106
Rhee, Syngman 11, 12, 14
Ridgway, General Matthew 13, 73, 157, 177, 189

Roper, Tony Trevor 70
Royal Artillery 31, 36, 61, 62, 77, 144, 145
Royal Engineers 45
Royal Military Police (RMP) 35, 37, 80, 112, 164
Royal Norfolk Regiment 50
Royal Ulster Rifles 39, 206
Russia 41, 71, 73, 76, 77, 85, 88, 94, 144, 155 160, 191, 192, 220
SAS 24
Seaforth barracks 52
Second World War 11, 20–2, 40, 80, 83, 88, 126, 136, 161, 174, 177–9, 187, 190, 194, 195, 197, 198, 210, 220, 221
Seoul 12, 52, 53, 56, 61, 81–3, 106, 140, 152, 154, 156, 165, 203, 204, 206, 220
Shearer, Georgie 214
Shinwell, Emmanuel 18
Singapore 19, 20, 22, 27, 31, 38, 50, 52, 60, 72, 170, 207
Skymasters 49, 79, 154
Smith, John 10, 33, 43, 84, 113, 164, 172, 179, 213
Southampton 19, 20, 22, 23, 31, 36, 37, 46, 50, 196, 198, 201, 204, 205, 207, 216, 217
Speakman, Bill, VC 53, 78
St James's Palace 154
Stirland, George 19, 28, 71, 75, 105, 159, 203
Suez 22, 31, 46, 50, 210, 211, 215
Sung, Kim Il 11, 12, 14
Sutherland Highlanders 116
Teal Bridge 107
Templer, General 39
Tokyo 70, 79, 83, 85, 142, 208, 210, 216
Truman, President 13, 21, 73, 157, 212
Turks 69, 70, 143, 185
Ulster Rifles 39, 69, 165, 206
UN High Commission for Refugee Agency 82
United Nations 10, 12, 14, 15, 21, 40, 71, 73, 89, 177, 189
USA 9–11, 186, 197
USS Montrose 35, 84, 216
USSR 11
Vaughan, Sarah 103
Victoria Cross 78, 141
Vietnam 14
Walker, General Walton 157
Wayne, John 84, 183
Williams, Ivan 30, 61, 114, 124, 126, 128, 129, 131, 138, 204
Wilson, Major General 157, 158
Windrush 22
Windsor Castle 24
Wing Dagger 24
Woolwich 31, 37, 38, 196, 202, 205
Wosan 51
Yalu River 92, 141, 156, 188
Yangtse 32, 33, 143
Yong-Yu 156
York 27, 28, 37